TALKING SCIENCE:
Language, Learning, and Values

Language and Educational Processes

Judith Green, *Series Editor*
The Ohio State University

Jay L. Lemke: Talking Science: Language, Learning, and Values

In Preparation

Marilyn Cochran-Smith, Jessica Kahn, and Cynthia L. Paris: Teachers, Children, and Word Processing: Making Connections in the Elementary Grades
Susan Dodge: Learning to Write in Kindergarten: Social Processes and Individual Strategies
Catherine Emihovich: Turtletalk: The Language of Learning in Logo Instruction
Luis Moll and Stephen Diaz: Challenging the Status Quo: Bilingualism, Literacy, and Educational Change
Christine Pappas: Genre from a Sociopsycholinguistic Perspective
Kenneth Reeder, Hillel Goelman, Rita Watson, and Jon Shapiro: Emergence of Language and Literacy in the Preschool Years
Deborah Wells Rowe: Preschoolers as Authors: Literacy Learning in the Child's World
Judith Sosken: Literacy, Gender, and Work in Families and in School
Jerri Willet: Negotiating Communicative and Academic Competence

TALKING SCIENCE:
LANGUAGE, LEARNING, AND VALUES

Jay L. Lemke
City University of New York
Brooklyn College School of Education

ABLEX PUBLISHING CORPORATION
NORWOOD, NEW JERSEY

Printed in the United States of America

Library of Congress Cataloging-in-Publication Data

Lemke, J. L. (Jay L.)
    Talking science : language, learning, and values / Jay L. Lemke.
        p. cm. — (Language and educational processes)
    Includes bibliographical references.
    ISBN 0-89391-565-3. — ISBN 0-89391-566-1 (pbk.)
    1. Communication in science—Study and teaching. 2. Science—
Study and teaching. 3. Language and languages—Study and teaching.
I. Title. II. Series.
Q223.L46 1990
501.4—dc20   89-78244
                                                                    CIP

Ablex Publishing Corporation
355 Chestnut Street
Norwood, New Jersey 07648

Table of Contents

PREFACE TO THE SERIES

LANGUAGE AND EDUCATIONAL PROCESSES

This series of volumes provides a forum for the exploration of how language in use influences and is influenced by educational processes. The volumes in this series reflect the diverse theories, methods, and findings about the roles and functions of language in educational processes. The common theme across these volumes is an understanding of the central role that language plays in education. Of particular concern is the need to make visible the often invisible influences of language on what and how students learn or fail to learn from participating in various educational processes throughout their lives.

Education and language are viewed as diverse and situated processes. Thus, to understand the role and function of language in the education of individuals and social groups, we must understand how language functions in and across various educational situations—in the home, in pre-kindergarten through high school, in college, in the workplace, and in post-graduate and professional education.

Scholars working on the nexus of language and education from the perspective of sociolinguistics, psycholinguistics, ethnomethodology, ethnography of communication, literary theory, sociology of language, cognitive psychology, linguistics and related areas are invited to submit monographs and edited collections of original papers to the series editor for review by the editorial board.

Judith L. Green
The Ohio State University

Associate Editor:
Ginger Weade
University of Florida

EDITORIAL BOARD:

David Bloome
University of Massachusetts

Carl Frederiksen
McGill University

James Heap
Ontario Institute for Studies in Education

Rebecca Kantor
The Ohio State University

Gladys Knott
Kent State University

Judith O. Harker
Veterans Administration Hospital, Northridge

Jay Lemke
Brooklyn College of the City University of New York

Luis Moll
University of Arizona

Christine Pappas
Univeristy of Louisville

Regina Weade
University of Florida

Amy Zaharlick
The Ohio State University

Introduction: Talking Science

This is a book about communication. It asks some fundamental questions and tries to give at least partial answers to them:

How do we communicate ideas?
Why does communication work so well sometimes, and fail so badly at other times?
What are the most basic difficulties in communicating scientific and technical concepts?

This is also a book about scientific and technical education:

How do teachers communicate science in the classroom?
Why do some students succeed in mastering science, while so many others find it impossibly difficult and frustrating?
What attitudes and values are transmitted in the science classroom along with the science that is learned?

Most fundamentally, this is a book about *talking science*: It asks how we use the specialized language of science to make sense of the world, and to make sense of and to one another.

"Talking science" does not simply mean talking *about* science. It means *doing* science through the medium of language. "Talking science" means observing, describing, comparing, classifying, analyzing, discussing, hypothesizing, theorizing, questioning, challenging, arguing, designing experiments, following procedures, judging, evaluating, deciding, concluding, generalizing, reporting, writing, lecturing, and teaching in and through the language of science.

Why the emphasis on *language?* Because language is not just vocabulary and grammar: Language is a system of resources for making meanings. In addition to a vocabulary and a grammar, our language gives us a *semantics.* The semantics of a language is its particular way of creating similarities and differences in meaning. We need semantics because any particular concept or idea makes sense only in terms of the relationships it has to other concepts and ideas. This web of relationships of meaning is woven with the semantic resources of language.

Semantics, fundamentally, is the study of meaning as it is expressed through language. In order to talk science, or any other subject, we have to express relationships between the meanings of different concepts, and semantics is the study of how we use language to do this. It is a profound and subtle field of study, and a very useful one. By the end of Chapter 4, I hope this important new perspective will begin to feel familiar and comfortable. Meanwhile, if something seems unclear, try interpreting the word "semantic" as just a technical synonym for the word "meaning".

The content of every scientific and technical subject can be expressed in language (and in specialized offshoots of language, such as mathematics). In fact, the same scientific ideas can be expressed in many different ways, because the semantics of a language always allows us to use grammar and vocabulary in different ways to express the same meaning. The wording of a scientific argument may change from one book to the next, one teacher to the next, even one day to the next in the same classroom. But the semantic pattern, the pattern of relationships of meanings, always stays the same: That pattern *is* the scientific content of what we say or write.

The semantic resources of language are the foundation for all our efforts to communicate science and other subjects. To understand how communication works, and what makes it succeed or fail, we need to analyze how we use language to *mean* something.

Communication, as I will use the term in this book, is always a social process. We do not communicate by the transmission of signs or signals, but by creating and manipulating social situations. *Communication is always the creation of community.*

When we talk science, we are helping to create, or re-create, a community of people who share certain beliefs and values. We communicate best with people who are already members of our own community: those who have learned to use language in the same ways that we do. When the people with whom we are trying to communicate use language differently, use it in ways that make sense of a subject differently than we do, communication becomes much more difficult. Science teachers belong to a community of people who already speak the language of science. Students, at least for a long time, do not. Teachers use that language to make sense of each topic in a particular way. Students use their own language to put together a view of the subject that can be very different. This is one reason why communicating science can be so difficult. We have to learn to see science teaching as a social process and to bring students, at least partially, into this community of people who *talk science.* Learn

Because communication and teaching are social processes, they depend on attitudes, values, and social interests, not just on knowledge and skills. In every chapter of this book, we will have to look at conflicts of interests and values in order to understand the successes and failures of communication in the science classroom. The classroom is not isolated from the attitudes, values, and social interests of the larger community. Teachers and students bring these with them into the classroom. Science education itself tries to teach certain values, and those values may not always agree with students' values or with students' views about their own interests.

In teaching the content of the science curriculum, and the values that often go with it, science education, sometimes unwittingly, also perpetuates a certain harmful "mystique of science." That mystique tends to make science seem dogmatic, authoritarian, impersonal, and even inhuman to many students. It also portrays science as being much more difficult than it is, and scientists as being geniuses that students cannot identify with. It alienates students from science.

This mystique does not benefit science teachers and scientists nearly as much as it benefits those whose power depends on public attitudes towards every form of "expertise." It is not in the best interests of students, or of most of us, yet it is subtly built into the way even the best intentioned teachers talk science. Analyzing how teachers and students talk science in the classroom can help us to understand how this mystique is perpetuated, why it is harmful, and what we can do about it.

The basic point-of-view in this book is that science is a social process. This is true even when a scientist is physically alone. Whenever we do science, we take ways of talking, reasoning, observing, analyzing, and writing that we have learned from our community and use them to construct findings and arguments that become part of science only when they become shared in that community. Teaching science is teaching students how to *do science*. Teaching, learning, and doing science are all social processes: taught, learned, and done as members of social communities, small (like classrooms) and large. We make those communities by communication, and we communicate complex meanings primarily through language. Ultimately, doing science is always guided and informed by talking science, to ourselves and with others.

Every scientific statement we make, every scientific argument, and all our reasoning as we do science are instances of talking science. In doing these things, we are marshalling the semantic resources of a powerful and specialized way of talking about the world. This book is about what we do, when, and with whom, when we are talking science in the classroom. It is a case study in communication, in the analysis of classroom teaching, and in the semantics of science. It is necessarily also about science and science education as social processes in the context of the larger society, and therefore about attitudes, values, and social interests.

Chapters 1 and 2 introduce the specific themes and methods of the whole book. Each analyzes a brief classroom episode, looking from two different points of view at how teachers and students talk science. The first point of view focuses on the patterns of social interaction in the classroom. Because communication is a social process, we need to understand how it creates and sustains a social situation: a set of relationships and expectations among its participants. Everything else that happens in communication depends on this basic framework of "who does what to whom." The second viewpoint emphasizes how science content is communicated in classroom dialogue: What are the semantic patterns of each science topic and how are they put into words?

The episode in Chapter 1 is a fairly "normal" example of classroom dialogue. In it, communication is working reasonably well. This episode provides a background against which we can view more unusual and revealing ways of talking science. The episode in Chapter 2 provides a first example: It is a debate in which students challenge a teacher's scientific explanations. This episode shows very well how communication breaks down when participants don't share the same ways of talking about a subject.

Chapter 3 is about the unwritten rules of the classroom. It is about the social situations that actually occur in classrooms and teachers' and students' strategies for attempting to control each other's behavior and the course of classroom events. I argue that there are important classroom rules which, even though students must violate them in order for learning to continue, are nonetheless maintained as rules because they help to preserve important mechanisms of social control that have implications well beyond the classroom. Chapter 3 describes the social contexts in which students and teachers talk science. It is about power, interests, and values in the classroom.

Chapter 4 describes in detail how the semantic resources of language are used in talking science. Specific examples from actual lessons illustrate the variety of strategies for communicating complex conceptual relationships through classroom dialogue. In many ways this chapter is the heart of the whole book.

Chapter 5 ties the language of the classroom to larger social issues of attitudes, interests, and values. It discusses the mystique of science, students' alienation from science, and a number of harmful myths about how science must be talked, how difficult it is, and what kind of truth it provides. This chapter also describes what students do and do not pay attention to in classrooms.

Chapter 6 is a brief discussion of the similarities and differences to be expected when applying the arguments of this book to subjects other than science. It raises critical issues for the analysis of curriculum in science and other subjects.

Chapter 7 summarizes many of the arguments made throughout the book by providing a succinct list of practical recommendations for changing the way we teach. It also points out that educational policy must always be based on value choices and honest recognition of conflicts of interest, not just on research findings, even those in this book. It tries to look beyond merely "technical" solutions to the more fundamental social causes of educational problems.

The main argument of the book really ends with the recommendations in Chapter 7, but it has been guided and informed all along by a general theory of meaning and social action. That theory, known as *social semiotics*, provides a number of alternative ways of looking at basic issues in education. For readers who are explicitly interested in theory as well as practice, I give an overview of social semiotics in Chapter 8.

I hope you will find these new perspectives on communication, science teaching, and language exciting. I also hope you will find them useful.

EXPLORING FURTHER

Many researchers in the field of education in the last decade or so have developed the view that learning is a social and cultural process in which language plays a critical role. A good introduction to this perspective is provided by the collection of papers edited by Cazden, John, and Hymes, *Functions of Language in the Classroom* (1972), by Edwards and Furlong's *The Language of Teaching* (1978), and the volumes edited by Green and Wallat (*Ethnography and Language in Educational Settings*, 1981), and by Wilkinson (*Communicating in the Classroom*, 1982).

At the end of each chapter of this book, I will provide further suggestions for reading in depth about the wider issues touched on in that chapter. Complete citations can be found in the list of References at the end of the book.

chapter 1

Two Minutes in One Science Classroom

Learning science means learning to *talk* science. It also means learning to use this specialized conceptual language in reading and writing, in reasoning and problem solving, and in guiding practical action in the laboratory and in daily life. It means learning to communicate in the language of science and act as a member of the community of people who do so. "Talking science" means observing, describing, comparing, classifying, analyzing, discussing, hypothesizing, theorizing, questioning, challenging, arguing, designing experiments, following procedures, judging, evaluating, deciding, concluding, generalizing, reporting, writing, lecturing, and teaching in and through the language of science.

How do we learn to talk science? We learn this language in much the same way we learn any other: by speaking it with those who have already mastered it and by employing it for the many purposes for which it is used. By the end of this book I hope to have shown that the language of science, like the language of each specialized field of human activity, has its own unique semantic patterns, its own specific ways of making meaning. For most people, if these ways are learned at all, they are learned in the dialogue of the science classroom. That is why I want to begin by looking at how we learn to talk science in classroom dialogue. The rules of that dialogue govern the activities through which we do, or do not, learn to talk science.

GETTING STARTED

Let's look first at the beginning of one science lesson:

1	*Teacher:*	Before we get started . . . Before I erase the board. . .
2	*Students:*	Sh!
3	*Teacher:*	Uh . . . Look how fancy I got . . . [looks at board]
4	*Students:*	Sh!
5	*Teacher:*	This is a representation of the one S . . . orbital.
6		S'pozed to be, of course, three dimensional. . . .
7		What two elements could be represented by such a
8		diagram? . . . Jennifer?

This opening dialogue was transcribed from a tape recording of a high school chemistry lesson. In an Appendix at the end of this book, I describe the research project in which this class and many others were studied. In addition to the recordings, there are detailed notes about each lesson, made by myself and another observer. They will provide useful background information when we need to interpret dialogue in the context of the larger classroom events of which it is always a part. (You will find the full transcript of this and other episodes in the Appendix. See DRS-27-NOV.)

A lesson is a social activity. It has a pattern of organization, a *structure*. Events of specific kinds tend to follow one another in a more or less definite order. It has a start and a finish. But like all other kinds of social activities, it is *made*. It is a human social construction. People have to *do* something to get it started, to enact one kind of event after another, and to bring it to a close. In Chapter 3 we examine some of the many standard kinds of events that occur in science classroom lessons. This chapter discusses one episode, lasting about two minutes, at the beginning of a lesson. We look at how the teacher and students get this lesson started, what patterns of activity then follow, and how science gets talked as part of classroom activities.

When our dialogue begins, the students are still talking to one another and the classroom is noisy. The "period" may have begun in the technical sense that the bell has rung, but the "lesson" as a social activity has not yet started. The teacher and the students have to do some work to get it started. They have to get one another's attention, focus that attention on the same activity, and begin cooperating to produce the sequence of events that we recognize as a Lesson.

The first thing the teacher says to the class as a whole (line 1) contains the very words "get started," but he doesn't say something more usual like, "O.K. Let's get started now." Some students, nevertheless, do stop talking and start to listen to him. Others do not. The teacher does not finish his first sentence; instead he pauses briefly (represented by . . . in the transcripts) and starts a new sentence. He doesn't complete this sentence either. There are still students who are not paying attention to him. But some of those who are now turn and start to "shush" the others (line 2). The teacher starts again, hesitantly (line 3), making a remark and pointing to a fancy colored chalk diagram of an atom on the blackboard. Some students are still talking, and again others urge them to be quiet (line 4). The teacher now starts to describe the diagram, and as he does so the class become quiet and attentive. A lesson has begun.

What happened that got the lesson started? It was not just the teacher's words, or what the teacher did. It was a joint effort of all the

participants. The teacher took the initiative by ending his private conversations with students at the front of the room. They went to their
seats. He turned from facing the blackboard to facing the class as
a whole and spoke for the first time in "teacher voice," that slightly
louder, public tone of voice so different from the voice he used in
private conversations a few seconds before. His whole action—turning
around, looking at the class, using a particular tone of voice, as well as
the words he spoke—constituted a *Bid to Start*. He was doing his part,
but the students also had to do theirs. No teacher can start a lesson
solely by his or her own efforts. Without the co-operation of the students, the lesson does not get started.

In this case more and more students act to ratify the teacher's Bid to
Start. They stop their other conversations, look up from their notebooks,
quiet other students and generally "pass the word" that the teacher
wants to get started. In doing so, they do their part to start the lesson. It
may not matter very much just what the teacher says, if the class is
expecting him to start. In some lessons there are even "false starts,"
when the class quiets down but the teacher turns out not to have been
ready to start and does not follow through. Students begin to talk again
and there has to be a new Bid to Start by the teacher, which the students
must again ratify with their cooperation.

The words the teacher actually does use here do fit the situation. The
words "get started" at least mention what is supposed to happen, even
if the unfinished sentence doesn't request or demand it. Even the words
"erase the board" *allude* to the starting of lessons because erasing the
board, like closing the classroom door, is an action that typically occurs
at the start of a period, if not at the exact moment when a lesson is to
begin. They are "cues" to the class. When the teacher changes strategy
(line 3) and directs the class's attention to his fancy diagram, he is
working to create a common focus of attention and interest, part of
getting started. Calling attention to something on the board is another
typical activity at the start of lessons.

By line 5 the teacher is ready to launch into the lesson. He completes
a sentence that says something in the language of science for the first
time. In fact, at this moment, not *everybody* in the class is paying full
attention. The class settles down during the course of the next few lines
and is fully attentive by the time Jennifer answers his question. The
teacher's final and strongest bid to start the lesson is his simply going
ahead with presenting the lesson content *as if* the lesson had begun.

There is no absolute criterion for when a lesson really does begin. In
many classes the lesson has begun even though not everybody is fully
attentive. In fact in most classes I have observed or taught it is *unusual*
to get perfect 100% attention from a whole class, and you don't neces-

sarily get it right at the start (see Chapter 5). In effect the lesson has begun when you can look back and realize that you are now in the midst of a sequence of events that makes sense only if the first event was, retrospectively, the start of a lesson. At the time the event is happening, there is no way to know that it will later turn out to have been the real start and not just a "false start."

All social activities are like this. They are "contingent" while they are happening, and definite only in retrospect. The contingencies of an event are the probabilities that different things will happen next. In real life, you never know for sure what is coming next, but if you can recognize that you are in the midst of a patterned, organized kind of social activity, like a lesson (or a ballgame, or a trial) you know the probabilities for what is likely to come next. All social cooperation is based on participants sharing a common sense of the structure of the activity: of what's happening, what the options are for what comes next, and who is supposed to do what. A lesson has this kind of *activity structure*.

The structure of a lesson as a whole is rather loose and complicated. It has a Start section, which has a structure of its own, consisting of Bids to Start by the teacher and Ratifications by students. It then typically has a series of episodes, some of which—like Taking Attendance, Going Over Homework, Class Announcements, and so on—tend to come first and be followed by events like Start Main Lesson (i.e., the teaching of the main content for the day's work, after all preliminaries), Reviews (of today's work, *after* the Main Lesson; or of yesterday's, *before*), and a Closing. Each of these is an activity in its own right, on a smaller scale than the lesson as a whole, and each has its own activity structure. In Chapter 3 we will survey the activity types of the science classroom.

Human behavior in structured activities is relatively predictable. For comparison with the Start of this lesson, here are some Bid Starts by other teachers in other lessons. One type is rather direct:

Come on people, let's go. We're already late.

All right, c'mon . . . focus!

All right, youth . . . let's get started.

Each of these is by a different teacher. Our teacher began less directly by alluding to typical start-of-lesson actions, like erasing the board. Here are some similar examples from other teachers:

O.K. Now open up [your notebooks] . . .

All right. Would you please find your seats.

O.K. As we can all see, we have three Do Now questions on the board.

Even the apparently strange *"Before* we get started . . ." finds. its parallels:

Two brief reminders and then we're ready to start.

I'd like to ask you a couple questions before we start.

In these cases, as in our episode, the teacher is not only working to get things started, but to let the class know that the first episode is a only a preliminary one and that the main business of the lesson will come afterwards. This is another very general feature of human action: The same words, the same acts often have more than one function. They do several jobs at once. In this case, the teacher's words were part of a Bid to start the lesson, *and* an announcement that this was only a preliminary activity before the main business.

THE UNWRITTEN RULES OF CLASSROOM DIALOGUE

Consider the lesson started. What is the activity structure of the first episode? It is a very common pattern in modern education, well known to teachers and students, a special form of question-and-answer dialogue. Various versions of it have been described by many other research projects (see, for example, the books by Sinclair and Coulthard, 1975, and Mehan, 1979 in References). We can get at the structure of a lot of classroom talk by examining it carefully.

5	*Teacher:*	This is a representation of the one S . . . orbital.
6		S'pozed to be, of course, three dimensional. . . .
7		What two elements could be represented by such a
8		diagram? . . . Jennifer?
9	*Jennifer:*	Hydrogen and helium?
10	*Teacher:*	Hydrogen and helium. Hydrogen would have one electron
11		. . . somewhere in there, and helium would have . . .?
12	*Student:*	Two electrons.
13	*Teacher:*	Two. . . . This is . . . one S, and . . . the white would be
14		. . .? Mark?
15	*Mark:*	Two S.
16	*Teacher:*	Two S. And the green would be . . .? uhh . . .
17	*Janice:*	Two P. Two P.
18	*Teacher:*	Janice.
19	*Janice:*	Two P.
20	*Teacher:*	Two P. Yeah, the green would be 2P x and 2P y.

The teacher's first question comes in lines 7–8, and we can take what Jennifer says next to be an answer to that question, even though she

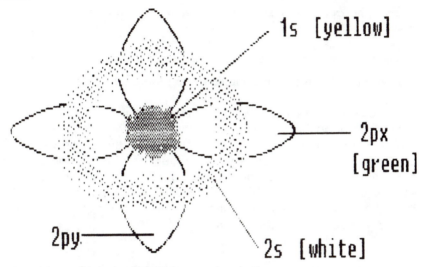

1s [yellow]

2px
[green]

2py

2s [white]

Figure 1.1.   Atomic Orbital Diagram

says it with a questioning (rising) intonation. Line 11 seems to pose the next question, and line 12 is its answer. But there is a lot more being said besides the bare questions and answers. They are embedded in a larger, more complex, and more interesting pattern of activity structure.

Before his first question, the teacher describes the diagram he has on the board (see Figure 1.1). He points to the central area of the diagram and identifies it as "the 1s orbital." He points out that the diagram does not show that it really looks like a sphere, that is, three- rather than two-dimensional as it appears on the board. Only then does he ask a question which refers directly to the diagram, and not to the whole of it, but specifically to the part of it he has just described. He has prepared a context for his question first. Without the preparatory statements, the question would have been ambiguous or confusing for the class.

Not every Teacher Question is preceeded by a Teacher Preparation for that question, but many are, and every one *could* be. As with lesson Starts, you can't know for sure that what the teacher is saying at any given moment will turn out later to have been a Preparation for a question. But when the question comes, the odds are good that what immediately preceded it (if they are linked semantically; see below) was, in retrospect, a Preparation and therefore relevant information for answering the question. Students who fail to connect Preparations and Questions are not in a good position to answer appropriately.

After the question, and before the answer, the teacher pauses and says (line 8), "Jennifer?" The pause marked the teacher's silent Call for

Bids to answer his question. This move in the dialogue structure is not usually verbalized. In many British classrooms, a teacher will say at this point, "Hands up." While it would only get a laugh in most American classrooms, its meaning is obvious enough in this context: Raise your hand if you want to be called on to answer. American teachers who silently wait for hands to go up, and don't see any, may say, "C'mon. Somebody give it a try." In that case it is a Second Call for Bids. But in this case Jennifer did raise her hand, and the teacher calls on her by name. This move is sometimes called the Nomination of the student. The whole Bid and Nomination exchange is optional in the structure, but teachers tend to prefer to have it occur.

We now get (line 9) Jennifer's answer. Or is it a question? That depends mainly on what follows it. In itself it is a little bit of both; it serves more than a single function, as so many actions do. But within the structure is it taken to be a Student Answer or not? Here it is, as we will see. The teacher might have said, "Are you asking me or telling me?" That would have been a question *and* an instruction to Jennifer to commit herself to her answer, not hedging as she did before. It would also retroactively deny her words the status of Answer. Jennifer's questioning answer subtly undermines the structure in an important way, as we will see later, but in this case the teacher simply ignores her intonation and treats what she said as a *bona fide* Answer.

He does so by repeating her answer with a firm declarative (falling) intonation. Other teachers at this point might have said, "O.K." or "Yes." or "Good." The teacher is confirming what she said as the Answer, giving it a positive Evaluation. This is the most characteristic feature of classroom dialogue of this sort.

Ordinarily, in conversation, or in any situation where one asks a question to obtain information, it is ridiculous or impolite to accept or reject the answer. An exchange like: "How old are you?" "35" "That's right" is condescending at best. The difference in the classroom is that the teacher is already supposed to know the Answer. He is not asking for information; he is testing to see if the student knows the information. We will need to ask later *why* it is, if the teacher knows and the students may not know, that teachers rather than students ask most of the questions, and students rather than teachers do the answering. When students do ask teachers questions, the students do not usually evaluate the teachers' answers (at least not out loud). There is, of course, another activity type in which students do ask the questions, but it has a very different organizational pattern, a different activity structure, from the one we are now analyzing (see Chapter 3).

The Teacher Evaluation move is not optional in the structure we are now analyzing. If the teacher does not give a positive Evaluation—for example, if he remains silent—the students will assume that this silence is tantamoumt to a negative Evaluation and will try a different answer. Teachers have to accustom students to a different activity pattern if they want to avoid this. Whatever the teacher does after an Answer is assumed to be an Evaluation, and a negative one if it is not obviously positive. Of course, there are other options teachers have at this point. They can give a neutral Evaluation, or a partially positive one (e.g., "O.K. That's interesting. I'd like to hear some other answers." or "O.K., Lynn. John, do you agree or disagree?")

Following a negative Evaluation, the teacher has a number of options which I will not discuss here. The dialogue tends to continue until a positive Evaluation is reached. After the positive Evaluation, the teacher has another optional move. In lines 10–11, what the teacher says about hydrogen partly serves the function of a Preparation for the next question, but it also functions partly as an Elaboration on the previous answer. In line 20 we have a positive Evaluation followed by an Elaboration on the answer, that has much less connection to the question that follows it. There are many cases where it may have no connection to what follows (e.g., at the end of an episode; see below). The Elaboration move adds more information to the answer.

What we find then, both here and pervasively in classroom dialogue, is not a simple two-part Question-Answer structure. Instead there is at least a three-part Question-Answer-Evaluation pattern, which I will call Triadic Dialogue. A typical round of this dialogue would be:

[Teacher Preparation]
Teacher Question
[Teacher Call for Bids (Silent)]
[Student Bid to Answer (Hand)]
[Teacher Nomination]
Student Answer
Teacher Evaluation
[Teacher Elaboration]

The moves in brackets are optional and often omitted. The essential triad of moves are shown in boldface. The moves come in the order listed, and the list shows the usual expectations about what precedes or follows a particular move. I have left out the other "branch" of this structure: the options following a negative Evaluation. A more formal presentation would look like a flowchart, giving the probabilities for each option following a given event (cf. Martin, 1985a).

If you look back at the episode so far, you will see that everything from line 5 to line 20 fits this pattern. But there is evidently something odd happening in lines 16–20 when Janice answers. Let's look at this in more detail.

SOME STRATEGIES THAT PLAY BY THE RULES

People are not slaves to the activity structures of their community. We do not just "follow the rules"—we use those rules as resources for playing the game according to our own strategies. There are many possible games of chess that conform to the rules, many possible English sentences that are "grammatical," and many possible sequences of classroom moves that fit the overall structures of lesson activity, including the triadic dialogue pattern. The differences between actual sequences of dialogue moves are like the differences between actual games: They are records of different strategies being played out move by move within the rules. Consider what happens in lines 16–20.

The teacher is asking students to identify the parts of his diagram by naming the atomic orbitals they represent. Mark has just identified the part in white chalk as the 2s orbital (lines 13–16). There is no Elaboration, and no additional Preparation for the question which follows, in which the teacher asks about the part done in green chalk (line 16). The new question is an exact parallel to the previous question, and in the pause, Janice answers it (correctly as it turns out) by saying, "Two P." We expect the usual positive Evaluation to come next in the form preferred by this teacher: a firm repeat of her correct answer. But this is not what happens.

The teacher's "uhh . . ." is a sort of verbal hesitation, a voiced pause in which he fills his turn to speak without advancing the action at all. Janice responds to this by repeating her answer quite loudly and clearly. Looking back, we could say that the teacher's "uhh" was taken by Janice as an indication that he hadn't quite heard her answer. But even now we do not get a positive Evaluation. Instead the teacher says, "Janice." In the tone of voice used this can only be taken as a Nomination (not, say, as an admonition, cf. Chapter 3). But according to the pattern of triadic dialogue, a Nomination should *precede*, not follow an Answer. If the teacher's move stands as a Nomination, then Janice's answers are demoted to the status of Bids to answer, and she must now Answer yet again.

There is no doubt that the teacher and all the students must have heard at least Janice's second clear answer. If she repeats it a third time, it would be strictly pro forma to acknowledge the structure the teacher wants to make, not the one she was previously following. In fact she does repeat her answer one more time, but much more quietly than before. And the teacher does not even bother to let her finish saying it before he overlaps her voice with his own, giving the positive Evaluation. (Note that when a line in the transcript does not begin at the left margin, it is to be read as simultaneous with the line above it. Otherwise each line follows in time the end of the line above.) This overlap is quite unusual, and would be impolite in other circumstances. But here it serves to acknowledge that Janice's last answer not only counts at last as the Answer, but that it was only a pro forma repeat.

But why? What is the teacher trying to maintain here, even at the risk of confusing Janice and the class as to what he is doing (and possibly even as to whether the answer really is correct)? He is maintaining the rule that students need to be called on (Nomination) before they can legitimately answer. Janice answered without being called on. This was not unprecedented, because in line 12 another student had answered under the same circumstances and his answer had been accepted. The teacher was not consistent about maintaining the rule that there should be Bids and Nomination before an Answer. In forcing Janice to observe this convention, he is maintaining "discipline." He is also maintaining his power in the class to decide who will answer. And in the context of this relatively easy review question, he is willing to sacrifice the continuity of development of the subject matter to maintain the structure he wants to see in use.

The teacher has used a "ruse," a *strategy* operating within the rules of the triadic dialogue structure, to achieve a certain result. He has made an unusual move, the late Nomination, which retroactively redefines the status of previous moves. Janice did not have to go along, of course. She might have said, after the "Nomination," something like an ingenuous "What?"—in effect declining to acknowledge it *as a* Nomination. Or she could have said, "I already said it," pushing to have her prior answer recognized as the Answer. In fact, she yields to the teacher, allowing his redefinitions to go unchallenged, and he as much as admits that this is what's happening by overlapping her answer and making it strictly an Answer pro forma. The low, quiet voice in which Janice gives her final Answer is her only protest, her bid to have it be known that the last repeat was just pro forma. So she has used a little strategy, too.

Students are quite good strategic players. In line 9, Jennifer's questioning intonation on her Answer hedges against it's being counted as wrong by the teacher. At the same time it expresses her uncertainty, and subtly turns the tables on the teacher by in effect asking *him* a question. The teacher does not respond in kind but simply sticks to the triadic dialogue pattern. Something different could have happened. Suppose Jennifer had said, "I don't know. Would they be hydrogen and helium?" and the teacher had said, "Yes." Then we would have come closer to shifting to an alternative dialogue pattern, one in which students ask the questions and the teacher answers. Another student might then have asked about the electrons or about what the colored parts of the diagram represented.

It's fairly common to get a series of student questions if the teacher accepts a first one and lets the dialogue pattern shift away from Triadic (see Chapter 3). But teachers don't usually deviate from the Triadic pattern because maintaining it gives the teacher many advantages. In this structure teachers get to initiate exchanges, set the topic, and control the direction in which the topic develops. They get to decide which students will answer which questions and to say which answers are correct. We have seen that they can even decide which answers will count as the legitimate Answer. In contrast, students have little or no opportunity for initiative, for controlling the direction of the discussion, or for contesting teacher prerogatives under Triadic Dialogue.

As we will see in the next chapter, students can get the upper hand by shifting to other dialogue patterns, where they have more latitude for strategic play within the rules. In Triadic Dialogue the deck is stacked against them. The rules heavily favor the power of the teacher, and this is no doubt one of the reasons why it has become such a popular style of teaching. We will return later to some of the troubling educational and value questions raised by the predominance of the triadic pattern in the classroom.

But first we need to look at this episode less from the viewpoint of the organization of its social interaction, its *activity structure*, and consider how the science content of the lesson is embodied in this dialogue.

FINDING THE SCIENCE IN THE DIALOGUE

A lesson is not just give-and-take between teacher and students. In the course of moves in the dialogue game, some science is getting talked about. The organizational pattern of the dialogue merely provides the structure within which teachers and students talk science in the classroom. The structure is important, but it does not tell us how to find the *science* in the dialogue. The lesson could be about atoms or about genes, about the weather or about earthquakes, and it could still have exactly the same activity structure of questions, bids and nominations, answers and evaluations.

Students also need to find the science in the dialogue. If they don't, they may learn how to play the classroom game, but they won't learn how to talk physics or biology. Most crucially, they need to learn how to separate and combine the science content and the dialogue forms in which it is expressed at any given moment. They need to know how to extract the science meaning from a Question-Answer-Evaluation triad and write it in their notes as a statement, or on a test as an answer. They need to be able to take a teacher's Elaboration on a previous answer and restate it as a question after class. To do this they need of course to undertand the relations of one move in an activity structure to another (e.g., how a Preparation helps determine the meaning of the Question, or how an Elaboration can modify the meaning of an Answer). But they need to use that understanding, even if only unconsciously, to piece together the pattern of meanings that we call the science content of the exchange, the episode, or the lesson.

The science in the dialogue is not just a matter of vocabulary. Classroom language is not just a list of technical terms, or even just a recital of definitions. It is the *use* of those terms in relation to one another, across a wide variety of contexts. Students have to learn how to *combine the meanings* of different terms according to the accepted ways of talking science. They have to talk and write and reason in phrases, clauses, sentences, and paragraphs of scientific language.

If you have ever studied a foreign language, you will know that reading definitions in a dictionary is not enough to tell you how to use those words properly in combination with other words. Even apart from correct grammar (endings, tenses, cases, articles, etc.), you need to learn the "semantics" of words: how their meanings fit together in different contexts. Definitions try to give a sense of the meanings of words, but to speak and understand, to write or read, you need to find the meanings of whole phrases and sentences, and not just of words.

When words combine, the meaning of the whole is more than the sum of its separate parts. To get the meaning of the whole, you need to know more than the meaning of each word: you need to know *the relations of meaning* between different words. A student may know the definitions of "electron," "element," and "orbital," but that does not mean he or she could use those words *together* in a sentence correctly, or say how their meanings relate to each other. To do so requires additional knowledge: knowledge of how these words are used in talking science.

The pattern of connections among the meanings of words in a particular field of science I will call their *thematic pattern*. It is a pattern of semantic relationships that describes the thematic content, the science content, of a particular topic area. It is like a network of relationships among the scientific concepts in a field, but described semantically, in terms of how language is used in that field. There is science in the dialogue exactly to the extent that the semantic relationships and the thematic pattern built up by the dialogue reproduce the thematic pattern of language use in some field of science.

The notion of a thematic pattern of semantic relationships is difficult and abstract at first. It will become more concrete and familiar as we use it to analyze classroom dialogues. In this chapter I just want to introduce the idea of the thematic pattern of a science dialogue. In the next chapter we will make more use of it, and in Chapter 4 we will see that it is a powerful tool for analyzing the language of science and science teaching.

Science dialogue, then, has *two* patterns: an organizational pattern, represented by its activity structure, and a thematic pattern. In all dialogue there are at least two different things going on. First, people are interacting with one another, move by move, strategically playing within some particular set of expectations about what can happen next (the activity structure). But they are also constructing complex meanings about a particular topic by combining words and other symbols (the thematic pattern).

Let's find the thematic pattern of the science in the dialogue of this episode.

So far as language goes, the science content begins in line 5. (Nonverbally, the teacher's pointing to the atom diagram, line 3, might also count as introducing science content.) Certainly the terms "1s" and "orbital" are technical terms, and the word "representation" has a semitechnical sense here, but could probably have been left out without changing the meaning much (e.g., "This is the 1s orbital," cf. line 13). The word "this," of course, refers to the center part of the diagram in Figure 1.1, to which he is pointing. Does the sentence tell us anything about the *relation in meaning* between "1s" and "orbital"? Actually, in a very subtle way it does. In the expression "1s orbital," as in so many expressions in science, the "1s" functions as a *classifier*. It tells us *which kind* of orbital is meant in some classification of orbitals. If a student is alert to this kind of semantic relationship, he or she will know that this is one kind of orbital and that there are other kinds. This is like understanding that "a grey squirrel" doesn't have to mean simply that the squirrel is grey, it can be used to refer to a *kind* of squirrel, and not specifically to its color alone.

Line 6 supplies a characteristic of the orbital; it is three-dimensional. All orbitals are three-dimensional; this is not a classifier, but a simple descriptive quality.

Lines 7–8 are in the form of a question, but even a question can provide thematic information. It can tell us something about the relations of the meanings of its key terms. This question implies that the parts of the diagram can be used to represent elements. The term "elements" is new, and we learn something about its use from this question. Of course, it takes many examples of usage before one can begin to extract the thematic pattern of a scientific field with any degree of certainty. But each example contributes something.

In dialogue a Question is often thematically incomplete without its Answer, and in triadic dialogue it needs the Evaluation of the Answer as well. In this dialogue, the teacher and Jennifer together, through the whole exchange of lines 7–10, tell us that the two elements, hydrogen and helium, can both be represented by the same part of the the diagram. If we add the information from the Preparation (line 5), we learn that these two elements can be represented by the 1s orbital. A specific relationship between the meanings of "orbital" and "element" is being constructed over six lines of dialogue. We also learn, from lines 7–10, that there is a particular relationship between the term "elements" and the terms "hydrogen" and "helium." The answer would not make sense in relation to the way the question was asked unless hydrogen and helium *were* two of the chemical elements. Each is a member of the class of elements. This too is a semantic relationship, and part of the thematics of the topic.

So far, then, we have the following special terms from the language of science used in the dialogue: *1s, orbital, three-dimensional, element, hydrogen, helium*. But in addition there are certain relationships among these terms that can be read from the dialogue:

1s	[is a type of]	orbital
orbital	[has quality]	3-dimensional
orbital	[can represent]	element
hydrogen	[is example of]	element
helium	[is example of]	element

These are semantic relationships. The thematic pattern of the dialogue is the pattern in which these relationships are joined together. If the relationships themselves and the pattern in which they are joined is the same as what we would find in science textbooks or the language of professional scientists, we can say that the thematic pattern of the dialogue is truly "talking science." We know that there is a larger pattern in this dialogue beyond just the relationships listed in the table because the dialogue has linked several of them together in order to tell us that the "1s [type of] orbital [can represent] the elements [known as] hydrogen and helium." As the dialogue continues and the pattern becomes more complex, we can draw a thematic diagram to show how the terms combine semantically in this field (see Figure 1.2).

Lines 10–13 introduce one new term, *electron*, and two new relation-

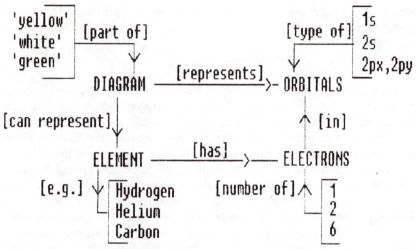

Figure 1.2.   Informal Thematic Diagram

ships to previous terms. One is the relationship expressed by saying that hydrogen or helium (that is, these two *elements*) "has" electrons. In fact, in both cases *electron* is preceded by a number. The general semantic pattern is:

    element [has] number [of] electrons

Different elements have different numbers of electrons. This is certainly part of the thematic pattern of physics and chemistry. But there is another semantic relationship implied here in line 11. Perhaps it is only in retrospect, or only if we are already familiar with the pattern, that it stands out. The phrase "somewhere in there" seems to connect electron to orbital in a *spatial* sense. That is also a semantic relationship. Since it is an important one, we ought to look for more evidence for it. It is an important characteristic of science dialogue that key semantic relationships, that is, those that do belong to the general thematic pattern of the subject matter, will be repeated again and again as they are used and reused in the dialogue. Look at the next few lines (21–24):

21 *Teacher:*   If I have one electron in the 2Px, one electron in the
22   2Py, . . . two electrons in the 2S, two electrons in the
23   1S, what element is being represented by this
24   configuration?

Even though the term orbital does not occur here, if we already know that, like 1s, the terms *2px, 2py,* and *2s* are types of orbitals, then we see that in each case *electrons* are said to be "in" *orbitals*. This is the semantic relationship:

electrons   [are located in]   orbitals

We also find out that certain numbers of electrons are said to be in each orbital. But how do we tell from the dialogue that, say, 2s is a type of orbital? Looking back at lines 13–16, the exchange with Mark, we see that the relationship between the Preparation, the Question, the Answer, and the Evaluation presumes that 1s (yellow circle in the board diagram) and 2s (a white circle) are two orbitals, each represented by a different part of the diagram (cf. line 5). The same applies to 2p (consisting of a vertical and a horizontal loop, representing the 2px and 2py, in green) in lines 16–20. You can begin to see here how the various semantic relationships *have to* form a pattern in order to make sense of what is being said here. We need to use links between several semantic relationships to piece together the meaning.

Not all of these relationships are part of the general thematic pattern of atomic theory. The fact that the 2p orbital is represented by a part of the diagram that is colored green is not part of the general conventions of atomic theory. It is an ad hoc convention of this diagram and this dialogue. It is not something that a student probably has to master. It is not part of the language of atomic theory and is not needed in order to talk science. The relationships between the orbitals and their colors in the diagram are part of the thematic pattern of this particular dialogue, but not part of the thematic pattern of the science field. On the other hand, the *shapes* and relative *sizes* of the parts of the diagram *are* part of the conventions of the field, even if their colors are not. This will become relevant at the end of the episode.

A very simple thematic pattern diagram, showing the links between the semantic relationships used so far in the dialogue, is drawn in Figure 1.2. So far, I have not been using formal semantic theory to describe these relationships. I will only do so when we really need it, but I am implicitly using semantic theory as a guide in identifying the relationships as we go through the dialogue. Figure 1.2 also uses only informal labels for the semantic relationships between the terms. If you follow the directions of the arrows, reading the diagram is like reading the possible sentences that use these terms together correctly according to the thematic pattern of the dialogue. With the understanding that the colors of the parts of the blackboard diagram represent the visual appearance of the parts, not colors as such, Figure 1.2 shows the thematic pattern of the science in the dialogue so far.

And so far the teacher has also obtained only right answers to all his questions. This has made it very easy to develop the thematic pattern of the dialogue bit by bit. The class, of course, is actually *reviewing* a thematic pattern that is already familiar. If this were the first time that the pattern was being taught, its parts would probably have been systematically developed one by one, then joined together. Here many of the linkages between semantic relationships have been indirect or assumed. In fact, it can be difficult or impossible to teach a thematic pattern one piece at a time because it often takes a mastery of the whole pattern before any of its parts seem to make sense. It is not just in science that we find concepts that can only be fully understood in terms of one another: Each piece of the puzzle makes sense only if you already have all the other pieces. This is one of the fundamental problems of science teaching, and indeed of teaching and communication generally, that analyzing thematic patterns can help us understand better.

This teacher has had such a smooth time so far that he could actually afford to sacrifice thematic development to the maintenance of discipline at one point (lines 16–20). When every move in the dialogue has meaning both as part of a thematic pattern and as part of an activity structure, it is not always possible to successfully carry out both a thematic development strategy and a social interaction strategy at the same time. Sometimes we must choose between them. In lines 16–20 the teacher chose to reinforce an interaction pattern that requires students to be recognized before they can legitimately answer. We have seen how that choice slowed up thematic development and could have potentially confused students. This sort of conflict arises again in this short episode, so I want to continue the analysis of the thematic pattern and the activity structure of the dialogue together.

TEACHING CONTENT VS. KEEPING CONTROL

Lines 21–24, as part of the activity structure of the episode, pose a Question. It is a long and relatively difficult one. After a brief interruption, the teacher returns to the triadic dialogue pattern with a Nomination:

27	*Teacher:*	Ron?
28	*Ron:*	Boron?
29	*Teacher:*	That would be—That'd have uh . . . *seven* electrons. So
30		you'd have to have one here, one here, one here, one here, one here . . . one
31		here—Who said it? you?

32 *Student:*   Carbon.
33 *Teacher:*   What's—
34 *Students:*   Carbon! Carbon!
35 *Teacher:*   Carbon. Carbon. Here. Six electrons. And they can be
             anywhere within those—confining—orbitals.

After the Nomination, we get an Answer (line 28), but then we do not get the usual positive Evaluation. Instead the teacher makes one of the possible moves that follow a wrong answer. He tries to show Ron why his answer could not be right, contrasting the features of Ron's answer with, by implication, those of the right answer. We'll come back to some of the details later. The teacher's response, however, is now interrupted by first one student (line 32) and then others (line 34) calling out the correct answer.

"Discipline," in the sense of the activity structure rules the teacher wants to see maintained, is now breaking down far more seriously than it did when Janice answered without being called on (line 17). There the teacher forced her to a third, pro forma repeat of her correct answer, just to maintain the rules. Now, not one but several students are calling out the answer. They are also interrupting the teacher. In Janice's case, answering without a Nomination was a possible option in triadic dialogue, and the teacher had already accepted this pattern once in the lesson already. Now, however, there is no option to cover what's happening. It is simply outside the rules.

The teacher's initial response (line 31) is to try to find out who said it first. If he had succeeded, he might have then Nominated that student for a pro forma repeat and gotten the action back into the triadic pattern. He tries to frame a question (line 33), perhaps one to which "Carbon" would be the answer, which might also have restored the interactional pattern. But other students are calling out the answer, and the teacher finally just gives a positive Evaluation (line 35), confirming Carbon as the correct Answer. He then gives a three-part Elaboration on the Answer, restoring the triadic pattern by completing it.

The teacher *could* have worked to restore the pattern when it broke down (lines 32–34). He could have insisted that the students answer one at a time, raise their hands, and not call out answers. He could have gone through a Bid-Nomination-Answer sequence before giving his positive Evaluation. He did this with Janice; he did not do it here. But circumstances were different here. Janice had given a correct answer to an easy question. It came at the end of a series of smooth dialogue triads with right answers. The teacher could afford the luxury of a brief delay in the thematic development, in getting on with the science in the dialogue, in order to restore a certain pattern to the activity structure.

This time, however, the question had been a difficult one. It was long and complex and represented a synthesis and application of much of what preceded it. The teacher had called on one of the brightest students in the class to answer it, hoping for another right answer and another smooth step at this more difficult point in the thematic development. The fact that Ron got the wrong answer likely meant that others in the class were having trouble piecing together the links in the semantic chain needed to get the right one. The teacher did not simply give a negative Evaluation of Ron's answer and call on another of the students who had raised their hands initially. He decided to provide more thematic links, to remind students of other parts of the thematic pattern that they could use to get the answer (lines 29–31).

In a sense his strategy may have worked, because several students do suddenly seem to grasp the answer. But if his thematic strategy worked, the result was to upset his interactional strategy. The appropriate next move in that strategy would have been for him to ask a Follow-up Question to Ron, hoping for a corrected Answer, a positive Evaluation, and so on. But confronted with the correct answer being called out, and seeing that a simple effort would not be enough to get the interaction pattern back on the standard triadic track, he chooses to complete the thematic pattern at the cost of the interactional one. He gets "Carbon" established as the correct answer at a moment when students seem to see why it is correct, that is, when they have fit it into the thematic pattern of the subject. And he ignores the breach of discipline, not even referring to it afterwards.

I would not disagree with this teacher's choice. It probably was much more important here to complete the thematic pattern than to enforce rules for the activity structure. But the situation illustrates the kinds of conflict that frequently arise in the classroom between teaching the science content and enforcing a particular set of rules for classroom interaction. The analysis of classroom dialogue must always take into account both of these two dimensions and how they relate to one another, moment by moment.

An activity structure like triadic dialogue is an important part of the "form" in which the science "content" is taught and learned. As we have seen, the relationships between Preparation, Question, Answer, Evaluation, and Elaboration often must be used to correctly piece together the semantic relations and overall thematic pattern of the science in the dialogue. In that sense they are not just "form," they are part of the content, part of the message. One needs to understand what they contribute to the message in order to extract the purely thematic pattern of the science content. How the science content is presented depends as much on interactional strategies and activity structures as it does on the thematic development strategy and the thematic pattern itself. These two aspects of the dialogue are intimately interdependent in the processes of teaching and learning through language.

What happens next? The teacher has just restored the triadic pattern by following his Evaluation with a series of Elaborations on the Answer, "Carbon." Notice that he can simply say "six electrons" with no other link to *Carbon*, because within the thematic pattern that has been established, we can deduce the semantic relationship, from the fact that carbon is an *element* and therefore "has" an appropriate number of electrons, in this case six. But this is the end of the triadic dialogue pattern in this episode. In the remaining lines, something quite different is happening:

35	*Teacher:*	Carbon. Carbon. Here. Six electrons. And they can be
36		anywhere within those—confining—orbitals. This is
37		also from the notes from before. The term orbital
38		refers to the average *region* transversed [sic] by an
39		electron. Electrons occupy orbitals that may differ
40		in size, shape, or space orientation. That's—that's
41		from the other class, we might as well use it for
42		review. [6 second pause]

In lines 36–37 the teacher makes a statement about the status of the discussion. This kind of talk about talk is called *meta-discourse* (after the term "metamathematics," which applies to mathematical theorems about how mathematics itself works), and so we can call this move a Metastatement. It is characteristic of the beginnings and endings of episodes and is part of the activity structure. It is one of the principal ways in which we control of the flow of activity by signaling boundaries. It also carries the message that what has been discussed is "from before," that is, something discussed more fully in a previous lesson and not new material.

From line 37 to line 40 we find another brief activity type, a Summary. Here this is perhaps best thought of as simply a section of the Review activity. How do we know that it is a summary? Because it highlights the most important term of the episode, *orbital*, by defining it (informally) and then it outlines the progression of the thematic development concerning orbitals. This last point might not be obvious unless you know, from the thematics of the subject of atomic theory, that the progression from *1s* to *2s*, from *2s* to *2p*, and then to *2px* and *2py* (in lines 5–20, in reverse from 21–24, and at the board in the aborted effort of lines 29–31) exactly illustrates pairs of orbitals that differ first in size, then in shape, and finally in spatial orientation.

Lines 40–42 are another Metastatement, marking the end of this Review episode, and naming it as such. Metadiscourse moves in an activity structure are powerful strategies of control. This teacher, having only just "rescued" the triadic structure (lines 35–36), immediately used such a move to signal the end of the discussion, and the end of triadic dialogue. He then shifts into a monologue structure, the Teacher Summary, which returns control and the focus of attention to himself. And finally he ends the Review episode altogether by this second metadiscourse move.

LANGUAGE, SEMANTICS, AND LEARNING

We have just analyzed a short episode of classroom dialogue. In it we found a regular pattern of interaction between teacher and students, within which they could play strategically off one another's moves. We also found that, through moves within this activity structure, the teacher and his students were developing a thematic pattern of relationships among the meanings of key science terms. In this episode we have seen one way of talking science. The thesis of this book is that the mastery of a specialized subject like science is in large part mastery of its specialized ways of using language.

What makes the language of science distinctive is primarily, but not exclusively, its *semantics*: the specific relationships of scientific meanings to one another, and how those relationships are assembled into thematic patterns. The work of assembling semantic relationships into larger patterns is done partly through grammar, partly through rhetorical structures and figures of speech, and partly through the moves of an activity structure.

The language of science has evolved certain grammatical preferences, especially in writing, but also in formal speech (including that of teachers). There is a lot of use of the passive voice, of abstract nouns in place of verbs, of verbs of abstract relation (e.g., *be, have, represent*) in place of verbs of material action. It also has its preferred figures of speech, like analogy, and rhetorical patterns (e.g., Thesis-Evidence-Conclusion). It also works through a variety of activity structures, whether triadic dialogue, ordinary question-and-answer, lecture, or summary monologues, or many others. It even has its own special forms of written texts: laboratory notes, reports of experiments, theoretical treatises, and so on. It has, in short, its own ways of organizing and presenting information and meaning, and its own patterns of meaning to present.

There is a lot of science in classroom talk, but most of it requires students to do the work of piecing together the meanings and thematic patterns. Once you have mastered those patterns, reading or listening to science is relatively easy, but before you have done so, when you are still trying to work out the patterns, much of what is said may seem to make very little sense at all. It is surprising how little classroom dialogue is devoted to the exposition of the patterns, to explicitly telling students just what the relationships of key terms are and how those relationships fit together into a larger pattern. Most of the time the patterns are simply there *implicitly*. They are assumed, presupposed, made use of. But rarely are they shown and explained directly.

Students are not taught *how to talk* science: how to put together workable science sentences and paragraphs, how to combine terms and meanings, how to speak, argue, analyze, or write science. It seems to be taken for granted that they will just "catch on" to how to do so, and to the thematic patterns of the topic. When they do, we are proud of them and praise their "understanding" and "comprehension." When they don't catch on, we conclude that they weren't bright enough or didn't try hard enough. But we don't directly teach them how to. We demonstrate to them a set of complex and subtle skills and expect them to figure out how we do it. Is it any wonder that very few succeed? Or that those from social backgrounds where the activity structures, preferred grammar, rhetorical patterns, and figures of speech that they are used to are least like those of science and the classroom do least well? We will look at these questions from a number of perspectives in later chapters.

The difficulty many students have in catching on to the semantic patterns of science is less surprising if you look at a few examples of the subtle language cues they have to go on. Of course, teachers do make meaning relationships explicit when they are first introduced, and occasionally afterwards during a review or summary. But that represents a small fraction of all classroom dialogue. For a far greater proportion of the time, teachers simply *use* the meaning relationships, and the outward signs as to what those relationships are can be quite subtle. It is these pervasive but extremely subtle cues that provide most of a student's opportunities for catching on to the semantics of the subject. The effect is to magnify the advantages of students who are used to language patterns, whether grammatical, rhetorical, or interactional that are close to those of classroom science dialogue. Let's take a few examples from this episode.

Compare, for instance, the wording of two superficially similar, but semantically very different Questions, those in lines 7–8 and lines 21–24:

| What two elements could be represented by such a diagram? | What element is being represented by this configuration? |

Grammatically, the differences are subtle. In one case *element* is singular, in the other case it is plural. In one there is a modal verb ("could"); in the other case, none. These differences are important cues to the differences in meaning between the thematic patterns that lie behind the two questions. Other differences, such as having the progressive verb in one and the simple verb in the other, or using the demonstrative "such a" vs. "this" don't really matter. In the first case the question is about an *orbital*, which *can* represent more than one element. In the second case, it is about a configuration of *electrons [in] orbitals*, which *do* represent one and only one element. The teacher uses the semitechnical term "configuration," but he could just as well have said "this diagram" again, since at the board he had just put in the electrons for Carbon. Then the *only* cues would have been the subtle grammatical ones.

When Ron misses the second question, the teacher tries to show him his mistake by describing some features of his Answer, "Boron," that don't fit the specifications of the question (lines 29–31). He begins by trying to get his own semantics right, switching from "be" to "have" to fit the pattern: *element [has] electrons*. But in both forms, he has used the subjunctive mood ("would"), which is a subtle cue that the answer "Boron" is wrong. Even subtler is the contrastive emphasis on "*seven*." We know that the underlying thematic pattern is that different *elements [have]* different *numbers [of] electrons*. The correct answer, Carbon, is an element with only six electrons, and if you read the full question carefully (lines 21–23), you can count up the number of electrons and see that they total six.

This subtle emphasis on the total number of electrons as being crucial, rather than the more complex sorting out of which electrons are in which orbitals (which is actually unnecessary to get the answer), is probably enough to cue the students in to the correct answer, Carbon. When the teacher does confirm this answer as correct, his Elaboration first points ("Here.") to Carbon on the Periodic Table of the Chemical Elements, a wallchart in front of the classroom, where the number 6 is prominently displayed next to the symbol C for Carbon. Then he emphasizes "Six electrons." As we have noted before, he does not fill in the rest of the sentence. The students are expected to use the thematic pattern to interpret this as "The element Carbon has six electrons."

Most teachers know, I think, that just giving a definition or explanation at the beginning when a new term or principle is first introduced, is not enough. Very few students will be able to use the term or relate it to other terms without having had more experience with it. Very few can guess how a principle is to be applied, just from knowing the formal statement of the principle. That is why there is a great deal of repetition, use of examples, and implicit use of terms and principles across a variety of contexts in good teaching. We know that it is only through and towards the end of this process that students seem to catch on to the semantic patterns of usage of terms and to the larger thematic patterns within which terms and principles are used. Successful students are learning through the *use* of terms and principles in context, by hearing and making sense of the subtle cues that accompany those uses. Those who catch on to the correct thematic patterns first have a much easier time making sense of the rest of what they hear.

In the next chapter we will consider what happens when students try to make sense of what the teacher is saying by fitting it to a thematic pattern that is *not* the one the teacher is using. In that episode, from a different lesson, we can tell what the students' own thematic pattern is because we hear them talking science a lot. In the episode we have just analyzed, and in most classroom dialogue, the students don't get much practice at talking science. This is partly the result of the pattern of triadic dialogue itself. It favors teacher dominance of the dialogue just as surely as the lecture method produces a teacher-dominated mono- logue. At least in triadic dialogue, the students have some small degree of active participation, even if only as followers of the teacher's lead. But lecturing often provides for more explicit teaching of semantic rela- tionships and larger thematic patterns. Triadic dialogue tends to keep the thematics of the science content implicit and effectively hidden from many students despite the best efforts and intentions of a good teacher.

In triadic dialogue and the other principal patterns of classroom learning, students mainly listen to and read the language of science. But they talk very little science and they write less. Just as with learning a foreign language, fluency in science requires practice at speaking, not just listening. It is when we have to put words together and make sense, when we have to formulate questions, argue, reason, and generalize, that we learn the thematics of talking science. If students cannot demon- strate their mastery of science by talking or writing, we can wonder if their test answers and problem solutions truly represent the ability to reason with science. For reasoning, too, is a way of talking oneself through a problem, a way of mobilizing the semantic resources of scientific language (including its diagrams and formulas) to make sense of a situation. In Chapter 4 we will see in more detail how scien- tific "thinking" can be better understood as another example of talking science. This chapter has done quite enough, I think, with one short episode. It's time to look at another classroom, where conflict rather than cooperation is at the root of the dialogue.

EXPLORING FURTHER

The linguistic analysis of classroom talk was pioneered by Sinclair and Coulthard in *Towards an Analysis of Discourse* (1975). Mehan's *Learning Lessons* (1979) describes many basic patterns of classroom talk in detail. Two more recent views of the subject are Cazden's review article ("Classroom Discourse", 1986) and Edwards and Westgate's book *Investigating Classroom Talk* (1986). My own work is also described in *Classroom Communication of Science* (1983b), which gives more detail on some topics, and *Using Language in the Classroom* (1985b), which presents a brief overview. I will suggest some references on the techniques of discourse analysis itself at the end of Chapter 2.

chapter 2
A Lot of Heat and Not Much Light

The most essential element in learning to talk science is mastery of the thematic patterns of each science topic. These patterns of semantic relationships among scientific terms are highly standardized in each field of science: Every science textbook, every science article, and all careful talk about science by the classroom teacher uses the same patterns. But students do not come to the classroom already using these patterns in their speech, and neither do they come *tabula rasa*, with no thematics at all for the discussion of a topic. In fact, in order for teachers to make sense to students, they must make connections between scientific thematics and the ways students already talk about a topic. A large part of the job of science education—and one in which it does not succeed nearly as often as we would like—is to provide students with new ways of talking about scientific topics.

In the classroom, there is always more than one thematic pattern woven into the talk. There is the standard scientific pattern of meaning relations, usually implicit in how the teacher talks, and there are one or more alternative patterns that are voiced by the students. Sometimes these alternative patterns are those of common sense or ordinary language; sometimes they are hybrids of common sense and students' past learning or mislearning of science.

Everything that is said in the classroom must be made sense of according to some thematic pattern. Thematic meaning, the sense or content of what is said, must be fit to some pattern in order for us to be able to restate it in other words or recognize it in another form. Thematic meaning *is* the shared semantic pattern common to all the different ways of saying the same thing. But if there is more than one thematic pattern that talk can be fitted to, then different meanings can be made of it, and those meanings can come into conflict. Everything the teacher says, and everything the students say, can mean one thing to the teacher and another to the students. This actually happens in the episode we are about to analyze.

It is not unusual for students to be confused in science class, to feel that what is being said, especially by the teacher, doesn't make sense. What is being said may not fit any thematic pattern they are used to. Sometimes, when this goes on for a while, a student will ask a question. Usually the question only asks for clarification, to fill in a semantic link in the chain needed to make sense of what's been said. If the teacher accepts the question and answers it, it often happens that another student will also ask a question, and then another, and then another. A new activity pattern begins, one with a structure very unlike that of Triadic Dialogue. Students ask the questions, teachers answer them, and it is teachers who check with students to see if the answers were satisfactory. In this activity structure, students acquire the initiative and the power to control the topic and direction of the dialogue, but they still defer to the teacher for correct answers. The teacher remains in control of the thematics. We will examine this activity type in the next chapter.

But sometimes a student finds, not a gap in the semantic chain, but a contradiction between what has been said and the thematic pattern he or she is trying to fit it to. Then a student may question or challenge what the teacher has said, claiming the initiative and direction of the topic *and* disputing the teacher's thematic pattern. It takes a lot of frustration, and not a little self-confidence, for a student to do this. Perhaps it happens more often silently than out loud, but when it does happen publicly we get a rare glimpse of the differences in thematic patterns that lie behind so many odd-sounding student questions and so much of the miscommunication and confusion that occurs in every classroom.

PLAYING BY ANOTHER SET OF RULES: TEACHER-STUDENT ARGUMENTS

Let's look at the beginning of another short episode. This is a different classroom, with a different teacher. We are not at the beginning of the lesson, but about 23 minutes into the period. The previous 5 minutes were spent discussing what happens to light from the sun when it hits the ground. Following his usual procedure the teacher had formulated this as a written QUESTION on the board for students to copy into their notebooks. The conclusion of the discussion was that the ground absorbs this light and gets hot. The teacher has just written a formal statement of this conclusion on the board (in the form of an ANSWER for their notebooks), then turns to the class and offers it aloud as a Teacher Summary:

1	*Teacher:*	The *ground* is now creating *heat* energy, *from* the light
2		energy. Eric, you have a question?
3	*Eric:*	Yeah, how can it be the ground creates the heat energy,
4		if the *sun* creates the heat energy?
5	*Teacher:*	*Well*, on the *sun*, and *in* the sun, the sun *is* creating a
6		tremendous amount of heat energy. But it's sending most
7		of its energy here as *light*, traveling through space.
8	*Eric:*	But light is *hot*, light is heat.

Eric has had time to read the written statement even before the teacher says it, for the first time, aloud. What the teacher says is phrased rather differently from anything actually said in the previous discussion (which was conducted by the rules of Triadic Dialogue, see Transcript LG-26–NOV). There the students heard that "light energy coming down from the sun" gets "absorbed" by the "surface of the earth" and that this "ground gets hot." The teacher then gives an example: Sand at the beach gets hot. When the teacher concludes the discussion by asking what kind of energy they are talking about, the answers that are called out include both "light" and "heat." He recognizes an answer "solar energy," which gets a positive Evaluation and the Elaboration,"originally," then nominates another student who answers,"heat energy," and gives that answer an unqualified and emphatic "Yeah." He then writes what we hear in lines 1–2 above on the board.

Eric now puts his hand up without any Teacher Question having been asked, so his signal is not a Bid to Answer, as in Triadic Dialogue, but rather a Bid to Speak. Teachers tend to assume that such Bids are Bids to Question in the alternate activity structure of Student Questioning (see Chapter 3), though in fact students Bid to Speak for a number of different purposes. In line 2 the teacher recognizes Eric for a Student Question. Eric does indeed form his words grammatically as a question, but semantically the pattern "how can X be [true], if Y [is true]" is as much an implied disagreement with what has been said as it is a request for clarification. Its status at the moment it is said is at least a combination of these two functions, but retrospectively, looking back from as early as line 8, we can see it as a Student Challenge.

The Challenge is the opening move of still another activity structure pattern: the Teacher-Student Debate. This pattern is less common than simple Student Questioning, and much less common than Triadic Dialogue. We will see examples from other lessons later. In line 8, Eric voices a Student Objection to what the teacher said in lines 5–7. He is no longer *asking*: He is *debating* the teacher, and this continues throughout the episode (see below).

In the Teacher-Student Debate pattern, students take the initiative with a Challenge to something the teacher has recently said. Students and teachers share control of the direction of the dialogue, and they compete for thematic control. We will see shortly how this pattern usually ends. The essence of a Debate is that the students have a different thematic pattern for the topic under discussion than does the teacher: They talk about it differently, using terms in different semantic combinations than the teacher does. This difference flares up into a full-scale Debate when the students also challenge the teacher's authority to simply assert what is right and sustain their objections and alternative thematics through at least a few exchanges with the teacher.

What are the teacher's moves in this structure? Retrospectively, after the Challenge, we can take whatever the teacher had said that got challenged to have been a preliminary move of the Debate, the Teacher Thesis. After the Challenge, we get a Teacher Response to the challenge, usually *defensive* in nature, justifying the thesis or reasserting it in different words. If the student challenger accepts the Response at this point, we don't really have a full-fledged Debate, but the challenger, or another student, may keep things going by offering an Objection, either to the original Thesis or to the Response. Then we are clearly in the midst of a Debate. In this episode, the Teacher Response in lines 5–7 uses a common strategy (Concessive-Adversative) in which the teacher first concedes that the Challenge is partly true, "but . . ." then points out that even so the original Thesis is still correct.

We now have a long series of Student Objections and Teacher Responses:

9   *Teacher:*   No! Some light is not hot at all. When I turned on these
10   flourescent lights today, I haven't roasted yet.
11 *Student:*   The bulb has heat.
12 *[Eric:*   Yeah, but when the bulb is on you get—the bulb gets hot.
13 *[Teacher:*   And essentially—
14   most energy from the sun comes here in the form of light,
15   and *not* heat.
16 *Eric:*   So the ground can't be *creating* heat. Because if the
17   ground wasn't dark, then it wouldn't absorb the light,
18   and the light, is heat, so it's not *creating* it.
19 *Teacher:*   No. Light is *not* heat. The light is light energy.
20 *Eric:*   Yeah, and *heat* is heat energy. [Students laugh]

The teacher Response to the Objection is to *contradict* it flatly. He supports the contradiction by a *counterexample* to what Eric had said in line 8. It is important to notice here that by arguing *against* Eric's Objection, rather than just arguing *for* the original thesis, the teacher has accepted that Eric has a Thesis of his own, that is, that he is offering an alternative, and unacceptable, thematics for light and heat. We will come back in a moment to look at just what that alternative thematics is, but first I want to survey the course of the activity structure of the Debate.

Another student now joins in on Eric's side (line 11), with an Objection to the counterexample (the flourescent lights). Eric picks up on this, making it more formally an Objection (by the phrasing "Yeah, but when . . ."). The teacher (line 13) has tried to interrupt Eric by saying "And essentially, . . ." as a prelude to a Reassertion of the Thesis, but Eric has refused to yield the floor. (Square brackets in the transcript mark lines that are spoken simultaneously.)

Under the rules of this activity structure, the Challenger can always reply to the Teacher, but the teacher's strategy seems to be to count the other student's rejoinder as the Objection and take his own turn next. When Eric has finished, the teacher continues (he does not restart) and does Reassert the original Thesis. A Reassertion is often also a Bid to End the Debate. Teachers generally get the last word in Debates (by virtue of their superior position of power in the classroom), and they have a number of strategies for closing off the Debate (see below).

But Eric does not ratify the Re-assertion as a Bid to End. He goes on to make a Counterargument (lines 16–18). This is still a form of Objection to the original thesis, as we can see by its opening and closing denial of what has become the key part of the thesis at issue (Does the ground create heat or not?). The teacher's Response to his Objection is another contradiction, followed by a Reason to support the contradiction (line 19). But Eric and the class do not take it as a Reason, but as a Tautology, and Eric responds in kind, with an Objection to it that is also a Put-Down of the teacher. At this point the teacher is clearly in danger of losing the Debate altogether. He resorts to another common Bid to End strategy, the Appeal to Authority:

```
21  Teacher:   And if you remember back—to the eighth grade—and you
22             should've learned a rule, and if you didn't it's OK,
23  [          we'll learn it now. You can change energy from one
24  [Eric:                       What was it?
25  Teacher:   form to another, but you can't create or destroy it.
26             Well, I don't know if that's true anymore either. But you
27             can change it, from one form to another. And that
28             actually happens. The ground creates heat energy, from
29             the light, which causes something very interesting.
30             [Turns and writes a Question for student notes on the
31             board]
```

His appeal is to a "rule," in fact, to the principle of Conservation of Energy. His Appeal to Authority is no longer a turn in the dialogue pattern of the Debate; it shifts over to a monologue pattern of Teacher Explanation, though in the larger sense we can consider it to still be part of the overall Debate episode.

Eric cleverly tries to subvert the teacher's strategy by interjecting a Student Question (line 24). This move, if ratified by the teacher, would have retained some measure of initiative for the students, by defining the new activity type not as a teacher monologue, but as Student Questioning dialogue. But the teacher does not in any way acknowledge Eric's question and in fact does not let him complete the question before saying what would have been the Answer to it. So what the teacher says doesn't count as an Answer in a dialogue, but as a continuation of his monologue. He ends the monologue with a Reassertion of the thesis and an Anticipation (line 29) of something that will build on the thesis. He then turns his back to the class and definitively ends the episode by making the next move in a much larger-scale pattern in the Lesson, writing the next topic QUESTION on the blackboard.

THE ROOTS OF CONFUSION: SEMANTIC CONFLICT AND SOCIAL CONFLICT

The Debate in this episode represents a double conflict. On the surface there is the obvious conflict of a pattern of social interaction in the classroom that pits teacher and students against one another. There is conflict in the activity structure of Debate itself and conflict between two opposed thematic systems, which give the Debate its impetus. These two conflicts, one interactional and the other thematic, reflect deeper conflicts that are present in less obvious ways in the classroom at all times. One of these is the conflict between teachers and students: between adults who wield authority and "children" who are subjected to that authority. The other is the confict between our commonsense ways of talking about topics and the specialized thematic patterns of science. First, I want to examine the thematic conflict in this episode; then we will look at some of the wider social conflicts that lie behind what is happening.

In this episode, as often in the science classroom, there is not one thematic pattern but two. As we saw in the last chapter, the way in which science is mainly taught today leaves these patterns *implicit* most of the time, so that the differences between the patterns rarely get talked about directly. This makes miscommunication more common and misunderstandings harder to straighten out. Few teachers pay sufficient attention to how students talk about a topic, or to the semantics of their usage of terms. Triadic Dialogue, the most common pattern of interaction in the classroom, also makes it difficult for teachers to hear how students talk about a topic. Most of what students say tends to be fit into the thematic pattern set up by the teacher's Preparation and Question moves, and students have little opportunity to make semantic connections in their own terms. As a result, teachers just don't hear their students' thematics very much.

Even when we do get to hear how students talk about a subject in their own terms, it can be very difficult to set aside our own thematic pattern and hear what they have to say on their own terms. To do a proper thematic analysis of this episode, we will have to construct two sets of semantic relations among what sound like the same terms. They may be the same *words*, but when they are used with different semantic relations to other terms, they represent very different meanings. As we will see, what "light" means for the teacher is not necessarily the same as what it means for the students.

The Semantics of the Debate

Look back to the first part of the Debate. In lines 1–2, the teacher makes connections among the terms *ground, heat energy,* and *light energy*:

ground   [creates]   heat energy   [from]   light energy

But there is also a subtler relation here. In line 1 he stresses *heat* in the phrase "heat energy, and he uses both the expressions "light energy" and "heat energy." The use of *contrastive stress* in line 1 and the implicit contrast between the two expressions invokes the standard thematic pattern of semantic relationships among the *three* terms *light, heat,* and *energy*. This pattern is not explicit here or anywhere in the episode, though it is crucial to it:

light   [is example of]   energy

heat   [is example of]   energy

These two semantic relationships are linked through the common term, *energy*. Together they tell us that that light and heat are two different forms of energy. In the technical language of semantics, *light* and *heat* are *hyponyms* of *energy*, and therefore "cohyponyms" of each other. This is the same semantic relationship we saw in the previous episode where *hydrogen* and *helium* were both hyponyms of *element*; that is, they are two different forms or kinds of chemical element.

With this pattern in mind, we can now interpret the Thesis in line 1. The teacher is saying that one form of energy is "created from" another. The meaning is that the light form of energy is transformed into the heat form of energy, by the action of the ground. But that is not exactly what the teacher said, of course. It is not obvious, unless you know that what he says must fit the thematic pattern relating *light* and *heat* to *energy*, that CREATES FROM represents a meaning relationship that might be better expressed as CONVERTS or TRANSFORMS. Knowing that, we can also see that the role of the *ground* is not that of Creator of *heat*, but simply that of an Agent in the transformation of light energy into heat energy. This is what the teacher *meant* by what he *said*, fitting it to the standard scientific thematics of light and heat. But what he *said* could be taken to mean other things if it was fitted to other thematic patterns, other ways of talking about light and heat that assume different semantic relationships among these terms.

Let's turn now to what the students say. In lines 3–4 Eric repeats part of the what the teacher has said, and makes a different contrast. He places contrastive emphasis on "*sun*" as opposed to "*ground.*" The terms he uses are *ground, heat energy,* and *sun*. He makes two sets of semantic connections among them:

> ground   [NOT create]   heat energy
>
> sun   [DOES create]   heat energy

I have substituted a NOT for the ? of what is said, since it is pretty clear from his whole subsequent argument that he is denying the truth of this relation.

Notice the differences from the teacher's pattern. There is no evidence that "heat energy" is being used as anything other than a synonym for "heat" itself. Eric never uses the term "light energy" and never indicates that he is using "heat energy" to mean heat-as-one-kind-of-energy. He has also dropped the FROM part of the semantic relationship term CREATE FROM. For Eric, so far as we can tell here, the sun *is* the Creator of heat energy, not just a middleman in the transformation of one form of energy into another. What is at stake for Eric is that is it the *sun,* and not the ground, which has the Creator role in the semantic pattern.

The semantics of the term *create* is very different in Eric's usage from the teacher's usage. For this reason it is actually necessary to treat CREATE as a semantic term in its own right, and not just as a link between other terms. Terms or phrases (e.g. *heat energy*) which must be treated this way, I will call *thematic items* from now on. So for Eric either the *ground* or the *sun* is the creator in a process that CREATES a result, *heat energy,* while for the teacher, the *ground* is only an agent in a process that CONVERTS a source, *light* [as a form of] *energy,* into a product, *heat* [as a form of] *energy.* Even though both use the *words* "heat," "energy," and "create" in ways that sound alike, what they mean by these words is very different. The meaning depends on the thematic pattern to which the words are fitted. (From here on I will use SMALL CAPITALS for meanings of thematic items, when I need to distinguish them from the particular words, in quotes or italics, used to represent them in a particular sentence.)

This is actually a very general and important point. Words do not necessarily "have" meanings in themselves. A word in isolation has only a "meaning potential," a range of possible uses to mean various things. What it actually means as part of a sentence or paragraph depends on which thematic item in some particular thematic pattern it is being used to express.

The meanings of sentences are not made up out of the meanings of words. We must arrive at both simultaneously by fitting words and their semantic relations within the sentence to some thematic pattern and the relations among its thematic items. And where do we find the thematic patterns? They are part of the common ways of speaking about a subject that we have heard, read, and used countless times in speech and in writing. It is only when we meet an unfamiliar pattern that we have trouble making sense of the sentences. Then we need to practice that pattern in the context of more familiar ones until we have mastered its use. In this case, of course, this is what I mean by learning to talk science. But the principle applies to all learning that involves language in speaking, reading, or reasoning about any subject.

Thematic patterns as complex as the ones we have just analyzed (and they are simple as such patterns go) are best expressed in the form of diagrams that can show the interconnected semantic relationships among several terms or thematic items. At the end of this chapter we will compare simplified diagrams of the thematic patterns of teacher and students in this Debate. Even the simplest diagram that makes use of formal semantic analysis takes some explaining, so I want to leave this until later. If you are curious now, have a look ahead at Figures 2.1 and 2.2. You will see that they resemble Figure 1.2 from the last chapter, which uses only informal substitutes for labeling semantic relationships. Locate the terms *ground, sun, create, heat, light,* and *energy,* and notice how they are differently joined to the terms around them in the two diagrams. The thematic *patterns* are different.

Let's continue to compare the way the teacher and the students speak differently about light and heat. In lines 5–7 we get the teacher's Response to the initial Challenge. He agrees with part of the Challenge's contention: that the sun is creating heat energy. Here he seems to have adopted the students' semantics for *create.* This term is no longer being used in any obvious way to mean CONVERT. But he adds a qualification to his agreement: the *location* where this creating is going on, "on the *sun,*" that is, not on the earth or ground that he is speaking about in the Thesis. He continues by saying that "here," that is, on the earth or ground, the energy from the sun is in the form of light. He actually says, ". . .its energy here as *light,*" where the word "as" expresses the implicit semantic relation of hyponymy, that is, that *light* [is an example of] *energy.* In terms of his own thematic system, he is just clarifying a difference of *location.* But if heard in terms of the students' thematics, he is both reinforcing their semantics of *create* and accepting a contrast

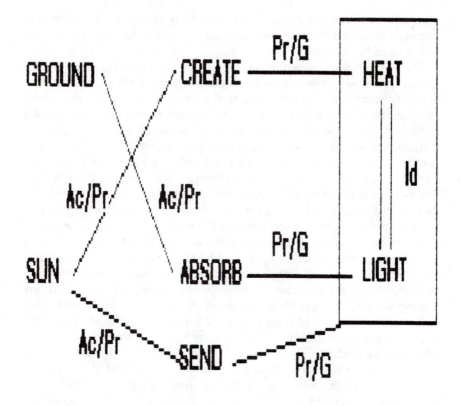

Ac/Pr = Actor, Agent: Process
Pr/G = Process : Goal
Id = Identification

Figure 2.1. Student Thematic Pattern

between *sun* and *ground*. What does not make sense from the students'
viewpoint is his contrastive emphasis on the word *"light."*

Eric objects to the teacher's Response by saying that light is hot,
which for him means that light is heat: There is no point in contrasting
them with each other. Eric has made a subtle semantic generalization.
From *light* [has quality] *hot*, he gets to *light* [is the same as] *heat*. This is
a very different relationship between light and heat than the teacher, or
the language of physics, constructs (i.e., that they are two different
forms of energy). The main point of the teacher's thesis, which is a key

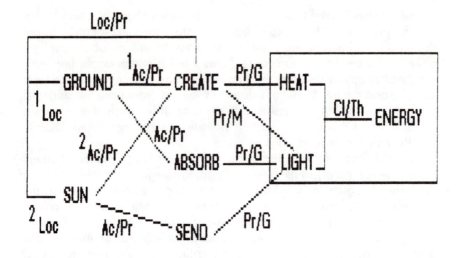

Ac/Pr = Actor, Agent : Process
Pr/G = Process : Goal
Pr/M = Process : Means, material
Loc/Pr = Location : Process
Cl/Th = Classifer : Thing

Figure 2.2. Teacher Thematic Pattern

point in the whole Lesson, concerns the conversion of light into heat. If they are the same, this would make no sense. So the teacher has to object to the equation of light and heat (line 9).

He follows up his contradiction of Eric's equation of light and heat with a counterexample: Flourescent light is not hot. The previous discussion, just before the Debate, has established pretty firmly for the students that sunlight is hot. Flourescent light is meant to contrast with sunlight and prove that not all light is hot, so light and heat cannot be the same thing. But the teacher has spoken not of light in the abstract here (lines 9–10), but of "these flourescent lights," for which the semantics is ambiguous. He could be speaking of the light, or of the bulbs that produce it. Another student therefore objects to the counterexample, maintaining that the flourescent bulbs do get hot (line 11), and this is picked up by Eric as an Objection.

The teacher knows that this is a digression which is not going to win him the argument. He would need to go into a long explanation about flourescent lights, and he wants to get back to talking about sunlight anyway. So we get his Response (lines 14–15) which again implicitly uses the hyponymy relation, this time worded as "energy . . . in the form of light, and *not* heat." But this doesn't seem relevant from the students' point of view. What is at issue for them is not how much energy comes as light or as heat, but whether the sun creates that HEAT-LIGHT-ENERGY or the ground does.

This is in fact the theme that Eric pursues in his long Counterargument (lines 16–18). Purely in its outward form, this argument makes more in the way of logical connections than anything the teacher says in the whole episode. Eric is *reasoning* with the language available to him, and using the form of a counterfactual argument (*reductio ad absurdum*), which is very sophisticated reasoning. He builds on the previous discussion about the ground absorbing light. It is not easy to follow Eric's reasoning, partly because he introduces an element that is extraneous from the point of view of the standard thematics (that the ground is dark), and partly because he uses a relationship from his own thematics that contradicts the standard view (that light is heat). He needs the bit about the ground being dark to establish a thematic connection with *absorb*. The previous discussion reviewed the fact that dark surfaces absorb more light from the sun than light ones do. The ground was cited as dark compared to the oceans. For Eric, since we know the ground is dark, we know it *absorbs light*. Since *light is heat*, we know that the ground is *absorbing* this LIGHT-HEAT-ENERGY, not creating it. Q.E.D.

The teacher hears the link in the chain that does not agree with scientific thematics, and contradicts it: "No. Light is *not* heat." Well, if it is not heat, then what is it? "The light is light energy." What does this sentence mean in his thematic system? What sense does it make to him? A paraphrase might be: "Sunlight is energy in the form of light. And not energy in the form of heat, which is a quite different form of energy." But the students again make sense of this by fitting it to their own thematic pattern. For them it is just a tautology, just a way of saying LIGHT-HEAT-ENERGY is LIGHT-HEAT-ENERGY. That sounds like an insult to their intelligence. Eric replies to nonsense with nonsense, to an insult with an insult (line 20): "Yeah, and *heat* is heat energy." Notice that for Eric this does *not* mean that heat is a form of energy different from light. It is just the same tautology twisted to his advantage rather than the teacher's.

At this point there is complete misunderstanding between teacher and students. Their semantic conflict over the thematics of light and heat has become a power conflict, a confrontation between assertions and egos. In wider social terms, the power conflict between those who assert the thematics of science and those who assert the thematics of common sense has reappeared in microcosm here. We will come back to these deeper implications of semantic conflict at the end of the chapter. For now we need only understand why it makes sense for the teacher to use an Appeal to Authority to put an end to the Debate. In many ways the Debate is as much about power and authority as it is about light and heat. What gets said in this concluding monologue?

The teacher shifts back to his original semantics for *create* as meaning CONVERT. The word he uses (lines 23 and 27) is *change*. And he makes it explicit that he means change of energy from one form to another. In the end, however, he simply reasserts the original Thesis, unchanged in its wording (lines 28–29). Having the last word here means keeping the original Thesis, which is already written (in stone) on the board. The students are left to unravel the actual contradiction between line 25 ("you can't create . . . it [energy]") and line 28 ("the ground creates heat energy") to see that "create . . . from" really means "change it [energy] from one form to another." And they still need to understand light and heat as different forms of energy. I doubt that very many students will have been able to solve this puzzle unless they already understood the teacher's Answer from the start.

Readers of this dialogue can usually make sense of either the teacher's viewpoint or the students', but not often of both. It is hard to formulate the exact differences between their views. But when you use thematic analysis, you can see the details of the misunderstanding from line to line. The most useful way to picture these differences is to compare the thematic pattern diagrams for the two sides in the Debate (Figures 2.1 and 2.2). Since we are now graduating from informal diagrams (like Figure 1.2 in Chapter 1), to diagrams that use formal semantic labels for relationships, I need to explain how to read a thematic diagram and interpret these labels.

Using Thematic Pattern Diagrams

Look first at Figure 2.1, which represents the simpler thematic pattern of the students. Ignore for the moment the labels on the lines joining the key thematic terms. These labels replace the arrows in informal diagrams like Figure 1.2. We could read the informal diagrams by following the arrows and supplying acceptable grammatical forms for the semantic relationship terms. Now those terms (like CREATE) are thematic items in their own right, and the labels will tell us what semantic relations we need to express grammatically to make complete phrases or clauses in reading the diagram.

Locate the term CREATE at the top center of the diagram. It has two lines joining it to other terms: one to SUN, and another to HEAT. We know from the dialogue that the thematic connection of these three terms for the students is represented by clauses like "if the sun creates the heat energy" (line 4; notice that this does not have to be a complete sentence, just a grammatical clause). The term GROUND is *not* connected to CREATE, because for the students the ground doesn't do any creating. We could, of course, put in a line with a NOT on it between these two (cf. line 16), but that would just clutter up the diagram here. Eric in effect only "quotes" the teacher's Thesis in line 3; it is not part of his own thematics. GROUND is connected to ABSORB, and ABSORB in turn to LIGHT. These connections lie behind lines 16–18, which tell us that for Eric the ground absorbs the light (this is true in the teacher's diagram as well). The diagram is not complete, of course. I have left out the connection of GROUND to DARK, and the whole business of the flourescent bulbs. What is shown is as much of the diagram as is needed to see the key differences from the teacher's thematics that are relevant to the Debate.

The labels on the lines that link these terms, or *thematic items*, stand for semantic relationships. Semantic relationships are more general and abstract than grammatical relationships, but in many ways similar. There is no complete semantic theory yet for English, but many of the important semantic relationships have been characterized by Michael A. K. Halliday (1985a) in his writings on functional grammar. Functional grammar is very different from Chomsky's formal grammar or traditional grammar. It describes every possible grammatical way of saying something in English in terms of the uses or functions of each grammatical pattern in expressing different kinds of meanings, that is, different semantic relationships.

The same semantic relationship can be expressed in different ways grammatically. For example we can say "the ground is dark" or "the dark ground" or "the ground, which is dark" or "as dark as the ground" and so on. Each of these adds a little semantic nuance of its own, but all express the relationship: GROUND [has quality] DARK. Most semantic relationships connect two terms, so if we draw a line between them in our diagram, we can label the line with abbreviations, borrowed from Halliday's terminology, for the kind of grammatical relationship that usually expresses their semantic relationship. The abbreviation usually consists of the semantic role of the first term, a "slash" mark (/), and that of the second term. These are listed in a key below each diagram.

For example, CREATE is linked to HEAT by a line labeled Pr/G. The key explains this as "Process:Goal." The process is CREATING; the

"Goal" of this process is Halliday's word for what gets created, namely HEAT. The usual grammatical relationship of Process to Goal is that of a transitive verb to the object of that verb. We can thus read:

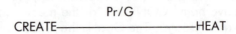

as "creating is a process that makes heat." On the other side of CREATE is a line labeled "Ac/Pr" that connects it to SUN. This stands for the relationship between the Actor or Agent that does the Process and the Process itself. CREATE is still the Process; SUN is the Actor, or "Creator"—and of course HEAT is what gets created. There are many ways to express this grammatically: "the sun creates heat" or "the sun is creating the heat energy" or "the heat is created by the sun."

We do not need arrows now to tell us that "the heat creates the sun" is *not* implied by the diagram. The labels tell us which is the Actor (SUN) and which is the Goal or result (HEAT). Sometimes the same term can be Actor for two different processes. Here SUN is Actor for SEND as well as for CREATE. And, of course, the Goal or result of one process can be the Actor in another process, and so on. This is how simple semantic relationships get linked together into complex thematic patterns.

There is one more important point about the diagrams before we go on to compare Figure 2.1 with Figure 2.2. The thematic items of a diagram are represented, of course, by words. But actually they are not words, they are the meanings that are expressed through the words. What I have loosely called "terms" so far are more like abstract "concepts," in that each can be expressed by many different words. For example, for the students, so far as we can tell, there is just one "concept" (which I label as HEAT in the diagram) that can be expressed by the word "heat" (lines 8, 16–18) or by the phrase "heat energy" (lines 3–4, 20). (For the students in this dialogue there is no evidence for a *separate* meaning for the word "energy," and so there is no separate thematic item ENERGY in their diagram.) The terms of a thematic pattern diagram should be called thematic items, or thematic terms, to distinguish them from words as such. In the last section of this book I will discuss more fully the relationships between words and meanings in a thematic analysis (see also Lemke 1983a).

Look finally at Figure 2.2. This is a diagram representing the teacher's way of talking about the topic. To make the comparison to Figure 2.1 more obvious I have used CREATE again as the thematic item at the top center. Notice, however, that it has *three* lines leading off from it. One to the Goal or result of the CREATING, namely HEAT; a second back to the Actor or Agent of this process for the teacher, the GROUND; and now a third line to the Means or Material *from* which the heat is created: LIGHT. This is a different semantics for CREATE than in the students' diagram. It is the reason why we have sometimes used the alternative name CONVERT for the meaning the teacher expresses by the word "create." The Goal is the *product* of the converting process; the Means is the *source*. And the GROUND is more like an Agent than a Creator.

There are two other major differences between the teacher's and the students' ways of talking science during this Debate. The teacher makes a distinction (lines 5–7) in the *location* of the CREATING. In the first place (superscript 1), the GROUND does the creating *on* the ground; in the second place (superscript 2), the SUN does it *on* (or *in*) the sun. The second major difference is much more important; in fact it is crucial to the entire misunderstanding between teacher and students. What *is* the relationship between LIGHT and HEAT? In Figure 2.1, for the students, "light is heat," and there is a relationship of Identification between them. Each is identified with the other. But in Figure 2.2, for the teacher, "light energy" and "heat energy" are two different *kinds* of ENERGY. The formal semantic relationship here is very common in science: "light" and "heat" are Classifiers of ENERGY (which is called simply the Thing classified). This produces the "hyponym" relation (technically it is HEAT—ENERGY that is the hyponym of ENERGY).

Now read the lines of the dialogue and trace them out on each of the two diagrams. See what the students must have made of lines 3–5, how they would have interpreted "heat energy" sent here "as light" as meaning heat and light were the same. Hear Eric's Counterargument as it would be traced out on the student thematic diagram, and then as it must have sounded to the teacher on his. Look finally at lines 19–20 in which the dialogue breaks down completely, to see how "the light is light energy" comes across to the students simply as LIGHT [is] LIGHT, a tautology, while for the teacher it was LIGHT [is a kind of] ENERGY (i.e., an important Classifier : Thing relationship).

Whether you think drawing the diagrams themselves is worth the effort or not, I hope you have seen the importance of the principles behind thematic analysis. Just as they are the key to misunderstanding and confusion, to disagreement and conflict, they can also be the basis for seeing the way to clarification and mutual understanding, even if in the end some disagreements will always remain. The diagrams themselves become essential when the thematic patterns get even more complex, and when the same meanings are expressed in very different words and different grammatical forms as well. I want to conclude this chapter by returning to the wider issues of social conflict that lie behind the patterns of classroom arguments and debates like this one.

AVOIDING EASY ANSWERS: CONFLICT AND VALUES

The pattern of the Teacher-Student Debate is not unique to this lesson. In other lessons as well, it begins with a Student Challenge that tends to contradict something the teacher has said. For example, in a geology lesson on evidence for movement of the earth's crust in prehistoric times, another teacher has just ended a discussion of why fossils of ocean-living organisms are found today in rock that lies on the tops of mountains. His conclusion is that the crust of the earth has been "up-lifted" by geological forces in the past. The Challenge is initiated by a student who says: "Couldn't the water go down?" Again in the form of a question, this Challenge takes the opposite point of view from a conclusion already stated and written on the board by the teacher.

We will study this episode in more detail in Chapter 5 when we talk about the fine line in many science classes between authoritative and authoritarian claims on behalf of established scientific views (see Transcript SC-20-MAR). Several students share the job of sustaining an alternative view to that put forward by the teacher, until one rather bluntly and skeptically asks: "How can you prove that that's a *fact?*" The teacher at this point makes an Appeal to Authority, naming a scientific principle in geology known as Uniformitarianism, and the Authority for it, James Hutton, one of the founders of modern geology. The Debate ends after this and reverts to triadic dialogue until the end of the episode.

In yet another classroom, a biology teacher discussing the limits to the physical size of a single cell has offered an argument that oversimplified the issue (Transcript JR-29-OCT). He has said that as the cell gets larger it will be harder for enough food to reach the center of the cell from the outside. A bright student Challenges this obliquely, "[but]. . . if it's bigger, then more food should be able to get in." The argument turns on whether a big cell is any different from a small one, if everything increases in the same proportion. The teacher does appeal to an authoritative principle, saying, "The thing that turns up here—I didn't want to bring it up because it gets into geometry . . . but . . .." and he goes on to state the principle of geometric scaling to back up his point.

In this case the strategy doesn't succeed in ending the Debate, and finally the teacher simply quashes the Debate by an appeal to his own authority, with the metastatement: "Well, let's not get into a whole type of cell theory." He then moves directly into a Teacher Explanation couched as an Answer to a Student Question which itself interrupted the Debate a short while before. The teacher manages to prolong a monologue long enough to offer a summary of the lesson so far, and write part of this on the board. But as soon as he is done the Debate resumes, ended again at the teacher's insistence: "Uh.. you're getting a little too picky." He then calls on a student not in the Debate who asks an ordinary Student Question. The students give up on the Debate after that.

Teachers do usually have the last word in these Debates, but few of them are deliberately authoritarian in the way they handle the disagreements. In some cases, the students just will not give in and simply invent more and more far-fetched objections. This situation usually ends by an appeal to the teacher's authority to control the topic of discussion. In other cases the teacher ends by appealing to an authoritative scientific principle (e.g., the Conservation of Energy, the Principle of Uniformitarianism, the geometry of scaling, etc.) which is relevant to the thematics of the debate. But the teacher may or may not explain the principle and its application to the issue in dispute. It may simply be used to overwhelm student objections. Analysis of Debate episodes generally shows that the authority of the teacher in the classroom and the authority of science to dictate the thematic pattern of a topic get inextricably linked in these episodes (see Chapters 3 and 5).

This is no accident. It is one of the pointers that should direct our attention to the larger social issues behind these Debates. I do not mean the scientific disagreements, but the twin social conflicts I have referred to before. One is the conflict between teachers (and adults generally), on the one hand, and students (and children generally) on the other. The second is the conflict between the specialized, especially technical and scientific, thematics of "experts" and the commonsense opinions of people in general.

Power, Prestige, and Authority in Science

Teachers and students have grossly unequal power in the classroom. The teacher is the representative of adult authority, and backed up, at least in theory, by the power of force as well as by the traditions of schools. That difference in power extends to control of the dialogue itself, both its form and its content, that is, both the activity structure and the thematics. The teacher has the power to decide what will and will not be talked about, who has the right to speak at any given time, and what is the "correct" way to behave and to talk about the subject.

This power difference biases the tenor of the dialogue away from a free discussion of issues between equals. Teachers do not *have to* explain their reasons or justify their decisions to students. They do not have to try as hard to understand the students' point of view on a subject as they would, say, their principal's. And students, too, are encouraged to accept the authority of the teacher, not just in matters of classroom organization and activity, but in matters of science as well.

Teachers, themselves, are not the ultimate educational authorities, and they often close off a discussion or debate prematurely in order to complete on time a syllabus that someone else requires them to. Classroom dialogue directly displays the power relations within which it is embedded, and those power relations derive from the wider social system—they are not features of classrooms or schools as such.

Just as students and teachers have unequal power, commonsense thematics and scientific thematics have unequal prestige in classroom dialogue. Not just in the Debates, but pervasively in science classrooms (see Chapter 5), students are encouraged to mistrust common sense and to accept the superiority of scientific thematics. This too is part of a larger social pattern: the acceptance of "expert views" on policy by people who do not understand the basis of those views.

A growing "technocracy" in the 20th century tries to control policy decisions by selective appeal to "experts," thereby neatly bypassing inconvenient disagreements about basic values. Science education, I believe, is unwittingly abetting this trend. It does so by successfully convincing most students that the experts, who talk science, are "smarter" than they are—and by failing, at the same time, to actually teach most students how to talk science. This encourages a rule of "experts," an alienation from science, a sense of inferiority, and ultimately a fear and hatred of this powerful "unknown." By its silence on questions of social values, science education also helps foster the misconception of science as value-free or value-neutral on which technocrats rely.

Science and Social Values

Science does not stand outside the system of social values. Like all meaningful human activity, it depends on socially shared habits, practices, and resources that each individual can mobilize only because he or she is a member of a community with a history and a system of basic values. With the language, activity structures, and thematic patterns we learn come values and a history of interests. We follow and further develop particular actional and thematic patterns in our community because we value them, and we value them because historically they have been of benefit to somebody.

Science, no more and no less than any other human activity, has had the history it has because people made choices to explore some areas rather than others, to invest in some kinds of research, to encourge some sorts of questions to be asked, some fields to be considered more important than others. Science, through its history, embodies value-choices and value systems. And it reflects the interests and power of those groups that have been in a position to influence, however indirectly, its history and course of development.

It wouldn't be necessary to say all this if we were not still burdened with the myth of the total objectivity and neutrality of scientific work with regard to all value questions. While science education does not actively promote that myth very much any more, neither does it do very much to give students a basis for countering it. The history of science is merely a footnote to the science curriculum, the lives and choices of scientists are rarely discussed, the actual nature of contemporary scientific work in government, corporations, and research institutes is hardly mentioned. There is very little concern for learning to talk science as part of the discussion of controversial issues, whether it's nuclear power and weapons, genetic engineering, or the control of sexually-transmitted diseases. Science is cut off from questions of social values by a curriculum that embodies an outdated view of what science is.

Education is always about values. What we choose to teach and what we emphasize always represents a choice based on certain values, beneficial to certain interests. How we pose the relationship between school knowledge and common sense, between talking science and talking in other ways about a topic, embodies certain values and prejudices. In the curriculum, we elevate one view of the nature of science over all others, just as we push one view of American history, one language (English) and its literature, and the accomplishments in all fields of people who happened to be, not by chance, mainly white, mainly male, and mainly of northern European descent. Science education is certainly not exempt historically from any of this.

Value Judgments and Value Conflicts

Let's take just one example close to home. I have called the student who Challenges the teacher in the Debate on light and heat "Eric." This is the result of finding more willingness on the part of many people, including science teachers, to give this student's arguments the benefit of the doubt when the student was called Eric, by a typographical error, than when she was called "Erin" in the original transcripts.

We have already seen that without an appreciation of the internal logic of the student's alternate thematics of the subject, it can be hard to follow her point of view (especially the Counterargument, lines 16–18). Many science teachers—and others with science backgrounds—in fact dismiss the Counterargument as "confused" or "unintelligible," having only the appearance of logic, but otherwise just being a sort of "rambling" by the student. It was hard to avoid the impression that for some readers this is just what would be expected of a working-class (Irish Catholic) teenage girl trying to argue with a trained (middle-aged, Jewish) science teacher. I found it was easier to get people to try to take her arguments seriously when they became Eric's arguments.

After having analyzed those arguments in far more detail than I have presented here, I find them quite impressive compared to what is typical under similar circumstances among her peers. Erin would be a promising candidate for a future scientist. But would she be as likely to be recognized as promising by a teacher who did not make the special efforts needed to understand her way of explaining things? And would the teacher be more likely to make that effort if the student in question were male, white, middle-class, and of a higher-status ethnic group?

I am not accusing teachers of conscious prejudice, though I am sure that some teachers do have such prejudices. I am saying that because students can be expected to "talk science" in nonstandard ways, with a different thematic pattern than the teacher's, an *effort* is needed to make proper sense of many students' points. If a teacher is more likely to stop and make that effort for some kinds of students than others, that in itself is enough to effectively discriminate against many students. Of course, students who are not native speakers of English, or of Standard Dialect, or who come from homes where arguments are differently organized in speaking, will be even less likely to talk science in a way that the teacher will recognize as making an unconventional kind of sense.

Discrimination does not have to be built on prejudice when so much of what impresses in the classroom is one very special way of using language among all the ways people in our community talk. It would take an almost superhuman teacher to be able to hear every kind of sense that students make. Can we blame a merely human teacher for being more likely to understand what sounds more familiar? Can we teach teachers more about what to listen for in the unfamiliar? We will have to return to this question later in the book.

Teachers clearly make value judgments about the worth of what students say in class. And they make those judgments for the most part in line with the dominant views and values of their own community. Whether we consider the content of the science curriculum or the way in which teachers and students communicate with one another in the classroom, we are concerned with questions of values. The conflicts between teachers and students over proper behavior and proper thematics are also value conflicts. Adults and teenagers or younger children have different values about conduct and freedom, different notions of proper discipline and behavior. They have different priorities as to what is more important when those values conflict. They also attach different values to the thematics of science vs. that of common sense, and to one topic in the curriculum vs. others.

These value conflicts are not peculiar to the classroom. They are ones which teachers and students for the most part bring to the classroom from outside school. They are the value conflicts in our society between older and younger; the middle-class and the poor; male and female; white and black; one ethnic tradition and another. Those value conflicts are most often the historical result of conflicts of interests between these groups, and differences in power between them. No analysis of what happens in a science classroom can be credible if it pretends that teachers and students talk science in ways isolated from wider social values and conflicts. Teachers know this better than anyone.

In the next chapter I want to look more carefully at the patterns of social interaction in the classroom and at how teachers and students work at controlling each other's behavior. We will look again at the activity structures within which students and teachers talk science, and return to questions of power and social values.

EXPLORING FURTHER

There are many approaches to analyzing classroom discourse and written text. The methods of interaction analysis and thematic analysis used in this book are similar to other techniques that call themselves "pragmatic" (or "speech act") analysis and "semantic" analysis, respectively. Good introductory surveys of techniques can be found in Coulthard's *Introduction to Discourse Analysis* (1977), Brown and Yule (1983) and Stubbs (1983), both called *Discourse Analysis*, and Gumperz' insightful book *Discourse Strategies* (1984).

The approaches that I myself have found most useful are described in Halliday and Hasan's *Language, Context, and Text* (1985).

These are all general-purpose books; more specialized references will be given after Chapters 3 and 4.

chapter 3

"If You Weren't Whispering to Scott, . . ."

In this chapter we will look at some of the common activity types of the science classroom, analyze the strategies teachers and students use to influence one another's behavior, and examine the values and interests that determine classroom rules. Let's begin by surveying some of the most important of the recurring activity structures of the classroom lesson.

WRITTEN AND UNWRITTEN RULES OF CLASSROOM BEHAVIOR

In Chapters 1 and 2 we have already seen examples of two predictable patterns of behavior in the classroom: Triadic Dialogue and Teacher-Student Debate. Triadic Dialogue is an activity structure: a sequence of predictable options for who will say or do what sort of thing next. It does not in itself have a particular classroom function, except to engage students in dialogue. It can be used, as we saw in Chapter 1, for the purpose of a Review, but it can also be used to discuss new topics, to go over the homework, and even to work step-by-step through the solution of a problem. Because it is used in all these ways, it is by far the single most common activity structure in many classrooms. Teacher-Student Debate, on the other hand (see Chapter 2 and below), is much less common. It also has a fairly definite sequential structure, but it serves a particular purpose or function: arguing disputed points of the subject-matter. Like Review, or Going Over Homework, it is a *functional* category of classroom activities, while Triadic Dialogue is a purely *structural* one.

The "unwritten rules" of classroom behavior can be described in these two ways: by activity *structures* that tell us what sequences of actions are expected to happen in particular contexts, and by the *functions* that these patterns perform in the classroom.

Categories like Dialogue and Monologue are only "structural"; they only tell us the sort of action sequences that may occur, but not their purpose or function. These activity structure patterns can be used for many different functions in the classroom. Other than Triadic Dialogue, the most important structure patterns are: Teacher Monologues, Exter-

nal Text Dialogue, Teacher-Student Duolog, Seatwork, Groupwork, and Boardwork. All the Activity Types of the Classroom are listed and briefly described in Appendix A of this book. Most of them have specific functions as well as their own activity patterns; for example, Demonstrations, Student Questioning Dialogue, Teacher Summaries and Explanations, and Teacher-Student Debates. A few are purely "functional" types and may be accomplished through several alternative possible activity structures. For example, a Review may be accomplished through Triadic Dialogue, Teacher Monologue, or even Student Questioning or Seatwork. Going Over Homework can also be done in various ways.

There is usually only one activity type going on in the classroom at any given time. Transitions from one to another are generally indicated by long pauses, signal words like "O.K." and "Now," or by meta-discourse (see Chapter 1). *This means that the structure of the Lesson as a whole is basically episodic.* It is usually possible to define distinct Episodes of one or two up to 15 or 20 minutes each. This can be done either by looking for changes in activity type (structure or function) or for changes in topic (see "Thematic tactics" below and Chapter 4). A typical Lesson may have anywhere from three or four to more than ten distinct episodes. The longer episodes will often be subdivided by shifts in topic while the same activity pattern is maintained.

There are many criteria that can be used to define the beginning and end of an episode, and they do not always agree. That is, the point when the new topic begins and the point when there is a change of activity type may not be exactly the same. Sometimes the topic will not change much at all as the activity type shifts, say from Triadic Dialogue to Teacher-Student Debate, as happpened at the beginning of the episode analyzed in Chapter 2. Sometimes an activity will persist (e.g., Triadic Dialogue, or Student Questioning) over many changes of topic. But there are usually several signals of a boundary between episodes: Students will shift posture, turn the pages of their notebooks, put down their pens, look around the room, comment to another student about something, look out the window, ask a question, and so on. The teacher will pause, or turn to write at the blackboard, or look down at his notes, or admonish student behavior, and then start the new episode with "O.K." or "Now."

The nature of Lesson structure and its analysis into episodes is discussed in detail, with many examples, in the original research report (Lemke, 1983b, pp. 21–25, 1–84) on which this book is based (also see Appendix D). In this rest of this section, I describe a few of the more important activity types. A fairly complete list will be found in Appendix A.

It is important to survey these activity types because they form the background, the ground rules for everything else that happens in the classroom.

In the broadest sense, a Lesson can be seen as a successful effort by teacher and students to maintain a common focus of attention and some shared activity structure(s) for as much of the typical 40–minute period as possible. The Lesson gets started (see Chapter 1) by their efforts, and it is sustained by them (except for occasional lapses: See notes on Interruptions and Liminal Periods in Appendix A and Lemke, 1983b, pp. 72–84) until, at the end, the Lesson dissolves back into the many separate conversations and activities from which it emerged.

In the course of a period we can observe: Pre-Lesson Activity, Getting Started, Preliminary Activities, the Main Lesson (with interruptions), Dissolution, and Post-Lesson Activity (which is much the same as the Pre-Lesson phase). Preliminary Activities include such routines as Taking Attendance, Class Announcements, and other class "Business," the "Do Now" (a Seatwork assignment on the board from the start of the period), Collecting Homework, on so on (see Appendix A). Some activities, like the Do Now or Going Over Homework, may help make the transition into the Main Lesson, that is, into the part of the period when new thematic content is being taught. A Review or a Demonstration may belong either to the preliminary phase (when its topic is not directly that of the Main Lesson) or to the beginning of the Main Lesson.

If there have been lengthy preliminaries, the Main Lesson may need to be "started" in much the way the Lesson as a whole was started initially. It is a sort of Second Start, signaling that preliminaries are over and that it is now time to get down to the main business of the lesson. Generally these Start Main Lesson activities are just like the Getting Started activities for the Lesson as a whole, except that they are especially likely to include the word "today" (or "yesterday"). An example of a very explicit signal of this kind is "Let's get to the main question for today," said by a teacher after 14 minutes of preliminaries, including a long Demonstration on a tangentially related topic (see start of Transcript LG-26-NOV).

The Main Lesson usually begins with Triadic Dialogue, an activity structure we have already analyzed fairly thoroughly in Chapter 1. Further analysis can be found in Lemke (1983b), and in the books by Mehan (1979) and by Sinclair and Coulthard (1975). It can also begin with a Teacher Monologue, usually in the form of a Teacher Narrative, that tells a story or anecdote to elicit student interest in the topic as well as introduce it. The Lesson on the "Giant Cell" that we will refer to later (Transcript 29-OCT-JR) begins with an account of a science fiction movie about such a giant cell. Teachers also sometimes begin with a

Review through Teacher Monologue, summarizing some information on which they plan to build during the rest of the Lesson.

More interesting, I think, are the other *dialogue* patterns. In addition to Triadic Dialogue and Teacher-Student Debate, there are the activity patterns of Student Questioning Dialogue, External Text Dialogue, Teacher-Student Duolog, True Dialogue, and Cross-Discussion. Dialogue patterns tell us more about how teachers and students interact in the classroom than do the patterns of teacher monologues.

In the same Lesson whose opening Review episode we analyzed in Chapter 1, there is a long period of *Student Questioning Dialogue* (DRS-27-NOV). In this pattern, it is not the teacher (as in Triadic Dialogue) but the students who ask the questions. They take the initiative and select the topics of the dialogue. What is especially interesting about this activity structure is that it is not simply a single exchange in the middle of the teacher-dominated dialogue. That is all it would be if a student simply asked a question and the teacher answered it and returned to the main topic. But what often happens is that other students take the teacher's willingness to answer the first Student Question as an invitation to ask whatever questions *they* have accumulated up to that point. So the Teacher Answer (usually followed by a Teacher Check-up to find out if the Answer was satisfactory to the student) leads to a second Student Question, another round of the dialogue, and then often a third and even fourth Student Question.

In the Lesson I just referred to, there is a sequence of *seven* Student Questions. The first two are from the same student, a main question and a follow-up to it. Of the remaining five, four are main questions and one is a brief clarification. The Student Questioning episode lasts a full five minutes; its seven questions range over three rather different topics. Its general pattern is:

[Student Bid to Ask]
[Teacher Nomination]
Student Question
Teacher Answer
[Teacher Check-up]
[Student Response]

Bracketed moves are optional, though the first two are strongly preferred by teachers (and nearly obligatory for the first Student Question in a series), while the last two are considered good teaching procedure and favor the interests of the student. Of these, probably only the Teacher Check-up move needs illustration. In the episode just cited, at the end of a long Answer to the first Student Question, the teacher asks,

"Does that answer your question, Cheryl?" In effect, this move creates an opportunity for the student that is analogous to the Teacher Evaluation move in Triadic Dialogue. The student is invited to evaluate the teacher's Answer for its responsiveness to her question, though not, it is understood, for its scientific correctness. (If a student does disagree with the answer, the Response can become a Challenge and initiate a new activity type, Teacher-Student Debate.)

In the episode of the seven Student Questions the teacher frequently shifts the activity structure back to Triadic Dialogue in the course of involving students in getting an answer to the Question, but this is Triadic Dialogue in one of its many special functions, as a means to an end within another activity structure.

External Text Dialogue is a variation on Triadic Dialogue in which a written text substitutes for an actual participant's "voice" in filling one of the roles in the Triadic Dialogue activity structure. For example, a teacher might read from the textbook the exact wording of a homework question, as if he were asking it as a Teacher Question in Triadic Dialogue. Generally teachers use a special inflection of their voices that distinguishes their own questions from those that are read out loud. But an External Text Question is then treated just as if it were the first move in Triadic Dialogue. It is followed by Bids to Answer, a Nomination, a Student Answer, and an Evaluation. Optional Teacher Preparation and Elaboration moves have slightly different functions than in Triadic Dialogue proper. The Preparation moves are usually just Orientations to the next External Text Question, such as identifying the number of the question in the textbook or on the test. The Elaboration moves, however, are now the teacher's principal means of controlling the dialogue and they tend to be much more frequent, longer, and thematically divergent from the Question and Answer.

Each External Text Question seems to initiate a new mini-episode of its own, having little continuity with what precedes or follows it. There are other special signals of this process besides the teacher's reading inflection. The teacher may refer to the textbook as "it" or its authors as "they." The number or letter of the question may be mentioned. Students, or the teacher, may comment on the nature of the question in a way they rarely do with "real" Teacher Questions. External Text may also fill the Student Answer slot in this pattern, as when a student reads an answer from his or her homework paper or test.

Let me cite some examples of External Text Dialogue from the Going Over Homework episode of the DRS-27-NOV Lesson:

Teacher: Question number 7 . . . A. "What-is-an-electron-cloud?" Sheldon?

Sheldon: "The portion of space about a nucleus in which the electrons may most probably be found."

The words which teacher and student read rather than say in their usual speaking style and inflection are enclosed in quotes. In addition, the teacher's reading of the question is in a rather staccato monotone, indicated by the hyphenation of his words.

A little later in the same episode, we find:

Teacher: Uh. . .*eleven.* "May two electrons in the same atom have exactly the same set of four quantum numbers?" Joanne.
Joanne: No.
Teacher: Thank you.
Student: "Why?"
Student: Why do they ask "why?"?

Here the teacher indicates an External Text Question by giving its number and by using a "reading inflection." Part two of this textbook item follows up on the first Yes-or-No question by asking "Why?" A student anticipates the teacher by reading this part out loud, and then another student comments, partly humorously, on the question (another example of metadiscourse). The teacher does not in fact yield his right to read the questions and repeats the "Why" before calling on a different student to answer. Had he not done so, the External Text Dialogue pattern would have diverged even further from Triadic Dialogue, weakening the teacher's control of the course of the discussion. In principle, however, there is no reason why a student cannot read the External Text Question, and in some classes the teacher may designate a student to do so (thereby retaining the controlling move).

Teacher-Student Duolog is a convenient term for another activity structure: the extended one-on-one exchanges between the teacher and just one student that sometimes occur in the classroom. This pattern seems to fall midway between Triadic Dialogue on one side and Teacher-Student Debates or Student Questioning on the other. Either teacher or student may hold the initiative, or it may pass back and forth between them. Either the teacher or the student may ask questions of the other, but no other student is recognized to participate, and usually other students stay out of these one-on-one dialogues.

The most common functional uses of duolog are of two kinds. Teachers maintain a duolog most often when they wish to make sure that a student understands a particular point. If a student's inital Answer is wrong, the teacher may ask a Follow-up Question of the same student, or give the student a Hint. A partially incorrect or incomplete Student

Answer may also lead to extended efforts by the teacher to elicit self-correction by the student. Teachers do not usually go beyond about three such exchanges with the same student, because other students, having been excluded, will usually lose interest and perhaps begin to talk among themselves or stop paying attention to the duolog. Longer duologs tend to be those initiated or maintained by students, sometimes as offshoots of Student Questioning or even Debate activities. It is harder, however, for a student to exclude others from joining in than it is for the teacher to maintain the exclusivity of the duolog for extended periods. Teachers tend to terminate these student-controlled duologs when the rest of the class seems to be getting restless, or when they no longer seem productive in relation to the teacher's own purposes in the Lesson.

Finally, we should mention the two rarest dialogue activity types: True Dialogue and Cross-Discussion. *True Dialogue* occurs when teachers ask questions to which they do not presume to already know the "correct answer." For example they may ask a student's opinion, or ask for a real life experience, or they may simply ask a question that has a very wide range of possible answers. In these cases, there is no basis for a Teacher Evaluation move, and so there is no Triadic Dialogue. There are Teacher Questions and Student Answers, and the teacher has an optional Teacher Comment move, similar to the Teacher Elaboration of Triadic Dialogue.

In science classrooms, unfortunately, True Dialogue tends to occur when the thematic subject is not science, but, say, Classroom Business, or some other matter. When discussing science, teachers tend to formulate questions to which there is presumably one and only one right answer. The habit patterns of Triadic Dialogue, and the extra control it gives a teacher, tend to favor this "quizzing" approach over a less dogmatic discussion of the subject. Many important issues of judgment and opinion in science are slighted in the classroom because they do not fit the dominant Triadic Dialogue pattern. They would usually be better handled by True Dialogue.

Cross-discussion is dialogue directly between students, with the teacher playing only a moderating role, or perhaps having equal standing with the students. It can happen that a teacher, having allowed Cross-discussion to begin, finds it difficult to regain control of the "floor." Usually, even when students are replying to what another student has said, they will address the teacher, not the other student. This makes the teacher the intermediary and leaves him with the option of taking a speaking turn in between the comment and any reply by the first student. Often the teacher will reply directly to the comment and exclude the original student altogether. In ordinary dialogue this would certainly be considered rather rude. The usual form of a Student Comment might be, "I think she forgot . . ." referring to a classmate in the third person. In Cross-discussion, this would become, "I think you forgot . . ." said directly to the other student. Teachers may tolerate spontaneous Cross-discussion briefly, but, in science classes at least, they rarely encourage it.

With this brief survey of activity types, we have set the stage for a more thorough examination of how teachers and students try to control one another's behavior and the course of the Lesson. Teachers and students have different and often conflicting interests in what happens in the classroom. It is no accident that Bids to Start are almost always made by teachers and only ratified by students, while at the end of Lessons, it is students who Bid to End the Lesson (by staring at the clock, closing notebooks, putting on jackets, etc.). Teachers ratify these Bids, or have to negotiate the Dissolution of the Lesson in relation to an official Bell or time for ending the period. This is a "symmetry of opposition" that reflects a very fundamental opposition of interests between teachers and students. In the next section we analyze the strategies and tactics that teachers and students use to pursue their frequently conflicting interests in the classroom.

TEACHER AND STUDENT STRATEGIES OF CONTROL

Particular activity types are sustained from moment-to-moment in the classroom only when teachers and students conform to their rules. As we have seen, those rules are fairly flexible and allow for a wide variety of teacher and student options within any particular activity structure. Teachers and students both tend to keep their classroom behavior within predictable limits. Even the ways in which they break the more explicit, or "written," rules of the classroom conform to a set of implicit, "unwritten" rules. When students break the rules, they do so only in a limited number of specific ways: They call out answers, throw paper, talk to a neighbor, stare out the window, start a fight. They do not speak in tongues, stand on their heads, or do push-ups in the midst of Triadic Dialogue! There are innumerable things they *don't* do, all of which would break the structure of a classroom activity type. The few things they *do* do are still integral parts of classroom life; they make sense as ordinary, expectable actions in the context of what typically goes on in classrooms.

The most implicit, "unwritten" rules of the classroom are completely taken for granted by both teachers and students. Like "laws of nature" they are hardly ever violated and have no need to be written down and enforced. The rules that are written down, violated, and enforced describe regular options within classroom activity structures that happen to go against the *interests* of those who make the "official" rules. Teachers tend to identify with these interests; students often do not. Students *resist* rules that they do not see as being in their immediate (and sometimes long-term) interest. Teachers and adults generally assume that the rules are ultimately formulated in the students' own best interests.

Later in this chapter, and in Chapter 5, we will see that the rules may not be all that good for students, or even for teachers or for society as a whole. Now I only want to point out that social rules which are frequently broken and need to be regularly enforced usually pinpoint conflicts of interest between social groups. In an important sense rule-breaking is not something that lies *outside* the recurring patterns of behavior of a social group. It is a *part* of those patterns. It serves specific social functions and interests. Very often it represents a competing, alternative pattern to the one that is dominant. It is foolish to dismiss rule-breaking as "immaturity"; it is arrogant to simply label it "antisocial." Students, and all of us, break specific rules in the same ways over and over again just as students did before us and will after us. Our rule-breaking has a pattern and this pattern's anatgonism to the rules reflects the differences between our interests as we see them and the interests of those who have the power to decide what the "official" rules will be.

We also need to bear in mind as we look at how teachers and students sustain classroom activities despite (and sometimes by means of) rule-breaking that students control teacher behavior just as much as teachers control student behavior. We have already seen in Chapter 1 that teachers require the active co-operation of students to get lessons started and to move through the routines of each episode. Students often effectively resist teachers' efforts to change routines or introduce innovations. They also enforce rules on teachers. Sometimes this may be as simple as enforcing on the teacher a preset agenda or agreement with the class, or (as we will see in Chapter 5) students may enforce on the teacher their own expectations about the proper teaching of a subject. Students also make explicit Requests and may Challenge teachers on points of the subject matter. They make use of many indirect (often nonverbal) means to let teachers know when they are bored, confused, or ready to end the lesson for the day.

Let's look first at some examples of what happens when students break the rules, and then we will consider some of the subtler tactics of control teachers and students use that lie within the rules.

RULE-BREAKING AND ADMONITIONS

The "official" rules of classroom behavior are presumably well enough known to older students that they hardly ever get stated explicitly in the course of lessons. A rare exception seems to prove the rule. In the lesson on solar heating of the earth (cf. Chapter 2), quite near the end of the period, when he was rushing to finish, the teacher asks a question about the sources of water and carbon dioxide in the atmosphere, a question to which there are many answers. In their enthusiasm, many students start to call out answers at once. The teacher interrupts this, saying: "Only one person at a time, 'cause we can't understand anything otherwise. Charley."

He states the rule against calling out answers in its positive form, includes a reason for the rule, and then uses his Triadic Dialogue power to Nominate one student to answer officially. He states the rule in a rather rapid and off-hand manner, as if repeating a well-known formula. It is not said deliberately or sternly, or even as if he were making a case in favor of the rule, but merely as a quick reminder. The Nomination serves to get the Triadic Dialogue back on track again. The teacher's statement of the rule is itself a normal move, a Teacher Admonition. Admonitions are the normal response to rule-breaking by students. They can take many forms other than an explicit statement of the rule, as we will see.

This particular rule violation, Calling Out, serves student interests, because it tends to reduce anxiety about speaking formally to the class and being on the spot if you're wrong. It reduces the teacher's direct power over the students by pre-empting his power to Nominate. It also diffuses the impact of his Evaluation, so that it becomes more strictly an evaluation of an Answer and not so much an evaluation of a student. Calling Out even tends to speed up the flow of the lesson and encourage a spirit of group cooperation and enthusiasm. It is especially likely to occur when that spirit is already present, and quashing this activity can also dampen that spirit of enthusiasm.

It should be clear that enforcing the rule against Calling Out enhances the teacher's power and is in his or her interest. But it is not necessarily true that Calling Out in itself inevitably leads to chaos. Teachers can and do sometimes tolerate it, and easily summarize or selectively evaluate, confirm, and repeat valuable contributions. Any rule, like this one, that is violated so frequently and with so little actual harm tends to remain a rule in order to strengthen someone's power in situations where there is a conflict of interest. It often also represents some wider social belief that may serve particular interests on a wider social scale, as we will see in the case of the rule against students talking to one other.

In the case of Calling Out the key belief may be the preference for individual over collective responsibility for success or failure, a preference which often runs contrary to common sense, but which isolates individuals and subjects them to control by power figures who could not dominate a larger group in the same way. Power often uses the strategy of "divide and conquer" by allocating individual rewards or credit for group efforts and assigning punishment to individuals when it would fear to do so to an entire group. Calling Out, on a very small scale, is a group response that nullifies the power of teachers in Triadic Dialogue to "pick on" individuals.

It is relatively rare for a teacher who is reprimanding a student to make the rule that has been broken fully explicit. More often a teacher, as happened in the middle of the "Giant Cell" lesson, interrupts the normal flow of the lesson momentarily by simply calling out the name of the offending student:

> ." . . all these people, all this living material, would be producing a lot of waste products. *Andrew!* And if you have a lot of waste produced, . . ."

Here the Admonition is inserted in the middle of a long Teacher Elaboration move in Triadic Dialogue. The Admonition is not itself part of the Triadic pattern. It belongs to a pattern of its own, the Admonition Sequence, which consists, in the simplest case, of: Student Violation, Teacher Admonition, Student Response. The Violation and Response moves are often nonverbal; the Admonition can be, too, but is more often verbalized.

An Admonition in its fullest form consists of Identifying the Violator, Declaring the Rule or Violation, and Directing Compliance. The first and last of these may stand alone as simplified Admonitions (e.g., "Andrew!," "C'mon!"), and the second and third are often combined (e.g., "Stop talking!" "Siddown!"). In this case, and many others where there is no Declaration or Direction that mentions what rule has been violated, the rule is usually assumed to be that against students talking to one another while another activity, like Triadic Dialogue, is in progress. Otherwise, a different rule is usually mentioned or alluded to in some way. "Talking" (which I will call Side-talk or "siding" as a violation) is the most common form of rule-breaking and we will consider the implications of this fact and of the rule itself later.

Consider a slightly more complicated example of an implicit Admonition from the same lesson:

"Yeah Ron? . . . Larry! C'mon, I mean I was looking at you when you did it. Be a little *subtle.* . . . OK, Ron."

The teacher is Nominating Ron in Triadic Dialogue, but interrupts himself with an Admonition directed to Larry. He Directs Compliance, but only alludes to the Violation by saying that it was what he just saw Larry do. In fact, Larry threw a wad of paper halfway across the room, probably a crumpled-up message to the classmate who caught it. This incident did not seriously interrupt or distract the class. It happened towards the back of the room and only a few other students seemed to notice it. The Admonition itself was a far greater interruption than the Violation. Apart from the past history of Larry's behavior we need to look at just what the teacher said to understand better what he was trying to accomplish with this Admonition.

The teacher's Direction to comply with the rule against throwing things in class is phrased ironically, as if it would be all right for Larry to throw paper around as long as he didn't get caught. The unusual feature of the Admonition is an optional indicator of the degree of seriousness of the Violation: the teacher's rather stern and annoyed tone of voice and his implication that it was especially bad that Larry did it when the teacher was looking right at him. Now in fact it's unlikely that these two had actually made eye contact, or that Larry noticed that the teacher was looking right at him. If that had been the case, the Violation would not have been simply Throwing Things, but it would have been a Provocation of the teacher. The teacher is cleverly implying that it might have been a Provocation, a deliberate act of disrespect, to impress on Larry and the class that he is tired of their "fooling around."

The very strong Admonition is softened somewhat by the ironic humor of the final "Be a little *subtle.*" Good teachers often use humor to soften serious Admonitions since this reduces the risk of a Student Response that could lead to a confrontation. The most common Responses are denials of the Violation. Interestingly, students rarely if ever challenge the rightness of the rule itself. Students tend to accept the rules even when their interests lead them to violate them rather frequently. In this case the student was trying to communicate with someone else in the class without side-talking. This is usually done by Passing Notes, another routine Violation. When no one is available to pass the note along, students may resort to throwing it, either crumpled up into a ball or even folded into a paper airplane. Students do not do this simply because they are bored with the lesson, but because they want to communicate with somebody and are hindered in doing so by the rules.

A different Violation elicits an unusual Admonition in the lesson on solar heating of the earth. The teacher notices a student out of his seat and says, "I guess you can see Erin in her riding boots." This line comes just as the teacher is trying to bring the class back to attention after the long pause (during which he was writing on the blackboard) that followed the end of the Teacher-Student Debate analyzed in the last chapter. He says it "aside" to the student concerned (thus Identifying him indirectly). The student is down on his hands and knees in the aisle next to his seat, probably retrieving a passed note that had been dropped.

The Admonition is meant to be humorous and to help settle the whole class, which has just finishing a period of side-talking. It implies that the student is down there trying to get a better look at the attractive legs and boots of a girl sitting behind him in the next row. Had this actually been the case it would have been very embarassing for the teacher to mention it publicly, but in fact this was just a comic fiction invented by the teacher. Other students laugh when he says it, but the student he is talking to didn't seem to understand it at all. Simply saying *anything* to a student who is out of his seat functions as an Admonition, and in this case resulted in the student sheepishly getting back into his seat.

Several minutes later in the same lesson, there is a sequence of control moves by the teacher:

Teacher: What is the ground giving off?
Students: Heat!
Teacher: But I wanna see a hand . . .. Ah! Yes, go ahead. . . .
Student: Me? I don' know uh—
Teacher: Oh, you're just waving "Hello, . . . How are you-" OK. *Ian.*
Rosie: *Heat?* [Students laugh]
Ian: Heat.
Teacher: I can't hear you, Ian.
Ian: Heat.
Teacher: OK. Rosie, don't be a ventriloquist now. Thank you.
Rosie: I'm *not.* [Students laugh]

The dialogue begins with a normal Teacher Question. It is actually a review question because he is asking about a diagram he has just drawn on the board to summarize the previous discussion. Students often respond to questions that seem obvious by a Chorus Answer, several speaking simultaneously, without Bids or a Nomination. A true Chorus Answer is one in which all or nearly all the class participates. In these cases the teacher usually accepts the Answer with a smile and goes on. In some cases teachers actually expect a Chorus Answer. But when only part of the class joins in, the teacher can instead define the response as Calling Out, a Violation.

He does this here by Directing Compliance with the rule that students should raise their hands to Bid to answer and wait for a Nomination. Several students do now raise their hands, and the teacher expresses his satistfaction with their compliance with a long, soft "Ah." But then he makes eye contact with a student whom he sees is not paying attention, has turned around in his seat away from the front, and has his arm up in the air for some other reason. He Admonishes this student by "nominating" him. The student responds as if he has actually been nominated to Answer and confesses that he can't do so (which in the context of this easy review question, already answered by the Chorus, is an admission that he was not paying attention). The teacher then confirms to him, humorously, that he was being Admonished, not Nominated (or Admonished *by* being Nominated, since behavioral moves as we have seen can have several functions simultaneously). The teacher jokes that he mistook the student's upraised arm (he may really have been gesturing to another student) for a Bid to Answer when the student must just have been waving "Hello" to the teacher. Waving "Hello" to the teacher in midlesson is certainly one of the innumerable things there are no rules against because it never occurs to anybody to do them.

The teacher next uses "OK" in its frequent function to mark a boundary in the activity structure. Here it signals a return from the Admonition Sequence to Triadic Dialogue. Then he genuinely Nominates Ian. But Rosie has not been paying close attention either (during an Admonition Sequence uninvolved students sometimes don't) and calls out the answer, with emphasis and questioning intonation. Rosie often gets the answer wrong, and tends to hedge, even in as safe a situation as this one should be. Ian, of course, also answers, but is drowned out by Rosie.

The teacher Admonishes Rosie indirectly by saying that he couldn't hear Ian. To the rest of the class this is clear, since they know that Ian was Nominated, and the Violation was what made it impossible to hear his Answer. Ian also knows this, but in addition takes the Admonition for a Request to Repeat, which is normal in Triadic Dialogue at this point, if not very common. The teacher's utterance effectively has both these functions. But it is ineffective as an Admonition for Rosie, since she obviously didn't hear the Nomination of Ian, though she should have been able to guess what was happening when the teacher seemed to Request a Repeat from Ian instead of following up on her Answer.

The teacher tries to make things clearer by Directing Compliance in a second Admonition, telling Rosie not to be a "ventriloquist," that is, not to speak for others or take their turn in the dialogue. Rosie still misses the point and may not be sure what a ventriloquist is. In any case her Response is a denial of the Violation, or at least of being a real ventriloquist (another action not specifically forbidden by the rules!).

The teacher had thought to forestall any Response by his preemptive "Thank you," anticipating compliance.

These examples should serve to illustrate the subtlety and range of teachers' responses to violations of the most common "official" rules of classroom behavior, and to show how the interpretation of classroom by-play depends on the unwritten rules of classroom activity structures. We will return to a further analysis of the significance of these common violations later, but first I want to survey the range of tactics teachers and students use to control the flow of classroom events, and each other's behaviors, in situations where there is no obvious rule-breaking. These are tactics for playing within the rules.

TEACHER AND STUDENT TACTICS OF CONTROL

Teachers do not usually control student behavior by directly telling them what to do. Explicit orders, directives, and even requests are fairly rare in the high school science classroom. Behavior is basically controlled by the expectations built into activity structure patterns. When teachers ask questions in Triadic Dialogue students answer the questions, and usually raise their hands to Bid and wait to be called on in a Nomination before doing so. Most classroom activity structures give teachers the initiative in changing from one routine to another and in leading the events of each episode. Teachers also tend to use their implied power in the classroom to define or redefine the status of events, even retroactively (cf. redefining Janice's Answer as a Bid in Chapter 1).

Teachers can indirectly influence the degree of student attentiveness or *engagement* (see Chapter 5) with the lesson by varying the pace and difficulty of questions and new subject-matter content. I will divide teachers' tactics of control, apart from direct use of their authority in Admonitions and Confrontations, into two types. *Structural tactics* are those which depend on the teacher's control of the activity structures of the lesson. *Thematic tactics* depend on their control over the way in which subject-matter content is presented.

Teachers do not just control "speaking rights" in the classroom through procedures like Nominations. They also tend to control *which activity structure* is in effect at any given time. Thus they can and do signal or declare *boundaries* between activity types or episodes, and can shift the Lesson from dialogue to monologue and back again. Teachers usually start episodes and indicate the close of an episode. They can shift the Lesson from a dialogue activity type to Seatwork or Copying Notes or Teacher Monologue. We have noted already that in the case of Teacher-Student Debates or Student Questioning Dialogue, where students initiate the activity and hold the initiative during dialogue, it is still ususally the teacher who *ends* these episodes.

Teachers signal a shift of activity type, or the end of one episode and the beginning of another, in a variety of ways. They tend to use verbal signals such as "Now" "OK" and "All right" often followed by explicit metadiscourse, including indications of the next activity:

"Please take out your homework"
"Where was I? Chemical Periodicity, Number 2"
"What we're trying to get at here is . . ."
"Now let's look at . . ."
"Let's get to the main question for today."
"And now we come to another question."

Teachers also use nonverbal signals for shifts from one activity type or episode to another. There are long pauses. Teachers may consult their notes. They often signal the end of one episode by writing on the blackboard something to be copied into student notes. Another episode begins when the teacher turns back to the class.

Teachers may explicitly *terminate* a student-dominated activity like Debates or Questioning with statements like:

"Well let's not get into a whole type of cell theory"
"Uh, you're getting a little too picky"
"I'm gonna try and tell you what happens. Just a second, Scott, just listen carefully."

These are usually followed by a shift of the activity structure to a teacher-dominated one such as Teacher Monologue or Triadic Dialogue.

Teachers also *interrupt* students during dialogue far more often than students interrupt teachers. They may interrupt a student for an urgent Admonition of another student, or to foreclose a student initiative in an extended Debate, Duolog, or Questioning episode, or to cut off a student who is rambling or expanding an incorrect answer, or even a correct one well past the point wanted. Especially in Triadic Dialogue the teacher acts as if the Nomination once given can be withdrawn at will. Teachers hardly ever *ask* to interrupt a student (e.g., *"Excuse me, John?"), though they do apologize occasionally when they interrupt one student to admonish another.

Teachers also control the *pacing* of lessons. This is mainly done by controlling the rate at which new thematic content is introduced by the teacher, but also by time limits placed on activities or episodes. Thus in one episode, a Going Over the Do Now, the teacher begins by saying "Now we won't be doing this type of work much longer. We're moving on to a new topic." The class proceeds to go over the solution of some complex chemical problems with confusing terminology (oxidation-reduction reactions).

The teacher controls the pacing by deciding how much time students get to write their solutions on the blackboard before he asks them to explain what they've written, and by how long he spends on one point before raising a new issue. He also has students dictate carefully word-ed answers for the rest of the class to copy into their notes and seeks to control how long this process should take. However, the students suc-cessfully bid to stretch out this phase of the episode. One calls out, "Wait wait wait. Hold on." Another: "Can she repeat it one more time?" These are Student Requests, the first directed to the dictating student, the second to the teacher. The first Request is directly honored by the student who pauses for ten seconds in mid-sentence. The second is ratified by the teacher: "Yes. Please, will you repeat it." There is some disagreement at the end of the episode as to whether the statement is correct as worded, but the teacher chooses to ignore this and forestalls the continuation of the discussion by going on to the next problem, "Now let's look at this one *here*."

Characteristically, teachers tend to manipulate pacing to speed up the lesson, and students to slow it down. You will rarely if ever hear a student say, "OK, Mr. Keeble, let's move on to something new." Teach-er control of pacing can be used strategically to create a sense of the "pressure of time" which can make it easier for a teacher to forestall student initiatives and keep to his or her own agenda for the lesson. Students' interests favor having the least material taught for which they will be held responsible on a test, and making sure they have thor-oughly mastered it before going on to a new topic. Teachers tend to feel that they have done a better job if they have covered more material in a lesson or a semester, and they tend to support the interests of those who write syllabi and curricula which demand that a certain amount of material be "covered" regardless of how well it is learned. Students' relative lack of control over pacing undoubtedly leads to too much material being covered too quickly for many of them to master it.

Why do curricula and teachers rush students through a difficult sub-ject like science? We will have more to say about this in Chapter 5, but for now it's worth pointing out that the effect of doing so is to confine the mastery of science to a relatively small fraction of the population and leave most of the rest feeling stupid. Too many science educators believe that science is intrinsically a subject only the favored few are capable of mastering. Those students can keep up, and it is thought that the others would never master the material at any pace. These beliefs serve interests which need to be challenged.

Pacing depends not just on structural control, that is, the regulation of the length of time alloted to activities and topics, but also on thematic control: the number of new thematic items and semantic relationships among them that the teacher introduces in each period. Can a teacher force students to be more attentive by speeding up the pace of a lesson? Usually this works only if the pace has been too slow to begin with, and has already led to boredom. Generally the pace is already faster than many students are comfortable with, and increasing it still further leads to frustration and withdrawal from active engagement with the lesson. The students give up and stop trying. There are, however, a number of other "thematic" tactics which teachers use to control student attentiveness and other aspects of the lesson. Basically, structural tactics are those that manipulate the activity structure itself, while thematic tactics manipulate the actual topical content of what is said within the course of that activity.

Thematic tactics include teachers' use of their power to control the topic and especially to decide what is relevant to it and what is "off the topic." One such common tactic is *Asserting irrrelevance* by labeling a student response "not an answer" (as opposed to a *wrong* answer) because it was not germane to "the question" (i.e., the previous Teacher Question), or to the immediate topic.

For example, at one point in the "Giant Cell" lesson the students, a little in doubt as to just what the teacher is getting at, answer his question about why a cell could not grow to giant size by saying that it would divide into two parts before it got that big. There is a lot of side-talk going on and the teacher is only just barely in control of the class. Students are calling out that they can't hear what other students are saying in answer to the question, and he has admonished them, saying that the reason they can't hear is because they've been talking so much. He finally gets the answer about cell division and says, a little impatiently: "You're not answering the question," followed immediately by a restatement of the question. Students stick with the theme of cell reproduction, a little frustrated with not being able to see where the teacher wants them to go. Finally the teacher intervenes with some extended metadiscourse: "We're not really dealing with reproduction now, OK? I know that's the next topic, so it's probably in your mind, but—uh—let's just look at a cell that's existed." He then restates the question yet again.

In fact this lesson *is* a lead-in to the unit on reproduction, motivating the phenomenon of cell division by pointing out that there are limits to the growth of a single cell. The teacher is trying to control not just the direction of the discussion, but also the excessive side-talk and inattentiveness by the tactic of asserting the irrelevance of what they are saying. This tends to force students to pay more attention to the clues he is giving them as he rephrases the question and otherwise indicates what he wants the topic to be.

In another lesson ("Oxidation-Reduction Reactions"), a different teacher resorts to the same tactic. A student is explaining his solution of a problem at the blackboard; he misinterprets a question from another student. She rephrases the question and there is a lot of side-talk going on. The teacher has his own notion of what the relevant question should be, and also a need to reassert his authority and quiet the class down a little. The student at the board answers the question as he interprets it, and other students then disagree with his answer. The teacher intervenes by saying:

> Look, we know it *gained* electrons, because it went from zero downwards, downwards in *charge*. Now the question is why, why not *two*, why four? Where did the *four* come from? That's the question.

The point of the teacher's intervention is not simply to come down on one side of the argument about which answer to the supposed question is *correct* ("*gained* electrons" vs. lost them). In fact he belittles the importance of that issue ("Look, we know . . ."). Instead he wants a different interpretation of the "the question." He states first what "the question" should be, and then emphasizes this by speaking the final clause ("That's the question.") with a special "soft" voice he characteristically uses for emphasis.

Marking Importance is another common tactic of control. When a class seems to be losing its engagement with the lesson, it is very common for teachers to in some way indicate that the current discussion is a matter of special importance. This is a thematic tactic because it in fact provides information about the topic itself and depends on the discussion of topical content for its effect, but it is as much used to control student behavior (mainly to increase attentiveness) as it is to actually identify the most important aspects of a topic. In the hands of the best teachers, it has a legitimately dual function. The teacher merely chooses the best moment to emphasize the importance of a topic in order to also produce the greatest effect on student behavior. For example, at a point in the "Atomic Orbitals" lesson (cf. Chapter 1) when there is a lot of side-talk because the students are a bit confused over how to draw "electron dot diagrams," the teacher is trying to answer a Student Question, and to use this as an opportunity to make an important point, but he can hardly be heard above the side-talk:

> You could put—Yeah, we write them in *pairs*. . . . Because—Hold it!—when we diss—*Class!*—when we discuss BONDING, it'll be important to know that they're in pairs, because, they like to have these opposite spins.

Here the teacher, who rarely uses direct admonitions, especially to the class as a whole, proceeds from a mild one ("Hold it!" that is, "down"), to a strong "*Class!*," and then to Marking Importance first by reference to a topic which the students already know is very important and are looking forward to learning about, Chemical Bonding, and then by explicitly saying that "it'll be important to know . . ." what he is trying to say in his answer to the Student Question. In the "Oxidation-Reduction" lesson, again at a point where there has been a lot of siding as students talk among themselves while waiting for a definitive summary conclusion, the teacher tries to get full attentiveness for a student's dictation of the summary by saying to that student, "Speak it clearly . . . your words of wisdom." This is meant not just for the student who is about to speak, but for the whole class to mark in advance the importance of what will be said and to focus the class' attention on it and get them to quiet down.

Marking New/Old Information is a similar tactic in which teachers get increased student attention to the current discussion by signaling that what is being said is providing new information for the first time, or alternatively that what is being asked about is "old information" which they are expected to already have mastered. The first version of the tactic stimulates interest (see Chapter 5); the second both puts pressure on students and suggests that perhaps they already do in fact know enough to participate successfully.

Regulating Difficulty is a behavioral control tactic that works entirely through the thematic development of content material. Asking a relatively easy question tends to increase the number of students who participate by trying to answer it, either by bidding to answer publicly or by silently comparing their own answer with what is said aloud. A question which is *too* easy, however, in the opinion of the class may provoke either a chorus answer, or no Bids. At the other end of the spectrum, asking a relatively difficult question tends to make students stop and reason silently, and so stop "siding." It also, as in the case of the long, complex question to Ron in the episode of Chapter 1, tends to preclude quick called-out answers (cf. earlier in that episode) and to force students to pay close attention to the question itself. Again, *too* difficult a question frustrates students and may lead them to disengage from any effort to answer.

Introducing Principles as a control tactic has already been illustrated in Chapter 2 as a common means (Appeal to Authority) for ending Teacher-Student Debates. The teacher cites a scientific principle which the students are not familiar with, asserting its relevance to the present discussion. Not only is this "New," but it is also something which the teacher is going to have to explain, thus justifying a Teacher Monologue and prompting student attention to it. It is a control tactic insofar as it is used at points when teachers need to reassert control over the activity of the class.

Creating Mysteries is another thematic tactic often employed by teachers to draw students' attention. The teacher creates a problem or dilemma to which the point of the lesson or episode will provide an answer or solution, but along the way suspense is created, and more and more hints or clues provided toward the eventual revelation.

This is the strategy of the Main Lesson on "Solar Heating of the Earth" (= "Terrestrial Radiation," Transcript LG-26-NOV). The teacher establishes early on that there is a key term or concept which explains this process. He builds steadily towards it, reminding students of it at key points, for example, at the end of the difficulties of the Debate about light and heat (see Chapter 2), when after restating his thesis for the last time, he adds, cryptically, .".. which causes something very interesting." He has introduced it as something that has "a *very* very special name," and even 10 minutes later, when he says, "Now we come to that fancy name. Look over here," he still has two more preliminary Questions to be answered before he will get to it. In fact, the bell rings before he ever does. Even a colleague who observed this lesson with me came away from it asking if I knew what this special term was.

In the "Oxidation-Reduction" lesson, when the teacher finally introduces a new topic after the preliminary problem-solving episode at the board, he does so at first covertly (it is only identified as the new topic later), posing a problem as if it might not have a solution at all: "If only there was a way to . . ." he says, and "Is it possible to . . .?" This again creates a mystery that holds students' attention at the crucial moment when he is shifting between episodes and activity structures and the class has taken this opportunity to engage in more than the ususal sidetalk.

Being Funny and *Getting Personal* are two tactics that are often used together. Humor is an important social lubricant; it minimizes the social friction that control moves produce when there are conflicting interests between teacher and students. Teachers often use humor along with

Admonitions (see above) to soften the blow to students' egos, and they are especially likely to use it when they resort to tactics that challenge students' competence or otherwise tend to control their behavior by embarassing them (i.e., by Getting Personal).

We have already seen many examples of this. Humorous admonitions to the whole class include those to cut out the "guerilla talking" or not to answer in chorus because "This isn't the Greek drama." A teacher refuses to give an inattentive student the pass to the restroom (implying she only wants to leave to avoid listening), but says it's because the pass is only available "on Christmas and Easter." These are thematic tactics because they introduce new, humorous themes for the purposes of control. Students do not often "get personal" with teachers, though they do take opportunities to joke at the teacher's competence. Teachers sometimes pre-empt and defuse this by indirectly joking about their own competence (as artists at the blackboard, or when their demonstrations fail, or the equipment for something is missing, etc.) In Chapter 5 we will look more at the role of humor in regulating student attentiveness. In the last section of this chapter I will describe a more personal Confrontation between teacher and student.

Finally, we should survey some of the tactics students use to control teachers and the activity of the lesson. In Triadic Dialogue, students can gain advantage, from their own point-of-view, by employing the standard alternatives to a straight Student Answer: Called-out Answers, Chorus Answers, Questioning Answers (turning an answer into a question), Declining to Answer, Asking for Clarification of the question (often a delaying tactic until another student gives them or the class the answer "illegally"). Students do this to avoid being held responsible for an answer, or getting embarassed for being wrong. We have also seen that students can enforce a prior agenda on the teacher, and this can be used tactically to keep the teacher from introducing a new theme or asking a tough question.

Students take the initiative most commonly with called-out Comments, but these are subject to Admonitions, so they do this more successfully with Student Questions, which can in turn serve as pretexts for Challenges (cf. Chapter 2). A student may sustain a Duolog with a teacher to make a point or keep attention focused on himself. Students also use metadiscourse to force teachers to clarify the activity structure, for example, when a student asks, "Are you asking which one of those four?" after a teacher has ruled several answers irrelevant to his Question, or when another asks, "What? are you doin' the homework for us?" when the teacher has proceeded to do a *sample* homework problem without an effective boundary signal from the previous episode.

Students also bid to override ordinary obligations to work in the class, for example, asking, "Do we have to copy this?" in the guise of a clarification. Students even, somewhat surprisingly, act to enforce the norms of scientific discourse on teachers. We will explore this phenomenon in Chapter 5. And finally, we should note that since students' speaking rights are rather restricted in the classroom, they often use nonverbal means to control the teacher's behavior. Most commonly, for example, they simply disattend to the teacher, by not looking at him or by staring out the window, or by restlessly shifting posture or turning pages in their notebooks to indicate that they are bored (e.g. when a duolog has gone on too long). Side-talk also puts pressure on the teacher to get more interesting, and at the end of the period, students may rush the teacher to end the lesson by closing their notebooks, putting on their jackets, and so on.

While teachers "officially" have greater power and authority in the classroom, and do generally hold the initiative, students retain an absolute veto over activities the teacher tries to impose. Even the threat of that veto, student noncompliance or uncooperative behavior, is enough to keep most teachers on the straight and narrow, that is, within the standard classroom routines and activity structures that students have learned to expect and have become comfortable with. One result of this is that teachers who try to innovate in the classroom can expect to meet with considerable student resistance, at least at first. For all their competition and conflicting interests, teachers and students still tend to hold each other to a common set of rules and expectations. We need now to analyze a little more critically why those rules are as they are, and what interests these rules actually serve. We need to examine the relation between behavioral control in the classroom and conflicting interests in the wider society beyond it.

WHY RULES ARE MADE TO BE BROKEN

Some classroom rules seem to be broken almost as often as they are followed. We have already noted the frequency of Calling Out and Side-talk in classrooms. They are probably the two most common active Violations. There are also some rather common passive Violations (in the sense of "sins of omission"): Not Paying Attention, Not Taking Notes, and Being Late. Each of these common violations represents a conflict of interest between teacher and student. The passive violations represent a kind of passive resistance, noncompliance by inaction.

Not Paying Attention can take many forms (including active forms like Side-talk or Passing Notes) but more often it is simply disengagement from the teacher's designated focus of attention (the Teacher

Question or Explanation, the Blackboard or Demonstration, another student) or from the activity itself. Students doodle, daydream, look around the room and out the window, and even fall asleep. In Chapter 5 we will analyze the rise and fall of students' engagement with the lesson and its relation to the activity of the moment.

Not Taking Notes is another very common form of passive resistance. Unless the teacher has directly told the class to copy something from the board and is watching to see that they do so, Not Taking Notes is easy to get away with. Students often see it as being in their interest to "write" as little as possible in class. For many of them writing is a burden; their writing skills are very, very poor and "copying" may mean copying almost letter by letter, a slow and tedious process. Students often complain "Do we have to write this?" or even "My hand's getting tired!" when they feel the teacher is writing more work to be copied from the board than is really necessary.

Being Late is the most serious of the passive Violations. For students it is an effective way to achieve their goal of minimizing worktime in class. Students arrive late, take as much time as possible getting to their seats, settling down, getting out notebooks and pens, handing in homework papers, and coming back to attentiveness for new episodes. They also, as we have seen, get restless well before the end of the period and try to get the teacher to end the lesson as soon as possible. Students who arrive after the lesson has started provide further opportunity for distraction and delays in resuming work.

The Functions of Side-Talk

Let's look more carefully now at the most common of the active Violations, Side-talk, or just "talking." Any time that a student talks at all during the period without having been called on by the teacher, the student is technically breaking the rule against "talking." There are scarcely any classes where this Draconian form of the rule is consistently enforced by teachers.

Teachers tend to tolerate Student Questions that are called out during pauses at the end of an exchange (e.g., after the Evaluation of an answer), if they are directly relevant. They also tolerate Called Out answers to easy questions, or Questioning Answers or Requests for Clarification when there are no Bids to Answer. They are most intolerant of Calling Out when it competes with Bids and so undermines their power to Nominate. But the rule against "talking" is primarily a rule against Sidetalk, that is, against students talking to one another during the Lesson. Again, it is most tolerated when it occurs before or after the "official" Lesson, or during Liminal periods (breaks between episodes or activities), and least tolerated when it occurs during official dialogue or monologue activity. It is the Violation that is most often Admonished, and so it is the rule that is most frequently enforced and thereby reinforced as being the rule. In fact it is the "unmarked" Violation, that is, when no indication is given as to what the Violation was, it is assumed to be "talking."

When the teacher just interrupts himself to say"C'mon" or "Hold it" or "Andrew!" or "Class!," these are Admonitions of Sidetalk. If a teacher merely pauses and stares in someone's direction, it is assumed that he is (nonverbally) Admonishing somebody for "talking," rather than for any other particular Violation. At any given time in any lesson, there are at least one or two active "sides," that is, pairs or groups of students paying attention to one another rather than to the official focus of attention in the class. It is not uncommon for up to 30–40% of a class to be "siding" at times in a lesson when engagement reaches a minimum (see Chapter 5).

Consider two examples from a lesson ("Solar Heating of the Earth," LG-NOV-26) taught by a very experienced teacher to a generally quite cooperative class. At one point, the teacher has just Nominated Monica to answer his Question, but interrupts her clearly audible Answer midway:

Teacher:	Frank. Did you hear Monica?
Frank:	No.
Teacher:	Why not?
Frank:	She hasn't—
Teacher:	Aahh. Always bored with a good lesson. Be quiet. [Students laugh] Monica, tell us again.

Frank has been siding with a friend in the back of the room. It would probably have been enough to have just said "Frank" to Admonish him for talking during the Triadic Dialogue exchange with Monica, but the teacher's actual strategy is more complex. He asks him if he heard Monica. This sort of question is also commonly used to remind the Nominated speaker to speak loudly enough for the whole class to hear. The expected answer is "No," which Frank supplies automatically and with no special sense of having been Admonished. The simple "Frank," taken as an Admonition might have led to a Denial from Frank.

Now, instead of doing what Frank expects by continuing with a Request to Repeat Answer sequence (e.g. *"Monica, can you say that again so Frank can hear you?"), he asks Frank why he didn't hear. This could also be part of the Request Repeat routine, with Frank expected to say "She didn't say it loud enough." In fact he may have been listening well enough to realize that she hadn't finished her Answer and been about to say "She hasn't answered it yet," but the teacher interrupts Frank, overlapping his voice with "Aahh" and adding the humorous comment "Always bored with a good lesson" followed by the overt Admonition.

The students laugh at how Frank has been trapped, at the implicit humor in stringing him along with an ambiguous activity structure (Request Repeat Sequence vs. Admonition Sequence), and at the irony of the teacher's comment about being bored with a good lesson. The final Request to Resume addressed to Monica ends the teacher's Interruption of her Answer, but by phrasing it with "again" the teacher keeps the illusion of the Request to Repeat Sequence alive and makes it appear that Monica had already answered once rather than been interrupted.

The teacher is smiling as he says "Always bored with a good lesson." The tone is very different from what we would expect from a teacher who was Admonishing a student or the whole class by saying, "Am I boring you?" The latter more directly carries a threat, for it implies that the students' talking is disrespectful, a personal insult to his competence as a teacher. Teacher competence is a very sensitive subject in many classes. Only very confident teachers joke about it; only rather angry ones raise the issue confrontationally. In fact students are probably bored with the lesson most of the time, in the sense of having little or no interest in its subject matter content. It is only the engaging personality of the teacher that may be holding their attention, or else their fear of his power.

About five minutes later a rather similar sequence occurs. The teacher has just asked and received a repeat of an answer, requested by a student who could't hear because his neighbors were siding:

Teacher: Thank you. Did you hear that Erin? Good. If you weren't whispering to *Scott*, YOU MIGHT'A HEARD HER IN THE FIRST PLACE! Thank you.

The first "Thank you" is to the student who has just repeated her answer. He then addresses the same functionally ambiguous question to Erin he had earlier used on Frank. She turns back to face the teacher on hearing her name and starts to say something which the teacher, as with Frank, pre-empts with his "Good" (which he would say in a Request Repeat Sequence if she had said "Yes"), and having got her attention, and "caught her in the act," he then proceeds to the Admonition proper. He names the Violation, identifies Scott by stressing his name and so including him in the Admonition as well, and then *very loudly* reminds her of the reason why she shouldn't be side-talking. His loud voice at that point also jokingly makes his normal beginning sound like a whisper by contrast. As he often does he pre-empts a Response by his final "Thank you," anticipating compliance.

If you ask teachers, or students, why they shouldn't engage in side-talk, they will answer in very predictable ways which we can anticipate from these two examples and from the others we have seen earlier. They will say that side-talk is disrespectful to the teacher or whoever else is speaking, that in doing it you miss important things that are said and interfere with other students' being able to hear the lesson.

All of these standard rationalizations for the rule accept teachers' interests. It is teachers who need respect from students and some evidence that they are not boring them. It is teachers who want to insure that students will not miss one precious word of what they want them to hear. These answers do not reflect the students' interests or point-of-view where these differ from the teachers' because the rule itself does not. If you ask teachers why there is so much side-talking in most classes, the answers are less satisfactory even on the surface. Teachers will say it is because students are "immature" or "restless" or, in some other teacher's classes, maybe even bored. The students will tell you that sometimes they just need to say something to someone or ask them something.

It is difficult to record side-talk during a lesson, and we actually know relatively little about what gets said. Observations during the lessons I recorded, and observations in many similar classes over the years, indicate that side-talk serves three main functions.

First, it provides a channel for repartee between students who are sustaining the dynamics of their personal relationships, whether friendly, joking, or hostile. This siding is essential to the development of a "class spirit," a functioning group dynamics in the classroom.

Second, side-talk serves students' needs to talk with someone other than the teacher about what is going on at the moment in the class. Students ask other students what's going on: What page are we on? Which homework problem is he talking about? What was that word he used? What does that say on the board? Do you understand that? What does he mean? Is this the answer? Should I ask him?

One teacher cannot respond to the need for these kinds of information on the part of 30 students, nor would students feel comfortable asking the teacher many of these things. I have frequently observed that a student will side just before raising his or her hand to ask the teacher a question. Many Student Questions and Student Comments grow out of Side-talk. Students first share their question, or confusion, or idea with another student, and only then do they go public with it and ask the teacher. Students, as we have seen already, get very little practice speaking the language of science. Just to phrase a question they need to get a running start, and dialogue is the practice ground for launching even as short a solo effort as a Student Question on the topic. Unofficial siding often replaces Cross-Discussion as an opportunity for wider student participation in discussing the topic. Much student side-talk, perhaps most, is directly related to "official" classroom activity.

The third major function of side-talk, of course, is to provide an option for students to disengage from the lesson activity altogether and talk with a neighbor about something else entirely. This is less common than the other uses of side-talk, and mainly occurs during pauses in lesson activities.

All three of these uses of side-talk are, I believe, essential to the effective functioning of the class as a social group. Without them, there would be less, not more learning taking place. Side-talk is an adaptive and functional form of classroom behavior. It does not always work in the teacher's interests, but the students' interests are also essential to successful education.

Too much side-talk can interfere with the progress of the main activities of the lesson, but it can also be a signal to the teacher that the class has become frustrated, bored, or disengaged from the lesson for some good reason. Siding at the wrong moment can be very distracting and annoying; students do not always use good judgment in deciding when they *must* say something to a neighbor. But I have seen a few classes where there was no siding at all, where such strict "discipline" was enforced by a teacher that all side-talk was effectively suppressed. In these classes there was no intellectual discussion in any meaningful sense of the term: There was attentiveness on the surface, but no real communicative or intellectual engagement underneath. There was also no humor or emotional color to the dialogue. Student participation was confined to nominated Student Answers and there were very few Student Questions or other student initiatives. For all I know, these classes did reasonably well on multiple-choice tests and standardized examinations. But they had almost no practice in talking science, they were not learning to enjoy science or find it interesting in itself, and they were learning to follow orders and do as they were told. The interests of the teacher in these classes were not balanced against those of the students in a dynamic compromise; they predominated to the exclusion of student interests.

In a classroom without side-talk, there is little or no group dynamics possible. All interaction is mediated through the teacher. There is also no True Dialogue or Cross-Discussion in these classes. The classes have very little spirit or enthusiasm. The students' behavior is almost entirely predictable and automatic, lacking the spontaneity which arises from responding to complex Others.

Without that dynamics, the classroom becomes a less than human place, and insofar as learning is a fully human activity, a social process, it suffers from the suppression of enthusiasm and all the other "contagious" emotions that arise from actively *shared* human experiences.

Without side-talk too many students are too often left confused, even if only for an accumulating number of small, sometimes critical, moments. Without the opportunity to get clarification or support from a peer, or to practice what they want to say, students are less likely to say anything publicly, or even to silently talk their way through the thematic pathways of the topic alongside the teacher's presentation. They hear only "teacher words," not their own, and learning is that much more alienating, that much further a jump from the familiar than it needs to be. Finally, without siding, students can only disengage from the lesson in ways least apparent to a teacher, providing less of the unintended but essential feedback by which good teachers regulate the pacing of their lessons to hold students' attention.

Strict enforcement of the rule against side-talk is educationally counterproductive. It is intellectually dysfunctional. Teachers implicitly acknowledge this by *not* consistently enforcing the rule. They do in fact frequently overlook siding when it is not disruptive.

Most siding does not get admonished. Siding occurs as frequently as it does in part *because* it is not always admonished, and it is not always admonished, in a deeper sense, because siding serves important and necessary functions in the classroom. But these are always "unofficial" functions; they are never officially acknowledged or sanctioned.

The irregular, somewhat unpredictable, occurence of Admonitions mainly serves to maintain the rule against siding as being the rule. Admonitions thus have an overt, dynamic function at the moment when they occur—to eliminate siding that has become or threatens to become disruptive—but they also have a covert, synoptic function, which is to remind students that there is still a rule.

Those Violations which are *not* Admonished serve even more important functions. We have already discussed their overt, dynamic functions for the students, but they also have a covert, synoptic function as well. Synoptic functions depend on the net effect of a pattern of action, quite apart from *how* they get accomplished in the moment-to-moment dynamics of the action. They tend to be relevant to larger social patterns of control beyond the immediate situation. The synoptic function of un-Admonished Violations is to prevent direct challenges to the rule itself, to head off critical debate over the basis for the rule. So long as enough siding is tolerated so that it can fulfill its immediate dynamic functions in the classroom, no one needs to make the effort to challenge the rule itself. If the rule were strictly enforced and every Violation were Admonished, frustration might build to the point where too many people would question the rightness of the rule and doubt the arguments in favor of it.

Does this pattern of convenient nonenforcement of a rule represent simple hypocrisy? If so, it is a pervasive pattern in our own and many other societies, a "Hypocrisy Syndrome". For there are many Rules that are frequently violated with impunity and only enforced just often enough to maintain them as Rules. They are not enforced strictly and consistently because they are in fact counterproductive and enforcing them stringently would build pressure for a challenge to the Rule itself. Such challenges can be dangerous to the power of those whose interests are favored by the rules.

The rule against side-talk seems a perfectly reasonable, neutral, "traffic-rule" that only gives everyone the opportunity to participate equally in the lesson. That is, until we examine it critically and ask why it forbids behavior that serves such essential functions that enforcing the rule strictly could be disastrous. We can see at a first level that this rule favors the teacher's power of control over the students' need to communicate with one another for a variety of reasons. But the rule in fact serves to maintain a more important fiction which serves much wider interests.

Why can we ignore students' needs to communicate with one another during the lesson? Presumably because they are there to listen to the teacher, not to each other. Because they can wait to talk to one another. What matters officially in the classroom is that each individual student pays attention to the teacher and speaks directly to him or to her. If the teacher designates another student as the speaker, that student, especially in Triadic Dialogue, is really speaking for the teacher. We have seen how the Question-Answer-Evaluation exchange, when it works smoothly (i.e, with correct answers) is a simple substitute for a Teacher Monologue. Despite the pseudodialogue, each student is supposed to be in an individual duolog with the teacher, learning on his or her own.

Of course we know this to be a fiction. Students learn a great deal from one another in the classroom. They mediate and translate for one another when the teacher's language is unfamiliar. They support and facilitate each other's learning in countless ways. Learning is not an essentially individual process in the classroom (or anywhere else, though that is a separate argument). Learning is essentially social. But the rule against side-talk is part of a general system of beliefs that ignores this. It presumes that each student learns as an isolated individual, even though part of a group. That system of beliefs represents an *ideology* of learning because it speaks of learning in a way that favors certain large-scale social interests (see Chapter 5 for a general discussion of social ideologies in the classroom).

If we know that classroom learning is an essentially social process, why are so many classroom rules formulated on the assumption that it is strictly an individual process? Calling Out and Chorus Answers are violations of the rules because they suspend individual accountability for correct answers. So for the same reason is "ventriloquism," when one student supplies the answer for another (a very common function of side-talk).

Viewing learning as an essentially individual process, and ignoring its social dimensions, helps to rationalize holding individuals solely accountable for their own right and wrong answers, their own success or failure at learning. When we fully recognize the social nature of classroom learning, it does not seem so surprising that students should collaborate in coming up with an answer to a question or a solution to a problem. In fact, outside school, we generally expect people to turn to others for help in solving real problems, and we reward those who know how to get the help they need and make use of it, including those who are good at working in groups and good at managing them. But in school, whatever the reality, the fiction is maintained that each student learns on his or her own and is individually responsible for success or failure.

Students of course are not individually responsible for how much they learn in a class. If a student is placed in a class where he or she has or makes friends, where there is good class spirit, where the person sitting next to you helps you out a little, where there is good participation and intelligent class discussion, the student will tend to learn more than if placed in a dull class, isolated from other help or opportunity for dialogue. Much research has shown that students with weak academic records do better in classes where their peers are somewhat more successful academically than they do in classes of other poor students. And that research is based only on test results that often do not measure a student's full development in the subject. What, how much, and how well a student learns depends very much and very directly on the social milieu of the classroom.

But there is one situation in which no exceptions to individual accountability for learning are allowed, one classroom activity structure in which the rule against side-talk is enforced strictly and totally: TESTING. During a quiz or test, students are totally isolated from all communication or collaboration with one another. It is in this situation that the ideology of individual learning reigns supreme, and it is in this situation, and only this situation, that the rule is consistently enforced.

The linkage between the rule and the ideology is made most clearly in this case. Despite all we know and acknowledge about the social nature of classroom learning, we still test students under conditions in which social skills become irrelevant (or confined to silently "psyching out" the teacher or testwriters). We justify this only by the belief that learning is individual, and by talking about how students must learn to perform on their own, without help. Yet we know that increasingly in our society most work is performed by groups or teams of people, that help is never far away, and that the best workers make use of these resources. Even on the factory assembly line the day of the isolated worker is largely passing, for good reasons. The advantages of the "divide and conquer" strategy of isolating individuals for reward or punishment are to a large extent outweighed by the greater productivity of teamwork. But the tests that matter most to a student's grade and to his or her future are predominantly tests of the ability to work in isolation. We do not even balance our evaluation procedures between individual testing and group project work in proportion to their realistic importance in adult society. Classroom learning is social; classroom testing is individual.

How many students would do much better in openly cooperative, collaborative projects than on tests taken in social isolation? How much better predictors of success in adult occupations would grades be if they were based to a greater extent on such projects? Whose interests are favored by the individualistic ideology of learning and testing? Obviously those are the kinds of students who do well under the present system. This does not mean, I think, students who are more self-sufficient or independent, as is sometimes claimed. If so, this system would produce disproportionate numbers of academically successful students who are loners and do not work well in groups. There are certainly such students, but they are relatively few in number.

More systematically, the present methods of evaluation favor students who find themselves in classrooms where most of the other students are well prepared by their family and social background for the activity structures and discourse styles of the average teacher. That means classrooms of mainly middle-class students. The present system of testing also favors students whose written language skills are relatively strong, and since written language is based on standard dialect, this favors middle-class students again. It favors students whose home cultures represent traditions in which individual action without the support of others is relatively more emphasized over collective or group activity, and this means again students from middle-class homes, and especially in the past those from North European, and even Protestant, traditions. (This is not to say that still other individual students, families, and even cultural groups do not happen to fit these requirements some of the time.)

Sociologically, it is no accident that the criteria for academic success seem tailor-made for the children of those groups in our society who have wielded the most political power for the longest time. It is the attitudes of those groups which have dominated the evolution of the curriculum, the formulation of teaching methods and classroom activity structures, and the development of the ideology of testing and learning that insure special advantages for their children.

But the ideological emphasis on individual learning does more than this. By holding each *individual* responsible for school successes or failures that are in large part the result of their membership in one or another social group (classroom, racial, ethnic, gender, or social class), it is possible to justify giving some students good grades, economic opportunities, and affluent lifestyles and leaving others to poor grades, poor opportunities, and lifetime poverty.

This "justification" of injustice in terms of individual "merit" conveniently ignores the fact that under the dominant ideology and its rules, it is the children of dominant social groups that turn out to have the most merit. Not in every individual case, of course. But on the average, in society as a whole, middle- and upper-middle class students do vastly better in school than do students from working class and poor families. The more a particular family raises its kids "middle class," regardless of its actual income or wealth, the better, on the average, they will do. Yet the ideology of individual learning, individual achievment, individual intelligence, individual self-discipline, and individual merit holds one single isolated individual student responsible for this result.

The rules that implement a dominant set of social beliefs are often meant to be violated, but not to be challenged. Despite, and indirectly *because* they are violated (and the violations admonished or penalized), they remain "the rules." They are selectively enforced, and remain always available to be used when it really matters (e.g., during tests). In the classroom, other commonly violated rules also have their wider social functions. "Paying Attention" is a rule that seeks to give the person in power (the teacher, or those who control the curriculum) the right to determine something as fundamentally a part of personal liberty as what we attend to and when. "Taking Notes" demands that we write what others tell us to write, and that we write mainly others' words, not our own. The rule against "Being Late" serves to enforce the middle-class (and ultimately North European) preference for punctuality, so important to our dominant "time is money" system of economic productivity. For each of these rules there is a ready justification, an overt function in the immediate situation. But each of them is also a pointer indicating the existence of covert functions that link the classroom to the wider society.

VALUES AND POWER

Teacher: Now let's look at longitudinal waves. [9 sec pause]
Control yourself! [aside]
All right. Now what if we take a spring and we
compress it, as we did here in class. You get a pulse
to go down the spring . . . that looks something like
this. [Draws on board]
Student: Wow. [ironic]
Teacher: And so forth down the string. [Continues to draw]
Student: We gotta draw that?
Another: No.
Teacher: Now I'm putting this up for *you* and not for *me*. If I
put it on the board, since you do not have as yet a
textbook, it's a good idea to put it in your notes.
You don't *have* to. I'm not making you. You'll be
taking it next term if you don't get it this term.
It's up to you. [13 sec pause] Now, *if*—Felicia,
please. Felicia.—If you compress a spring, ...

This class is doing a lesson on Wave Motion. It's a ninth grade class in its first term in high school (see Transcript EL-20-NOV). The teacher is accustomed to teaching eleventh and twelfth grade classes and is a little exasperated with these students. At the beginning of the period he made comments on the number of students who had failed the last test and told a brilliant little parable about a "snow goose" whose moral was that he was there to help the students, while the troublemakers in class were just making it harder for them all.

After about 9 minutes he began the Main Lesson, picking up from his introduction of Wave Motion the day before. He does a Review by Triadic Dialogue, but is interrupted by a student who wants the pass to the restroom. He asks her if she can answer the first review Question. She can't, and he declines to give her the pass. Finally he gets an acceptable Answer and writes a review statement on the board, at length (half a minute).

One of the several students who did not get the first Question right then tries to get his attention (for a Student Request), but the teacher refuses, explicitly, to recognize him. The student insists, makes the point that he can't see the board from the back row seat he's in, and this leads to a Confrontation with the teacher, who put him there in isolation because he couldn't keep quiet when seated next to anyone. As the Confrontation builds to a climax the teacher announces that the student is flunking the course. He softens the blow a bit at the end telling Jimmy that "if you change your way of living, you'll pass." He then resumes the lesson with a long Preparation for the next Question, beginning with the dialogue I've transcribed above.

He uses a boundary signal "Now let's" to mark the start of a new episode, and introduces the theme "longitudinal waves," which was the answer to the main Question of the previous Review episode. As he goes to demonstrate waves on a long coiled spring (a "Slinky"), two students start talking on the side. The Confrontation with Jimmy had left the class briefly subdued and quiet, but siding is now starting again and he admonishes one siding student with "Control yourself."

As he then talks his way through the Demonstration and draws a diagram at the board, a student mocks his artwork (a common student move), and then another one asks whether the class has to copy this fairly complex picture. A student answers his question, as if in a public side-conversation. The Student Question had been called out, with no recognition or even eye contact with the teacher, so its status was ambiguous. The teacher now responds to the Question, speaking to the class in general. He emphasizes that it is for their own good that they cooperate and work in the class, and he uses the not-so-veiled threat that if they don't, he will fail them and they will have to take this required course over again. As he continues to draw at the board and give the class time to copy, the students start to side again. He resumes the dialogue with another boundary signal "Now" but immediately has to interrupt himself again to Admonish Felicia for talking. Finally he returns to the Preparation for the next main Question.

This teacher is getting less than normal cooperation from his class. They have not been learning the material very well so far during the term, and the teacher is trying to "crack down" before it's too late. The teacher wants the students to share his view of what is good for them, his values about hard work and achievment, failure and success. He wants the students to cooperate for their own good, because they should see that it is in their own interest to do so, but the "bottom line" is that if they don't he will use his power to fail them, and the school system and the larger society will penalize them in other ways for "their" failure. The doctrine of enlightened self-interest is throughly intermixed here with coercion by the threat of superior power. For the teacher there may be no contradiction between his belief that hard work brings success and his power to define what success means. But his students are in fact caught in a conflict of values and unequal social powers.

There is a lot of conflict in this classroom. It is on the surface and easy to see and hear. But conflict between teachers and students is a constant element in classrooms. Events happen constantly that make sense only when seen in terms of that conflict. We have already come across many examples of this. To understand the nature of this conflict, we need to see two quite different points-of-view at once.

Most of us probably subscribe in large part to the teacher's values, for teachers' values derive from the dominant attitudes and beliefs in our society. We believe that education and all its rules are constructed for the good of students and in their interests. We justify and rationalize every restriction on students' rights and freedoms as being "necessary" in their own interests. We believe that the use of power and even force to compel students to do as we wish is justified by their natural irresponsibility and the good we are doing them. We fully accept that the ends justify the means.

But what adult would submit willingly to the rules of classrooms and schools? Having no say in what we must learn. No right to speak unless given that right. No right to communicate with others for any reason. No right to come and go as we please. No say in who our teachers will be or the criteria by which we are judged. Being subject to public embarrassment and admonition by a person we may not respect. Threatened with loss of opportunity of further learning and even with social disrespect and poverty for the rest of our lives if we do not accept the values and conform to the styles of behavior of people we may not want to identify with.

Adults do not accept these conditions, and are not expected to. College students and adults choose their courses and teachers, cut classes, arrive late and leave early, and are rarely admonished for Calling Out or Side-talking. They are not taught by pseudodialogue for the most part either. Many of them pay high tuitions and can take their money elsewhere. Even so, we recognize that many regulations are made in the interest of the faculty, the administrative bureaucracy, or the institution rather than in the interests of the students. Because adults tend to have more power, they are subject to fewer indignities and can insist more effectively that education serve their interests as *they* see them, not as others see them.

The claims of public education to altruistic service to students are compromised by its fundamental reliance on coercion. Educators do *not* take student's own values or estimations of their own best interests into account in curriculum planning, in teaching methods and classroom rules, or in testing and evaluation. They do not do so because they do not have to. The "necessity" of every restrictive or coercive educational practice can be called into question. The convenient belief that their age in years in and of itself disqualifies some people from being taken seriously or insures their "natural irresponsibility" is surely as fundamentally immoral as the similar beliefs about race, gender, and nationality that were long held to be indisputably obvious truths.

Adults are taught to expect that children will act irresponsibly because they are "young" and "immature." There is no more scientific basis to this belief, in my opinion, than there has been to the belief that some people were irresponsible simply because they were black, or female, or elderly, or peasant, or working-class. People in dominated social categories are very often *made* to act the way they do by how they are treated. They thus seem to confirm a belief that they are inferior by nature, a belief which only serves to rationalize their domination by those who keep them acting as they do.

There is *no* scientific evidence I know of to prove that brain development in adolescents differs from that of social adults in ways that neurologically prevent them from acting responsibly, nor any to show that the many who do act perfectly responsibly are neurological freaks. Loose talk about "hormones" and "puberty" is often simply a smoke screen for ignorance about the relationship between biology and behavior. In many other societies there is no "adolescence" at all. There is also often no economic need to keep youngest adults from competing in the labor market, and full social rights are conferred at about age thirteen (the age of *biosexual* maturity).

The only basis of social justice is that *everyone*'s values and views of their own interest be taken as seriously as we wish *our* own to be.

Students resist classroom rules because they find it in their interest to do so. We have seen in this chapter that in many cases it is also in the interest of better classroom education that they break some of these rules. There is conflict in the classroom because there are fundamental conflicts of values and interests between students and teachers. These are not simply conflicts-of-the-moment, over getting the pass to the restroom or judging the right moment to talk to someone, they are fundamental conflicts that have their foundation outside the classroom and the school.

Many students do not share teachers' predominantly middle-class, North European values about individual effort and achievement, acceptable levels of noise or emotional expression, punctuality, or proper dress and decorum. They resent the derogation of their values, their dialects and languages, their cultural preferences. They do not believe, and with good reason, that the curriculum is designed to benefit them in life when they leave school for any destination other than a liberal arts college. They believe that school is wasting their time, keeping them off the streets and out of jobs, confining them against their will under insulting and intolerable conditions in schools that are often ugly and physically unsafe. Most of these students would not come to school at all unless coerced, especially if they had another neutral place to meet their friends. From their point of view they are being forced to memorize useless facts and told they are useless when they refuse to do so.

The fundamental conflicts of values between teachers and students are not just conflicts of class, race, or ethnic group, they are also conflicts of age and generation. Adults oppress children in our society just as surely as Whites have oppressed Blacks and men have oppressed women. As many myths are told against children and young adults to justify the subordination of their interests to those of parents and older adults as have been told about non-Europeans and about women. The older deprive the younger of economic opportunity and political rights, they control and abuse their property and their bodies, they coerce them with force and the threat of force. It is not true that all parents, perhaps even that most parents, love their children or even like them. As soon as they are able to deal emotionally with their feelings, many children decide that they do not like their parents, or adults generally. The conflicts of the classroom play out in microcosm much larger social conflicts, which our society has persistently refused to face up to for a very long time. We will return to these fundamental questions again in later chapters, especially in Chapter 7.

EXPLORING FURTHER

This chapter has focussed on the social interactions of the classroom and raised many questions about their wider significance. Recent work analyzing classroom discourse from a social and cultural perspective is well illustrated in the collections of research studies in Green and Harker's *Multiple Perspective Analyses of Classroom Discourse* (1988) and Emihovich's *Locating Learning: Ethnographic Perspectives on Classroom Research* (1989). In addition, important questions of linguistic and cultural diversity, and the social perspective on literacy are addressed by a number of writers in the collections edited by Trueba, Guthrie, and Au (*Culture and the Bilingual Classroom*, 1981) and by Bloome (*Literacy and Schooling*, 1987 and *Classrooms and Literacy*, 1989).

Further references on these topics will be given at the end of Chapter 5.

chapter 4

The Science in the Dialogue

In this chapter we look at how teachers and students build up the thematic patterns of science in classroom dialogue. We have already seen, in Chapters 1 and 2, that the give-and-take of classroom activity structures tells only half the story of science teaching. We must also identify the specific science content that is being taught, and show how its particular pattern of conceptual relationships is being gradually built up and repeated throughout the dialogue.

To find the science in the dialogue, we need to identify what I called the *thematic pattern* of its science content. A thematic pattern shows what many different ways of saying "the same thing" have in common. It describes a shared pattern of semantic relationships. This pattern gets repeated at different points in the lesson, and from one lesson (and even year) to the next. It is the same pattern found in the textbook and the test. It is the pattern that students must master in order to "talk science" acceptably on this particular topic. And it is the pattern they must use to reason their way through a problem, or give the expected answer on a test.

How exactly do teachers communicate thematic patterns? What strategies do teachers and students use to weave these patterns of semantic relationships into their classroom dialogue? How are students to tell, from among all the things said in a lesson, which ones form the pattern they must learn? What, in short, are the most fundamental ways in which the science content of a lesson is taught?

In the sections that follow I first discuss thematic patterns themselves: how they relate to actual classroom dialogue and other expressions of curriculum content (textbooks, tests, syllabi, etc.), and how they are described by the semantics of language. Then we survey the most important strategies teachers and students use to communicate thematic content in actual lessons. And finally, I briefly consider how we use thematic patterns in reasoning and in arguing about what makes sense.

THEMATIC PATTERNS AND CURRICULUM CONTENT

[March 19:]

Teacher: What happened was, more than likely is, the crust was pushed up. OK, and when we say the crust was pushed up, we say that it's *uplifted*. And that's why we find these marine fossils up on high mountaintops.

[March 20:]
Teacher: I'd like to go on with what we were talking about. And we were talking about *fossils*, that are used as *evidence*, that the earth's crust has been moved. Now what did we say about these fossils, how do they help us . . . *know* that, uh, the earth's crust has been moved?
Student: Like, if y'find, *fish* fossils on top of a mountain, you know that once there was water . . . up there, 'n the land *moved* or somethin'.
Teacher: OK, and what else besides . . ..

These two short excerpts come from lessons to the same class on two consecutive days. On March 19 the teacher introduced the notion that parts of the crust (surface) of the earth have been lifted up or have sunk down at different times in geological history due to forces inside the earth. He gave two important examples of geological evidence that this has actually happened. One of those arguments is based on the fact that fossils of marine life originally buried beneath the sea can now be found at high elevations above sea level. The conclusion was that the rock strata in which the fossils were embedded must have been lifted up. The next day, the teacher begins with a review of these points.

In the first excerpt, the teacher is stating the conclusion of a discussion, bringing that discussion to a close. The next day, he asks a Review Question and gets the answer given in the excerpt. He then gives a Positive Evaluation of this answer. In terms of the science content, what do these bits of dialogue from two different lessons have in common? How do they differ?

The two examples have only two actual (science content) *words* in common: "crust" and "fossils." No direct relationship of meaning is made between these words in either case. But the examples have at least three more *thematic items* in common: MOVED ("pushed up" "uplifted" "moved"), MARINE ("marine" "fish"), and HEIGHTS ("high mountaintops" "top of a mountain"). We also have CRUST ("crust" "earth's crust" "land") and FOSSILS. Among these five items the two excerpts construct the same semantic relations:

CRUST—m/pr—MOVED
MARINE—cl/th—FOSSILS
FOSSILS—loc—HEIGHTS

CRUST is that which moves (the Medium) in the Process MOVED, abbreviated here as—m/pr—for the Medium/Process semantic relationship (see below for more on these relationships). MARINE is a Classifier or type of the Thing FOSSILS (—cl/th—). And HEIGHTS is the Location (—loc—) of [MARINE FOSSILS].

Notice that in the second excerpt it is the *whole exchange*, including Question, Answer, and Positive Evaluation, which is needed to construct the same set of relationships that are made by the first excerpt. To see that the two excerpts have this much of a thematic pattern in common first requires identifying synonyms, that is, realizing that "crust" and "land" here are two ways of saying the same thing (which I arbitrarily label CRUST). To see that "marine fossils" and "fish fossils" say the same (or closely related) things we must see that one is an example or *hyponym*, rather than synonym, of the other. Similarly for the variant forms of HEIGHTS. It is the business of semantics to help describe the nature of the various kinds of meaning relationships (synonyms, antonyms, hyponyms, classifiers, locations, etc.) that we can make with our language.

But individual semantic relationships do not yet make up a full thematic pattern. We must look at how they are joined to each other in each excerpt. Obviously in both,

[MARINE—cl/th—FOSSILS]—loc—HEIGHTS

and

CRUST—m/pr—MOVED

are made to relate to each other in a specific way. In the first excerpt one is said to be "why" the other is true. In the second, we find the words "know" and "evidence." No simple relationships among these words from the two different excerpts tell us that both excerpts are saying pretty much the same thing overall. A more complex semantic analysis, one which looks at the grammatical relationships of the clauses and at the rhetorical structures of the two arguments is needed to show this systematically. But we know intuitively that it is true, and we could now draw a diagram of the thematic pattern shared by these excerpts, linking the two lines just given by a relationship we could call Cause/Consequence, or perhaps in this case, Evidence/Conclusion.

I have compared many more such excerpts from the two lessons and constructed a slightly larger thematic pattern diagram (see Figure 4.1) that includes the one we have just come up with (Lemke 1983a). In these other excerpts, HEIGHTS, for example, is also expressed by "elevations" and "high mountains" and "heights"; MOVED by "changes," "a regional uplift," and in a parallel example by "sank" "subside" "subsidence" and even (a slip of the tongue) by "subsistence." Processes don't have to be expressed by verbs (e.g. uplift, subsidence), so long as they get put in the same relationship to the Agent or Medium ("the crust

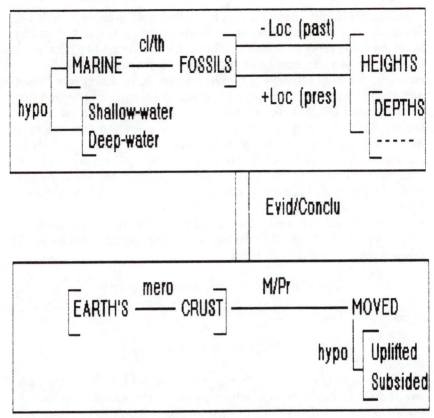

Figure 4.1.   Crustal Movement: Thematic Pattern

was pushed up" or "there was a regional uplift" that is, of a region of the earth's crust). Semantic analysis has no trouble explaining the similarity of the resulting meanings. The most complex case here is the great variety of ways of expressing the Evidence/Conclusion relationship that ties the diagram's parts together: "help us know" "if . . ., [then] y'know" "that's when . . . happens" "this suggests that" "used as evidence that" "and that's why" and so on.

But despite all these changes and variations, the same basic thematic pattern is repeated over and over again, at different points in each lesson, and from one lesson to the next. If you put all the expressions of this pattern in the two lessons side by side, it is very easy to see just what they all have in common. Many of them provide clues to the pattern. For example, at one point on the first day the teacher says, "they were *marine* fossils, they were *fish* fossils." This introduces the possibility of substituting "fish" for "marine" as a Classifier of FOSSILS. In our excerpt from the second day, this is just what happens.

In other excerpts we also find the same thing said in two slightly different ways in the same sentence, but in contexts that make it clear that they do mean the same thing. As we go from one example to the next, not *everything* changes at once. There may be two examples that have hardly any words in common, but between them will be other examples whose specific wording shifts gradually, item by item or relation by relation, to create an almost continuous series linking the most differently worded examples together. All are instances of the same thematic pattern. This is how we learn to *abstract* from the different ways of saying something their common or shared *meanings*.

In teaching science, or any subject, we do not want students to simply parrot back the *words*. We want them to be able to construct the essential *meanings* in their own words, and in slightly different words as the situation may require. Fixed words are useless. Wordings must change flexibly to meet the needs of the argument, problem, use, or application of the moment. But they must express the same essential *meanings* if they are to be scientifically acceptable and, in most cases, practically useful. This is what we mean when we say we want students to "understand concepts."

I will argue later that for the most part "concepts" are just thematic items and their customary semantic relationships, that is, they are just bits of thematic patterns. We never use them one at a time; their usefulness comes from their connections to one another. So it is really the thematic patterns that we need and use. Purely "mental" notions of what a concept is tend to mystify how we talk and reason. They ignore the essential role of language and semantics in teaching and learning *any* subject.

Thematic patterns are also needed to make sense of much of what is said in the classroom (and elsewhere). In many cases what is said is missing key elements of the pattern because it assumes that listeners can fill those pieces in. Without the pattern, what is said may be unintelligible. Even when there is a slip of the tongue or an uncorrected mistake (e.g., "subsistence" for "subsidence"), if we know the pattern, we can guess very accurately what was *meant* and supply for ourselves what should have been said. In practice, of course, it is not the *abstract* pattern itself that most of us use to make sense of what is said from moment to moment. Those patterns are needed only for systematic analysis of the successes and failures of teaching and other forms of communication. Ordinarily, we simply use what was said (or read) on one occasion to fill in the gaps in what we heard (or read) on another.

We learn by comparing and interrelating what is said in this part of the lesson to what was said in that part, and both of those to what was said yesterday, or what we remember from last year. And we add in what we read in the textbook and maybe even even the answer to a question on last week's quiz. That is, we do these things if we are successful students. As teachers, we are constantly trying to remind students where to look for the missing pieces they *always* need to make the most sense out of anything they hear or read.

Even writing, even the most careful and explicit textbook, and certainly all spoken language (in the classroom and elsewhere) provides only clues to its full meaning. The words we hear, or read, represent only the tip of the iceberg of meaning. What we hear must be fit to some familiar thematic pattern (scientific or everyday) to make any sense. That is because making sense *means* identifying the semantic relationships between the words and phrases used, that is, hearing them in the context of a thematic pattern. Another way of saying this is that making sense of anything we hear means somehow connecting it up with something else we have heard before. And those connections can go on and on. Thematic patterns easily link up with one another, and we can expand the context in which we interpret something in many different directions.

The simplest example of this was described in Chapter 2, where we saw how the same sentences could be interpreted in very different ways by the teacher, who fit what he heard to one thematic pattern, and by the students, who fit it to a very different one. We will return to the issue of differing thematic contexts of interpretation at the end of this chapter. Here, however, what is important is to see that one person may make connections to one thing heard or read in the past, while someone else may connect to something quite different. You can be sure that students in classrooms frequently make very different connections, and therefore have very different interpretations. The differences may be great enough that they infer from the same classroom dialogue quite different thematic patterns for a particular science topic.

It is impossible to avoid this problem. You cannot be fully explicit and still intelligible. There is no way to define every word in every sentence, to make explicit and unambiguous every semantic relationship, every synonym and alternative phrasing. To try to do so is to go against the basic nature of language as a form of communication and a tool for making meanings. This is one reason why it is so difficult to program computers to speak colloquial English (not just synthesize "canned" speeches, which is much easier). Even mathematics, which sometimes tries to escape from language, needs to retain some level of ambiguity, some vulnerability to differing interpretations, in order to remain a flexible tool for reasoning and creativity (see below).

In every case, we have to learn how to take advantage of the flexibility of language. As speakers and writers and teachers, we need to learn how to evoke the thematic patterns we want used. As listeners and readers and students we need to learn to make the most possible meaning we can, including, but not limited to, our best guess about the thematic patterns we are *supposed* to use. As teachers we have at our disposal the enormous advantage of two-way dialogue and the opportunity it gives us to build up with our students *shared* thematic patterns for better communication and for more effectively talking science together.

CLASSROOM DIALOGUE AND THE CURRICULUM

Analyzing thematic patterns always means comparing different bits of language to see what meanings they all have in common. Those shorter or longer stretches of talk or writing are customarily called "texts" even if they are not written. (To avoid possible confusion, I will not use "text" as an abbreviation for "textbook.") The principle that we make sense of any text by relating it to some specific group of other texts is called the *intertextual* theory of meaning. It is discussed in more detail in Chapter 8.

When we are trying to make sense of the thematic meaning of a text, whether it is an excerpt of spoken dialogue or a passage of writing, we naturally look for other texts to connect it to that at least partially share the same thematic pattern. We also customarily connect it to other texts in the same activity structure (e.g., we connect an Answer to the corresponding Question) or in the same larger unit of speaking or writing (e.g., Evidence to Conclusion in an argument, Chapter Summary to Chapter in a textbook). Usually, these texts will also share the same thematic pattern, up to a point.

I have said this in order to make clear that the idea of a thematic pattern applies to all language, spoken and written, and not just to classroom dialogue. We can pick a paragraph in the Geology or Earth Science textbook that will have the same thematic pattern as our last example about the uplifting of the earth's crust. We want our students to be able to see the same meanings there that they heard in the classroom dialogue. Since the thematic patterns of science are highly standardized, we could pick any of a dozen different textbooks, for high school or for college, and somewhere in them find one or more stretches of text again with that same thematic pattern, though obviously each will again have its own particular wording of the common meaning. We could look in on another teacher in another school and if this topic was covered in the curriculum, we would expect to again find the same thematic pattern repeated there.

Classroom dialogue and textbooks are not the only places the pattern will turn up. We expect to see it on a test sometime as well, perhaps in the form of a multiple choice question, hopefully as part of the answer to a short-essay item. The answer to an essay question could be graded quite precisely by matching its thematic pattern to the standard one written by the teacher. The same thematic items should show up with the same pattern of semantic relationships connecting them. If students have a field trip or time in the laboratory, we may hear the pattern being used as part of an explanation of what is seen there. In some classes we might hear students using the pattern to argue or debate with one another or to reason their way to a conclusion about a problem. If we could listen in on their "inner speech," we might hear the same pattern even in their silent reasoning to themselves.

We can probably find this same thematic pattern in the teacher's class notes somewhere and in a formal Lesson Plan. We could even find it on an official syllabus. Maybe some of these versions will be incomplete, because they were written for people who are expected to be able to fill in any missing parts.

What all these examples show, of course, is that a thematic pattern is a small piece of the *curriculum*. If it describes the actual dialogue of lessons, it will also be part of the "lived curriculum" of students' actual classroom experience (as opposed to just being part of the "official curriculum"). Comparing the thematic patterns of classroom dialogue with those of tests, for example, can tell us if we are testing what we teach and teaching what we test. Comparing these with the syllabus can tell us how closely what happens in the classroom corresponds to what the "official" curriculum prescribes.

Curriculum, of course, is much more than just the content that is taught. There are often nonverbal skills as well, and curriculum may also include activities better described by activity structures than by thematic patterns (e.g., in laboratory work). But thematic patterns are pervasive in every aspect of the curriculum (including attitude and values objectives, evaluation criteria, etc.). The whole content curriculum of a course could be specified by one very large thematic pattern diagram that showed how each little bit is connected up with all the rest. It would be a sort of two-dimensional abstract of a complete textbook. More useful, perhaps, are large thematic diagrams for instructional Units comprising perhaps a few weeks' class work. At a glance one could see all the major topics and their relationships to one another, the prior content which is being built on, the possible pathways through the diagram (representing different sequencing of topics), and the possible directions for further work. All connections and transitions are shown as well.

We will have reason to discuss some aspects of curriculum later in the book, though it will not be a major focus. Apart from considering some of the possible applications of thematic analysis to curriculum issues, however, what seems most important here is simply to recognize that what we mean by most curricular content is essentially a mastery of certain ways of using language. Mastery of a thematic pattern, large or small, means being able to mobilize a system of semantic relationships to talk your way through a task. And that we do almost entirely by means of language, by "talking science."

DESCRIBING SEMANTIC RELATIONSHIPS

When I first introduced the notion of a thematic pattern diagram in Chapter 1, we identified the thematic items that seemed to be important to the episode we were analyzing ("Atomic Orbitals"). Most of these would be found in any discussion of this topic in a physics or chemistry book, in classroom dialogues in most schools, and on teacher-made and standardized tests of the subject. Moreover, they would be found to have the same semantic relationships to one another, expressed inevitably in slightly different ways. The only exception to this (see Figure 1.2 in Chapter 1) are the colors of the parts of the DIAGRAM. Orbital diagrams are standard, but there are no established conventions to color-code them (or even to color them at all), so that much of Figure 2 is specific to this lesson and not part of the accepted thematics of science. I briefly discuss the interplay between language and visual representations of thematic relationships towards the end of this chapter (see also Lemke, 1987a). The rest of Figure 1.1 is fine as it stands except for its use of informal descriptions of the semantic relationships rather than the systematic ones introduced in Chapter 2.

In Appendix C, "Semantic Relations for Thematic Analysis," I list and briefly describe some of the most important and frequently encountered semantic relationships. Each relationship is a specific relation of meaning between two thematic items, or two sets of linked thematic items (cf. the two sets linked in Figure 4.1).

It is very common in scientific language to take a small thematic pattern, give it a name (e.g., "orbital configuration"), and then link it to other thematic items as if it were a single item itself. This is the phenomenon of *thematic condensation* which makes scientific language often seem so "dense" and impenetrable to the nonexpert who does not know how to expand these condensed items to recover their full meanings (see below and Chapter 5; cf. Lemke, in press-a). So a semantic relationship may connect simple items or condensed items. But while thematic items are myriad, and condensation enables us to add new ones all the time, all semantic relationships tend to be variants of a relatively small number of basic ones.

These basic semantic relationships are actually "families" of relatively similar meaning relations. Halliday (1961, 1985a) has used the term "degree of delicacy" to describe how finely we distinguish similar shades of meaning. At a low degree of delicacy, the relationship between APPLE and RED or OLD in "the red apple" or "the old apple" is the same. RED and OLD are in each case Attributes of APPLE, the semantic relationship is that of Attribute to Carrier. At a higher degree of delicacy we might want to distinguish these as two different kinds of Attribute relationship, and only consider the relationship to be the same in the case of "the red apple" and "the yellow apple" or "the old apple" and "the new apple."

Even at a low degree of delicacy, however, "the Macintosh apple" represents a very different relation between MACINTOSH and APPLE, since MACINTOSH is a *type* or class of APPLE. The relationship is that of Classifier to Thing [Classified]. An apple can be "very red" or "very old," but it cannot be "very Macintosh" for just this reason (see Halliday, 1985a, pp. 163–165). There can be more delicate divisions of many of the basic semantic relationships listed in Appendix C.

The basic semantic relations can be roughly divided into five groups. First there are those, like Attribution, that typically relate qualities, quantities, and types to a central thematic item (Nominal relations). All are used in "the three red Macintosh apples." Then there are those that relate an item to another that is being presented as its synonym, antonym, hyponym, and so on. These present one item as an example or instance of another, or as a special case or a part of another, or as equivalent to or contrasting with another. They are sometimes called the "taxonomic" relations (see Halliday & Hasan, 1985, pp. 80–81, Hasan, 1984a).

The third group are the relations between various processes or activities and the objects or agents that participate in them (Transitivity relations; see Halliday 1985a, pp. 101–157). In this group are the relations of Process to Agent, to Target (the affected thing or participant), to Medium (a single, essential participant), to Beneficiary, to Range or Extent, and so on. Also included in this group are the relations of Identification (e.g., A is B) and Possession (e.g., A has B).

The fourth group are the Circumstantial relations of an item (including a Process item) to its location, time, manner, reason, material, means, and so on. And the fifth group comprise relations that tend to occur between whole sets of linked (or condensed) items: Cause/Consequence, Evidence/Conclusion, Generalization/Instance, and so on. There is some argument in semantic theory about which relations in this last group are the basic ones, if any.

Semantic relationships can be very abstract, which means that they are also very general. This is especially true if we do not distinguish subtypes within the basic "families" very delicately. It is also possible to be so delicate that there are as many relationships as there are pairs of thematic items, but that defeats the purpose of distinguishing items and relationships to start with.

Thematic analysis is most useful when it operates with a limited number of basic semantic relationships. For example, it helps us to understand analogies and metaphors. When a teacher says "Electron comes to town, wants to go into the cheapest hotel," semantic analysis helps us to match this up with its more standard version, "Electron enters an atom, needs to occupy the lowest-energy orbital." The key thematic items may be different, but the basic semantic relationships are not.

Thematic analysis has to abstract away from the specific wording in any particular text that constructs a specific thematic pattern. That means that in identifying semantic relationships we have to ignore many of the fine points, not just of word-choice among synonyms, but even of grammatical patterns. The thematic pattern is the same whether we say "the diagram represents helium" or "helium is represented by the diagram." It is also the same whether we say "regional uplift occurred" or "the region was uplifted" (see Halliday 1985a, pp. 319–345 on Grammatical Metaphor). For more details, you can consult a short article, "Thematic analysis: Systems, Structures, and Strategies" (Lemke, 1983a) as well as Halliday's *Introduction to Functional Grammar* (1985a). Halliday's book is mainly about grammar, but most of his grammatical relationships are designed to correspond to semantic ones.

If we now reexamine the informal thematic pattern diagram of the "Atomic Orbitals" episode from Chapter 1 (Figure 1.2), we can see how its informal labels for semantic relationships indicate the formal ones we can now assign. Thus [parts of] is Meronymy, [type of] is Classification, [e.g.,] is token/type, [number of] is Quantification, [in] is Location, and [has] is Possession (though, more delicately, it perhaps also implies meronymy, or whole/part relation, in this thematic pattern).

[Represents] could be taken as a thematic item in its own right REP-

RESENTS, in which case it would be a process, with some transitivity relations to DIAGRAM and ORBITALS. In fact, if we are not too delicate, we can consider [represents] as a member of the Identification family, with the parts of the DIAGRAM being identified as types of ORBITALS. They are also, in this text at least, tokens assigned to types (of ORBITALS). The relation of the parts of the DIAGRAM to specific ELEMENTS is much the same, except that [represents] now has a Modality, called the Potential modality [can]. In many thematic patterns we can ignore Modality, but in this case, there is a systematic contrast between [represents] and [can represent] which is part of the meaning of these relations.

In the next part of this chapter we are concerned with how thematic patterns get talked out in classroom dialogue. We are concerned less with abstract semantic relationships, and more with the verbal strategies (*discourse strategies*) that are commonly used to build up those relationships by simply "talking science." In many ways this is the heart of this book and the essence of science teaching.

BUILDING THEMATIC-CONCEPTUAL SYSTEMS WITH LANGUAGE

A thematic pattern is a way of picturing the network of relationships among the meanings of key terms in the language of a particular subject. Those terms and their synonyms amount to ways of saying the thematic items of the pattern. The grammar and rhetorical forms used in speaking or writing provide the means of expressing the semantic relationships among these items. As I argue in Chapter 8, the terms *get* their meanings *from* the ways they are used.

This point of view turns our traditional notion of the relation between words and meanings, language and concepts, upside down. Concepts and meanings do not exist in the abstract. They are not in some sense "already there" in our Minds, or in Plato's realm of pure Ideas, *before* they are expressed in words (or pictures, or *some* system of symbols or signs). In fact they are not, then, "expressed" at all. Rather, they are *constructed by* our speaking or picturing, constructed through our use of words or other signs.

Of course, when we construct a meaning, or a meaning relation between thematic items, using language, we are probably just *reconstructing* it on the model of how someone else constructed it before us. We may not use exactly the same words, but we produce the same meaning pattern. Someone else makes sense of the words we say by constructing their own meaning pattern from the words (i.e., by "interpreting" them). To the extent that both of us are members of the same community, and to the extent that what is said is not too unusual in our experience, we will tend to come up with the same meaning pattern for the words.

The ways in which members of a community tend to use and construe words on a particular subject similarly from one text or occasion of speaking to another (cf. the "intertextual" principle, above) is represented by a thematic pattern. Of course there are also differences within communities in how members of different groups speak about a subject (different theories, different opinions, different value systems). Those differences, and their conflicts, are represented by having more than one thematic pattern for a subject (as we saw in the Debate in Chapter 2).

We are accustomed in science and science education to speak in terms of "concepts" and "conceptual systems." We know that scientific concepts are interlinked in their meanings, and that it is the use of systems of linked concepts that gives scientific reasoning its power. It is not unusual to say that teaching science is teaching the use of its conceptual systems. But just what are "conceptual systems"? Where do you go to find one? To study one? How do you build one? Communicate one? Learn one?

If concepts do not exist as Ideas in their own separate, nonmaterial reality, they must be patterns of relations among phenomena and events that can be perceived and studied. Undoubtedly, there are physiological relations among processes in the brain and the rest of the body as it interacts with its physical environment that correspond to what we call "using a conceptual system." But the fact is that we know next to nothing about the rules of that correspondence, and even if we did, the study of relations among neural impulses, levels of blood chemicals, and environmental interactions, would tell us little of interest unless they could be related to their conceptual *meanings*. On the other hand, there are a large number of easily observable phenomena for which we do already know how they correspond to meanings that are important to us in science or other fields: speaking, writing, drawing, calculating, experimenting, and so on. Of these, we know the most about processes of action that make meanings by using language. And we know that scientific theories and "conceptual systems" are mainly taught through language, supplemented by diagrams and mathematics, and by practical hands-on experience.

In terms of language, we *do* know what a scientific theory or conceptual system must be. It is a thematic pattern of semantic relationships in a subject, one that is reconstructed again and again in nearly the same ways by the members of a community. That community may be a small scientific elite, or it may be a broad cross-section of the educated public. The job of science education is, at the very least, to teach students how to use language according to the thematic patterns of science, flexibly and for their own purposes. This means, at least, teaching them to "talk science" in class, on tests, in talking their way through to the solution of a problem (aloud or to themselves), and in writing or speaking about issues to which science is relevant.

How, in a classroom, do teachers and students use language to build up thematic patterns that correspond to the conceptual systems of a subject like science? What strategies are used to make it easier for students to correctly infer semantic relationships from the words that are actually heard? How, in short, can we *teach* thematic patterns in the classroom as we *use* them? I call the strategies by which teachers and students come to share a new thematic pattern in their classroom dialogue *thematic development strategies*. The next few sections describe some of the most important and useful of these strategies, as actually observed in science classrooms. Appendix D provides a more comprehensive list of thematic development strategies.

DIALOGUE STRATEGIES

I want to discuss first a number of strategies for building up thematic patterns by using the resources of the common activity structures for classroom dialogue. We will then consider some of the common monologue strategies, that is, those used in Teacher Summaries, Teacher Narratives, and so on. Finally we will survey strategies that can occur as part of almost any activity structure.

The most common activity structure of science classroom *dialogue*, as we have already seen in Chapters 1 and 3, is Triadic Dialogue. And perhaps the most important and obvious thematic development strategy used in Triadic Dialogue is that of the *Teacher Question Series*. In using this strategy, a teacher plans a sequence or series of thematically interrelated Teacher Questions which, as a whole, construct a set of semantic links that are important to the thematics of the topic being discussed.

We have seen an excellent example of this in the episode on "Atomic Orbitals" analyzed in Chapter 1 (see Transcript DRS-27-NOV). The first Teacher Question (lines 7–8) links DIAGRAM to ELEMENT, the second (lines 10–11) links ELEMENT to NUMBER and ELECTRON (and incidentally ELECTRON to ORBITAL), and the third (line 13) and fourth (line 16) link the parts of the DIAGRAM to the types of ORBITAL. Finally, the fifth Teacher Question (lines 21–24) links all the thematic items together at once. This question is an example of a *thematic nexus*: a point in the dialogue where several thematic relations are all interconnected. A *nexus* is always a key point in the thematic development of an episode or a lesson. By bringing all the parts of a thematic pattern together at once, it not only articulates their semantic relations to one another, but it makes sense only if students can interpret it using the whole pattern. Often, as here, they cannot, or it takes them a while to figure out what is being said or asked.

Later in this same lesson, the teacher asks a series of questions about similarities in the properties of certain groups of elements (copper, silver, and gold; chlorine, bromine, and iodine). Then he asks a series about similarities in their electron orbital configurations. The two come together at a *nexus* only when he first says "the outermost electron shell is similar. They have, therefore, similar properties." This is the main point of the whole lesson, the climax to which it is building. It links CONFIGURATION to PROPERTIES, but each of these is already a *condensation*, that is, a name for a whole little thematic pattern (e.g., CONFIGURATION is [NUMBER—Quantification—ELECTRONS]—Location—[TYPE—Classification—ORBITALS]). There is a full analysis of this episode in Lemke (in press-b).

We have already seen in Chapter 1 that the Teacher Question Series in that first episode also implicitly develops the three Attributes of ORBITALS: SIZE, SHAPE, and ORIENTATION. It does this by asking questions in a sequence that compares first the "1s" orbital with the "2s," which differ from each other only in size (not in shape or orientation), then the 2s and the 2p, which differ in shape, but not in size, and finally the 2px and 2py, which differ only in orientation. These Attributes are explicitly mentioned only in the episode Summary (lines 39–40), but they are visible in the blackboard diagram (Figure 1.1 in Chapter 1), and the question series calls attention to them in this way. But the actual thematic development, that is, the explicit verbal mentions and linkages of terms corresponding to thematic items (e.g., 1s, 2px) do *not* always appear in the Teacher Question move itself. In this case, "1s" is mentioned as part of the Teacher Preparation move for a question, "2px" is part of a Teacher Elaboration on a Student Answer, and "2s" and "2p" are part of Student Answers.

None of this is too surprising, of course, because the teacher has been controlling the thematic development through his Preparation and Question moves. So long as the students provide the thematically correct answer, Triadic Dialogue provides efficient exposition of thematic relations. It is, as we have seen before, a transposition of a teacher lecture or monologue into dialogue form. The students play "straight man" for the teacher's routine.

What happens in Triadic Dialogue when students do *not* give just the answer the teacher, and the standard thematic pattern, expect? Sometimes a teacher may hear several answers and simply *select* for approval and repetition the one that fits the thematic pattern he or she is trying to develop. This happens for example in the episode on "Longitudinal Waves" (EL-20-NOV) when in answer to the question, "Can you give me an example of a longitudinal wave?" students call out answers: "Waves" "Wave motion" "Sound" "Sound wave." The teacher replies to all this:

Teacher: Yeah! Who said "sound" first?
Gary: Me!
Teacher: Y'did? Alright, Gary, you're right. It's *sound*. Sound wave
            is a perfect example of longitudinal wave motion.

The teacher has first selected Gary's "sound" (with his Evaluation move) and then the slightly better answer "sound wave" (in his Elaboration) to incorporate into the thematic development. "Sound wave" is better thematically because it implies that sound is a wave, a kind of wave, that is, SOUND—token/type—WAVE.

In other cases the teacher cannot simply select, but has to *modify* the Student Answer to fit the thematic pattern. This can be a simple modification, as for example when the teacher in the lesson analyzed in Chapter 2, before the Debate episode, had asked "What form of radiant energy do we get from the sun?" A student answers "Sunlight." But the teacher says, unusually explicitly: "I'm gonna kinda capsulize that, and write down *light.. energy.*"

A moment later another student gives a belated answer of "solar energy," and the teacher responds: "OK. That's another way of saying light energy from the sun." And finally still another student answers "Heat." To this the teacher responds, "Well, I'm not—Yeah, you're right, but a very *small* amount, compared to the light, OK?" He tries to explain what he means, and this exchange is a probable precursor of the Debate, as you can well see. There has been selection here, of "light" to represent [LIGHT—hyponymy—ENERGY], and modification, into "light energy."

A little later in this lesson the teacher asks, "What determines the amount of absorption, or the *amount* of reflection? [that is, of sunlight by the earth]" As answers he gets "the seasons" and "the color of the object." He asks for an expansion of this second answer and gets a long reply which includes, "And if it's a cloudy day, (. . .) the earth's surface isn't going to be absorbing that much because the clouds are reflecting some of the light." The teachers gives a positive evaluation saying, "You hit on a key idea." Then he writes at the board the official answer and reads it aloud, "The surface composition. Is it *water* we're talking about. Is it *land*? (. . .)" He has extracted just the phrase "earth's surface" from the Student Answer, which was certainly not the main point the student was making, but which did link briefly into the thematic pattern the teacher is trying to develop. And he has modified it into "surface composition." These examples should serve to illustrate the important thematic development strategy in Triadic Dialogue of *Selection and Modification* of Student Answers.

A related strategy is that of *Retroactive Recontextualization* of Student Answers. This has a fancy name because it is of considerable importance to the theory of meaning (see Chapter 8). In essence, it means simply that *after* an answer has already been given, which had one meaning in the context of the dialogue that preceded it, the teacher says something to alter the context and make it seem, retroactively, that the Answer had quite a different (or additional) meaning. In a way this happened when the teacher modified "earth's surface" to "surface composition" and connected it to the LAND *vs.* WATER contrast. It happens more strongly in the "Crustal Uplift" geology episode discussed at the start of this chapter (Transcript SC-20-MAR). The teacher asks a rather oblique review question on the second day:

Teacher: We talked about *elevations*. What *about* elevations?
Monica: You can tell whether they were under water, or *above* water by the *fossils*.
Teacher: OK, we talked about finding *marine* fossils (. . .) at high elevations, in high mountains.

Whatever thematic pattern Monica may have been constructing for herself, the teacher borrows "under water" and shifts it from a Location to a Classification as "marine fossils" and puts them in a clearer relation to "above water" by expressing HEIGHTS differently. We have already seen the thematic pattern the teacher is trying to develop here. He has retroactively made Monica's answer seem to fit it more closely than her words taken by themselves, without what he says afterwards, might have lead us to.

An even more extreme example of retroactive recontextualization comes at one point in the "Atomic Orbitals" lesson when the teacher has asked the class whether a circular motion he is making with his hand is clockwise or counterclockwise. The context has been that electrons in the same orbital spin in opposite directions, one clockwise, the other counterclockwise. The students intelligently recognize this as a "trick" question and reply that from their viewpoint it is counterclockwise, but that from the teacher's viewpoint it would be clockwise. The teacher, pleased, responds: "Relativity! That's how Einstein made his fortune."

The teacher has suddenly altered and expanded the thematic context from electrons spinning in orbitals, to relative motion generally, and introduced the new thematic formation of Einstein's theory of relativity (which does have to do with relative motion, the viewpoint of an observer, and even electron spins). The teacher is mostly making a joke, a kind of clever pun on "relative," but at the same time he places the Student Answer in a context that gives it a much wider meaning than it had before his Elaboration.

Finally, there is one more important dialogue strategy that I want to discuss, *Joint Construction*. It sometimes happens that the thematic development of a dialogue is so closely shared between the student and teacher contributions that they complete one another's sentences or one another's meanings. This works best when both teacher and students are using the same thematics, as when Student Answers complete Teacher Question sentences in the "Atomic Orbitals" episode (lines 10–20). When the fit is less perfect, the teacher's contributions shift the final meanings toward the desired thematics.

This can also be illustrated from the end of the episode in this same lesson in which the class has been going over their last night's homework (Transcript DRS-27-NOV). Mario answers the last textbook question ("Distinguish between an atom in its ground state and an excited atom.") by reading an answer copied from the book. The teacher asks him if he knows what he's saying (a good example of the difference between just saying words and really making meanings thematically), and then asks if anyone else can "say it differently," that is, in their own words. This is much harder, and the teacher helps out:

Cheryl: Um. . the ground state is at a lower energy—
Teacher: No *added* energy. Yeah?
Cheryl: —and the excited is—
Teacher: You add something, like thermal energy, like heat.
          Electrons jump to another shell, another kind of higher
          energy orbit, and, uh, they're *excited*.

One could imagine a student having said, or written: "The ground state is at a lower energy (no *added* energy) and the excited is, you add energy." In effect, this is said here by the student and the teacher together, jointly constructing an Answer. In terms of the *activity structure*, that is, the social interaction, the teacher is *interrupting* the student; but in terms of thematic development, a single set of thematic relations is being built by the two together.

It is perhaps worth a moment to analyze the thematic development here a little more closely. The Textbook Question has set up a Contrast relation (See Appendix C) between the meanings of GROUND STATE and EXCITED (by saying "distinguish between") and has implied that these are possible Attributes of an ATOM. Cheryl's first contribution picks up GROUND STATE and gives it an Attribute, LOW ENERGY, at the same time implying a Comparison relation to something else ("lower energy"). The teacher now chimes in with the theme of ADD (a Process) and its Range, ENERGY. It is said in such a way that his whole comment could be taken as a parenthetic Elaboration of "at a lower energy." This sets up an Equivalence between two meaning structures: ADD ENERGY to an ATOM (or not), and: ATOM with Attribute LOW (or HIGH) ENERGY. The Equivalence is between NOT ADD ENERGY and LOW ENERGY, of course.

Cheryl continues by giving the other item in the Contrast Pair, EXCITED, and is about to give its Attribute, which, to complete the Comparison relation, would probably be HIGH ENERGY, say, "is at a higher energy." The teacher simply completes this for her using *his* wording of the thematics: ADD ENERGY. What he actually says first omits the word "energy," then gives a Hyponym of ENERGY "thermal energy" (THERMAL is a classifier of ENERGY, the whole phrase is a hyponym of ENERGY). And again using the vague linking term "like" he adds a Synonym of THERMAL ENERGY, namely HEAT.

That much is not really thematically different from what the student was presumably about to say, except for the thematic potential of ADD as a process, to link to more thematic items at once than an Attribute can. What is really new is his Elaboration on their joint answer, which brings in ELECTRON. In fact he transfers the Attribute EXCITED from ATOM to ELECTRON, and by doing this manages to make the link back to ORBITAL, which now takes the Attribute HIGH ENERGY, formerly given to ATOM. In this way the teacher has shifted from a simple contrast between two possible attributes of an ATOM (GROUND STATE/LOW ENERGY vs. EXCITED/HIGH ENERGY) to a thematic linkage of two Processes: ADD ENERGY and ELECTRONS JUMP.

With the flexibility of these Processes and the thematics of an ATOM as ELECTRONS—Location—ORBITALS, he can and does proceed to construct a new contrast JUMP vs. FALL BACK, and connect that to ADD vs. LOSE ENERGY, and finally to the atom's emitting the lost energy in the form of a photon of light energy "with a special characteristic wavelength." We can begin to see here how thematic development can take a simple semantic relationship (Contrast of Attributes) and extend it into a rich and complex thematic pattern. We will see more details of how this is done later in the chapter.

There is much more to be said about how teachers use the relations of different moves in Triadic Dialogue (e.g., Preparation to Question, Elaboration to Answer) for thematic development, but the discussion here and in Chapter 1 should already have given a fairly good idea of the most common strategies. In other classroom dialogue activity structures, such as Debates, Student Questioning Dialogue, and External Text Dialogue, there are similar strategies (see Lemke, 1983b, Chapter 3). In activity structures where the teacher cannot control the thematic development as easily through his questions, he or she does so through Teacher Answers (Student Questioning Dialogue) or even through Elaborations (External Text Dialogue; see Lemke, 1989b).

Having said enough for now about dialogue strategies, we have still to consider some of the strategies specific to classroom *monologues*.

MONOLOGUE STRATEGIES

The emphasis on student participation in classroom dialogue has led, at least in junior and senior high school science lessons, to a great reduction in the amount of monologue. Teachers do not lecture much; in fact, many of them do very little explaining or even summarizing. Teachers tend to organize lessons predominantly in terms of Triadic Dialogue. But there are still moments of monologue, when the teacher provides information, explains a point, tells a story or anecdote, gives a long answer to a student question, or summarizes a discussion. There are certain thematic development strategies that tend to be associated with each of these functions of teacher monologues. Student monologues are very rare indeed, occurring mainly in the form of long answers to Teacher Questions, or occasionally when a student is trying to clarify some point which was misunderstood in a briefer form.

One of the most common strategies in teacher monologues, *Logical Exposition*, occurs when teachers are trying to make a logical argument that requires a number of logical connections between points. This cannot be done very efficiently through Triadic Dialogue. At one point in the "Atomic Orbitals" lesson, while the class is going over the homework questions, a student answers a "Why?" question about the fact that two electrons in the same atom cannot have the same four quantum numbers (quantum numbers are Attributes of ELECTRONS):

Sam: I think it has something to do with the electron spin? . . .
           that they always run, ah, *spin* in opposite directions.
Teacher: It happens to be called the *Hund* rule, that if two
           electrons had exactly the same four quantum numbers in an

atom, it would mean that they were in the same place at
the same time. . . And in reality two things cannot be in
the same place at the same time. So that if they were—had
the same quantum numbers, that's what they would be. So
they have to be slightly different.

The connection back to electron spin gets made just a little later.
Notice that Sam corrected himself from "run" to "spin" corresponding
to his having mastered a distinction between two ways of talking about
the possible movement of ELECTRONS; in some contexts they MOVE
(i.e., "go" "travel" "run"), but in this one they SPIN. The Teacher Monologue is fit into the dialogue as a long Elaboration, or perhaps a Cor-
rection, to Sam's answer. The teacher Names a Rule, then States the
Rule. He then proceeds to Apply the Rule to the present case, constructing a logical argument (basically a *reductio ad absurdum*).

The thematic content of the argument is just that ELECTRONS in the
same ATOM do not have the same four QUANTUM NUMBER Attributes and are not in the same PLACE at the same TIME. The Logical
Exposition constructs this content by arguing for it according to a time-
honored rhetorical pattern of classical logic: A implies B/ not B/ therefore, not A. The rhetorical structure is not itself thematic (see Genres
and Rhetoric below). It is more like an activity structure, a way of using
the thematics to reach a conclusion. The same thematic pattern can be
expressed in many different logical and rhetorical sequences of statements or questions, just as it can be expressed through many activity
structures.

As a second example of Logical Exposition, consider the lesson on
the "Giant Cell" (Transcript JR-29-OCT). We are in the midst of a
Teacher-Student Debate over whether size alone impairs the efficiency
of a cell. A student has just argued that if we make the cell bigger,
everything about it gets bigger in proportion, so it should be just as
efficient as a small cell. The teacher responds:

Uh, that's a good point. The thing that turns up here—I didn't want to
bring it up because it gets into geometry, and I don't know if you've had
this in geometry yet—but as the area of—we're talking not about a circle
now, we're talking about a *sphere*, OK? a *ball*—as the area of a ball- as
the size of the ball gets bigger, the *volume*, the space *inside*, gets larger a
lot faster, than the surface area, OK, the area along the *outside*. So that,
even though the outside would be getting bigger, maybe, a greater proportion of material in the middle—

At this point he is interrupted by a student objecting to a part of his
argument and the Debate continues. Again the teacher Introduces a

Rule (Proportional Scaling), not by naming it, but by introducing a new thematics, that of Geometry. He again seeks to Apply the Rule using a logical argument. As in the previous example, the logical connector "so" turns up to signal Logical Exposition. The key element of the thematic pattern is UNEQUAL PROPORTION, expressed once in the Rule by "larger. . .faster" and once in the Application by "greater proportion." The students can be expected to understand the argument only insofar as they interpret these two ways of saying that VOLUME ("inside") increases in GREATER PROPORTION than AREA ("outside") as having the same thematic meaning. As a Logical Exposition of the thematics, the Application amounts to a restatement of the Rule, and so as an additional opportunity for the students to master the thematic pattern common to both (see Repetition and Variation below).

Another important monologue strategy is the use of *Narrative*. Like a logical argument, a narrative is also a rhetorical structure that provides a framework for the systematic expression of a thematic pattern. It should be obvious that thematic patterns, as we see from their complex diagrams, are not *linear*. That is, thematic items are interconnected in loops, with some items being joined to many others, and therefore there is no unique path through a diagram, no single natural way to say it as a sentence or paragraph. Instead we have to choose some sequencing strategy to decide in what order we will say its various parts. Narratives, like logical argument patterns, provide sequential frameworks for expressing thematic patterns.

A Narrative tends to proceed chronologically, rather than by logic alone, in its sequence. It narrates a sequence of events, aiming at a Climax, or End Result, rather than at a Conclusion in logic. Teachers use Narratives to tell anecdotes, stories, and jokes, and sometimes to produce extended analogies (see below). Often these have thematic systems of their own that are not related to the topic of the lesson. One case in which they do contribute to thematic development, however, is when they are used in Teacher Explanations of complex processes, that is, those that have several stages.

For example, at one point in the lesson on "Longitudinal Waves" the teacher decides to explain how a SOUND PULSE travels by "compressing" and "stretching apart" air MOLECULES first in one place and then in another next to it. He draws the sequence of events at the blackboard and narrates each stage. He begins by setting up the situation when there is AIR but no SOUND (the "Initial State" in the Narrative structure); he then introduces a SOUND PULSE (the Complication, in narrative terminology), and proceeds to narrate a sequence of "Episodes" or events.

This narrative does not end with a Resolution; its Final State is the repeating cycle of the sound pulse traveling on indefinitely. One could, of course, continue the narrative in a different way and end with a return to silence. What is important for thematic development is that students are familiar with the conventions of narrative or story telling, even in this simplest form. The teacher can use the format of a narration to link the thematic Processes and other Items of one narrative event or episode to those of the next, creating a complete exposition of the thematic pattern.

Let's conclude this section with a brief look at monologue strategies in Teacher Summaries. Essentially there are three strategies that seem to be common to most Summaries: *Selection, Foregrounding and Backgrounding*, and *Connection*. Summaries are extremely important to thematic development because they both *select* and *synthesize* thematic content.

Selection refers to the fact that a summary does not repeat everything that was said in the dialogue that is being summarized; a summary is selective, it includes only the essential or important thematic items and relations. This is crucial for students, because they usually do not know, as the dialogue proceeds, what is going to turn out to be important in the end and what is not. The summary also synthesizes the different thematic relations by directly linking them to one another; that is, it is a thematic *nexus*.

Foregrounding, and its complement, Backgrounding, carry the process of selection one degree further, by emphasizing *within* the summary, and therefore within the thematic pattern, just *which* relations are the most important. This is usually done in summaries by vocal emphasis (verbal stress or highlighted intonation) on key words expressing the foregrounded items or relations. What is not foregrounded in this way is, relatively speaking, backgrounded.

Finally, summaries are not usually totally isolated and self-contained. They will contain some elements, or be introduced or immediately followed by elements, that connect the thematics they describe to some still larger thematic pattern, or some related thematics. These Connections are not only to what has been said previously, but they often also prefigure or preview what is to come in the lesson. These strategies are illustrated by examples analyzed in Lemke (1983b, Chapter 3).

We can now conclude our survey of thematic development strategies by looking at what are probably the most fundamental ones, those which can be used in almost any activity structure, dialogue, or monologue.

ESTABLISHING THEMATIC PATTERNS: FUNDAMENTAL TECHNIQUES

In this section we are going to look at examples of the techniques by which some of the most essential semantic relations are *implicitly* communicated. Only rarely (see Metadiscourse below) do teachers or students make *explicit* the semantic relations in their talk, by naming, describing, or commenting on them. We will see how teachers and students communicate the fact that two expressions are meant to be equivalent to one another or to be in contrast with one another. We will see how semantic relations are established by analogies and grammatical patterns, and how thematic patterns are communicated by the strategy of repetition-with-variation. We will look at examples that occur over a stretch of a few words and we will discuss patterns that stretch over whole lessons and beyond.

Equivalence and Contrast

The two most basic semantic relationships for thematic development are Local Equivalence and Local Contrast. Equivalence is not simply based on synonyms, nor Contrast on antonyms. Those are only one means of establishing that in a particular discussion, or for a particular thematic system, two expressions are to be interpreted as meaning in effect the same thing, or as having opposite, complementary, or contrasting meanings. Some of the key strategies can be illustrated from the Teacher Summary quoted earlier concering the geometry of scaling (JR-29-OCT):

> Uh, that's a good point. The thing that turns up here—I didn't want to bring it up because it gets into geometry, and I don't know if you've had this in geometry yet—but as the area of—we're talking not about a circle now, we're talking about a *sphere*, OK? a *ball*—as the area of a ball- as the size of the ball gets bigger, the *volume*, the space *inside*, gets larger a lot faster, than the surface area, OK, the area along the *outside*. So that, even though the outside would be getting bigger, maybe, a greater proportion of material in the middle—

In the fourth and fifth lines the teacher sets up a Local Contrast between "circle" and "sphere." He uses two techniques to do this. First he places them in *Parallel Environments*, "we're talking (not) about a . . .." Parallel environments means that the words or expressions to be contrasted (or marked as equivalent, see below) occupy the same or corresponding "slots" in similar or identical grammatical constructions. The strongest parallelism, as here, has exactly the same words preceding or following the contrasted, or equated, ones. Even if the words are not quite identical, if the grammar is the same, there can be a slightly weaker parallelism, and in the weakest case, only the thematic relations of each term to its own neighbors may be the same, with different actual wordings and grammar. In the last case you have to already know the thematic formation used to establish the parallelism to get the additional information about the contrast or equivalence.

When the technique of parallel environments is used to establish Contrast, of course, it is common to have a specific verbal signal, such as "not" "but" or "on the other hand" in addition to the parallelism. In this example, as frequently, there is also a second technique used to signal Contrast, the *Contrastive Vocal Stress* or emphasis on one of the terms (*"sphere"*). We saw many examples of this contrastive stress technique in Chapter 2 during the Debate.

Notice that "circle" and "sphere" are *not* normally antonyms. They are placed in contrast here only for the purposes of this lesson, though that contrast is based on a thematic system in geometry which contrasts geometrically similar figures in two- and three-dimensions.

Immediately after establishing this local contrast (i.e., contrasting "locally," in *this* discussion), the teacher introduces a local equivalence between "sphere" and "ball." He uses three techniques in doing so. First, the words "sphere" and "ball" *are* commonly synonyms of each other. It is still necessary, however, to establish that they are thematically equivalent in this particular discussion. Every thematic pattern defines its own set of equivalent and contrasting terms; any two synonyms *can* be made to contrast for the purposes of a particular discussion, and even antonyms can have their opposition in meanings neutralized temporarily in a discussion or suspended generally in the thematics of a particular topic. Here we know that "sphere" and "ball" are being made equivalent because they are also in *Apposition* to one another, and they have the same stress given to them (called *Tone Concord* in linguistics). Apposition and tone concord are the two most common techniques of establishing thematic equivalence of expressions, even when they are not synonyms.

Apposition is often used in a technique called *Glossing*, in which a teacher restates what he has just said in a way that informally defines it or gives its meaning, usually by making it equivalent to a more familiar expression. This is most often done with unfamiliar terms, but it can be done just to make sure an expression is understood. For example:

> Remember I told you that we might find *shallow* water fish, fish that are known to be found in shallow waters, very low waters, we find these *fossils* in deep oceans.

First there is an appositional gloss on "shallow water fish" and then there is even a gloss on "shallow waters." In the second case, "shallow" is made equivalent to "very low" by the strategy of parallel environments ("... waters"), as two expressions for the same thematic Classifier SHALLOW. There are also two Contrasts here. There is contrastive stress on the first *"shallow"* to indicate that these are SHALLOW-WATER fish as opposed to DEEP-OCEAN fish. The second is on *"fossils"* to indicate FOSSIL FISH as opposed to LIVING FISH. Here the contrasts have already been established for the thematic pattern being used in the episode, now they are being *used*. But every use of a thematic relation is also a reinforcement of it, a part of teaching it so that it sticks and students come to use it for themselves.

As a final example of establishing Equivalence, consider:

> How did you know it *lost* electrons? How did you notice that it's minus an electron here?

Even though there is contrastive stress on *"lost"* to indicate that LOSE in in contrast with GAIN here, an equivalence is set up between "lost" and being "minus an" by the parallel environments. Notice that the environments are not exactly parallel in either wording or grammar, but they are two Teacher Questions in apposition, one restating the other, and they express the same thematic relations of ATOM, LOSE, and ELECTRON. This is enough to establish the equivalence.

I want to illustrate, finally, one other common technique for establishing contrast, *Self-correction*. In the "Atomic Orbitals" lesson we find:

> Notice here at the bottom, Lanthanide and Actinide. Those are the f shells being filled up—the f orbitals being filled up.

The teacher has made a simple mistake and corrects himself in mid-sentence. In some contexts, "shells" and "orbitals" could be taken as synonymous in the thematics of atomic theory, but *not* when the Classifier "f" precedes the term. Then only "orbitals" is correct. The self-correction here helps establish that in this context SHELL and ORBITAL are in thematic contrast. A little later:

> The electron dot notation I mentioned is the outside orbital—uh, *wrong*—is the outside *shell*.

Again the teacher makes this easy mistake and corrects himself, but here he uses an explicit verbal sign of contradiction (*"wrong"*), as if evaluating an Answer, and also the vocal contrastive stress on *"shell."* This is the less common, if more obvious, case of contrast by self-correction. Our first example is more the norm, but because it is less obvious, the clue it gives to an important conceptual distinction remains very subtle and implicit.

It is obviously extremely important to clue students in on whether two expressions are meant to say the same thing in different words or to say two different things. You can perhaps imagine the difficulties non-native speakers of English, or even speakers of English dialects other than those of the teacher, can have interpreting clues as subtle as the ones I have been describing. Nevertheless, these are the only clues available most of the time. (See Metadiscourse below for the rare exceptions.)

Repetition with Variation

Although Equivalence and Contrast may be the two most basic semantic relations, obviously there are many more and there need to be ways for teachers to help students abstract from any one particular wording of the relations of a thematic pattern to the pattern itself. Only in this way can they become free of parroting back fixed wordings and begin to use thematic *meanings* flexibly to answer questions, talk their way through problems, and so on.

The fundamental technique for helping students see that there are many different ways to express the same thematic relations is the use of Repetition with Variation. In this technique, over the course of a few minutes, or a whole period, the same thematic relations are expressed in slightly different wordings. If repetition were exact, students would be dependent on fixed wordings and might or might not interpret their thematic meanings. With variation, it is possible for students, even unconsciously, to do intertextual comparison, to hear each expression in the context of the others. This not only leads to mastery of meanings, rather than memorization of wordings, it also gives students models of different, and so flexible, ways of constructing the thematic relations with words. Of course, just listening to the teacher do this is not enough; they need practice at doing it themselves, at putting things into "their own" or "different" words.

We have already seen one excellent example of Repetition with Variation at the beginning of this chapter. We analyzed a number of ways in which the relation of MARINE FOSSILS to CRUSTAL UPLIFT were expressed. We could construct the thematic pattern there precisely because we had not just fixed words, but variations that enabled us to extract their common thematic meanings: the items and semantic relations that each expressed in different ways. It is for that very reason that all lessons use this technique constantly.

I will analyze just one further example of this pervasive teaching strategy, from the lesson on the "Giant Cell" (JR-29-OCT). The teacher is summarizing the previous discussion on why a cell cannot just grow indefinitely in size. He gets interrupted a few times by questions and objections and so has to restate his summary several times. He also constructs a final "official" version, which he writes on the blackboard and reads out loud. In all there are five versions of the same summary in less than two minutes. Here are some of the repetitions with variation:

> The reason the cell size is limited is because as the cell gets larger and larger and larger, the proportions in—the living material in the very center of the cell is deprived of food and oxygen. So a cell can't just become larger and larger and larger. . . .
> And we saw that the cell size was limited because as the cell got larger, the center of the cell had a harder and harder time getting the things it needs to stay alive. . . .
> So the reason the cell size is limited, [is] because as the cell *gets* larger . . . it becomes harder and harder for the central part of the cell to get the things it needs to stay alive. . . .
> It becomes harder for the center of the cell to get the necessary material. Materials like food, oxygen. . . .

It is easy enough to see by comparing these examples that there are variations in word choice for the same thematic item: "the living material in the very center of the cell" "the center of the cell" "the central part of the cell" for CELL CENTER (or maybe NUCLEUS), "deprived of" "harder time getting" "harder to get" for DEPRIVATION, "food and oxygen" "things it needs to stay alive" "necessary material" for MATERIAL. There are also differences of grammatical construction, and different ways of expressing semantic relations such as Cause/Consequence, and Token/Type (e.g., FOOD to MATERIAL). In the course of the whole episode, there are even more variations expressing the basic thematic relations of the topic's thematic pattern.

Structural Strategies

The last major category of fundamental strategies are those that make use of grammatical, syntactic, rhetorical, and generic structures. Analyzing these techniques often requires formal training in linguistics or discourse theory (see Chapter 8). Fortunately *using* them does not, just as we can all use English syntax when we speak without studying it formally. It is only if we wish to *change* the way we use these techniques, to accomodate to the needs of our students, or to become more aware of what we are doing that we need to learn more about the basics of language itself. I think that many of us who try to contribute to society by teaching and communicating effectively, may *want* to learn more about language. It is, after all, the principal tool and resource we have for what we want to accomplish. I will discuss this issue further in Chapter 7.

Meanwhile, I can sketch out how and why structural strategies are important for teaching thematic-conceptual systems, and give a few examples. First of all, linguistic theory shows language as being organized into structural units (that is not the only way it is organized, of course). A sentence is a kind of structural unit, and so is a paragraph. Within sentences, individual *clauses* (which generally contain a verb) are structural units, and within clauses there are (among other units) noun groups (like "shallow water fish") that are also structural units. An Exchange in Triadic Dialogue (i.e., one set of Teacher Question, Student Answer, Teacher Evaluation, and any other optional moves in the same set) is a structural unit. A syllogism (Major Premise, Minor Premise, Conclusion) is a structural unit.

All these different structural units are not necessarily units of the same system of organization. Noun groups and clauses are part of the syntactic organization of language. Sentences and paragraphs are part of the organization of writing (people do not actually *speak* in sentences and paragraphs, cf. Halliday, 1985b). A syllogism is part of the rhetorical organization of language, and an Exchange in Triadic Dialogue is part of the activity structure organization of language. The written equivalent of an activity structure is called a *Genre*, such as a sonnet, a limerick, a simple narrative, and so on. In the sections on monologue and dialogue strategies we have already discussed some of the common classroom uses of genre structures and activity structures in thematic development.

What do all these structural units have in common that makes them useful for thematic development? Essentially, each one consists of a number of specific *parts* (e.g., Clause Subject, Teacher Elaboration, Minor Premise, Narrative Complication, Topic Sentence, etc.). Each part has a specific *function* within the overall unit, and a specific functional relation to each of the other parts within the unit (e.g., Teacher Question to Student Answer). Those functional relations of the parts imply relations between the *meanings* of whatever is said in each part, and therefore provide clues to semantic relationships. How do we know, for example, who hit whom in "Maria hit Jesse"? That is, how do we decide, knowing that HIT is the Process, whether Maria or Jesse is the Agent, and who is the Target? We know because an English clause of this kind is a structural unit with the following three functional parts:

Clause Agent/Subject—Process Verb—Clause Target/Object

They happen to always come in this order when the Process Verb is in the Active Voice—as opposed to "Jesse was hit by Maria," which is in the Passive Voice, where the parts come: (a) Clause Target/Subject, (b) Process [Passive] Verb, (c) Clause Agent. You may or may not know how to do this grammatical analysis of the clause, but you do know that it was Maria who hit Jesse and not vice versa. So you do know that the thematic pattern would be MARIA—Ag/Pr—HIT—Pr/Tg—JESSE. You know it because you are so used to the structural pattern of this kind of clause that you automatically infer the correct semantic relationships.

Something similar happens with all the other kinds of structural units in language. We use the familiar patterns of meaning relationships among their parts to communicate the semantic relationships of thematic items in the thematic pattern of the subject we are talking about. The structural pattern of a certain kind of clause is always the same whether we are talking about giant cells, crustal uplift, or the weather. And so is the structural pattern of a syllogism or an analogy, a Triadic Dialogue or a Teacher-Student Debate.

In Chapter 1 we already saw that there was a very subtle difference in the thematic pattern of the "Atomic Orbitals" episode that was signaled only by a difference in grammatical structure. In one line the teacher asked, "What two elements could be represented by . . ." and in another, "What element is being represented by . . .?" The important difference here is a difference in the Modality (cf. Halliday, 1985a, pp. 85–89, 332–341) of the Clause Verb, represented by the auxiliary verb "could." The difference of singular vs. plural (a difference of Number in the Noun Group) on "elements" is also thematically significant here (see Chapter 1).

In that same episode, there is an even subtler thematic relation that is marked by a minor point of grammar. When the teacher gives his Positive Evaluations of answers like "Two electrons," he only says "Two." But when the answer is "Two P," he does not, and could not, just say "Two." He has to say "Two P." Why? The answer depends on two things. First, the rules of *ellipsis* in English, that is, the rules that say when you can and cannot leave something out and still be understood (see Halliday & Hasan, 1976, Chapter 4). And second, the fact that the "two" is in one case semantically a Quantifier and in the other case a Classifier.

The quantifier is grammatically a *cardinal* number (one, two, three, and so on), but the classifier is actually an *ordinal* number (first, second, third, and so on). Does it matter? It may not matter if a student misses this little point here, but sooner or later the student must learn how to talk this science correctly, and that includes treating the TWO in TWO—cl/th—S one way in speaking and reasoning, and the TWO in TWO—quantif—ELECTRONS another. How is the student to learn this? Mainly from just such subtle clues as this one, repeated many times in many ways.

As an example of a technique that uses a more obvious kind of structural pattern, consider the rhetorical pattern we call an *Analogy*. This is a favorite device of teachers, and one which is very effective. *Why* is it effective? More to the point, *when* is it likely to work well or not so well? What makes a good analogy? What makes an analogy work is very simple in thematic terms. An analogy sets up a simple correspondence between two thematic patterns. The patterns have different thematic items, but the same semantic relations between them. One pattern is already familiar, the other is new. Students learn to transfer semantic relationships from the familiar thematic items and their pattern to the unfamiliar items and their pattern.

The principle behind Analogies applies also to Metaphors (where unexpected words are used to express a thematic item because those words also express the corresponding items in some other, analogous thematic pattern). We have mentioned already the case of the teacher who said:

> Electron comes to town, wants to go into the cheapest hotel. It goes into the cheapest one that's available. If the 1s is there, if it's empty, *fine*. If the 2s is there, empty, fine. 2P? Great. What's the *next* lowest?

Here we have an extended metaphor (a Conceit), which is based on an implicit analogy between the familiar thematic pattern in which we connect the items PERSON, ARRIVE, TOWN, CHEAP, AVAILABLE, and HOTEL. We know what the semantic relations among these items normally are. What the teacher actually says sometimes substitutes common words for these items to express the less familiar items: ELECTRON, ENTER, ATOM, LOW-ENERGY, UNOCCUPIED, ORBITAL. To a not very high degree of delicacy, the semantic relations of corresponding items in the two patterns are the same. Notice that the teacher mixes expressions from the two patterns, starting for example with "cheapest" and ending with "lowest" though the meaning in both cases is that of the thematic item LOWEST ENERGY.

In the discussion of the "Giant Cell" and why it can't grow larger indefinitely, the teacher introduced an analogy between the cell and a large crowd at an outdoor political rally (JR-29–OCT). A systematic analogy is developed, with the student providing the details of the problems that might be faced by people in the center of the crowd (heat, smells, need to eliminate wastes, need to get food and water). Each of these is then transferred to build up the new thematic pattern of the argument that is summarized in four versions in the section on Repetition with Variation above. The semantic relations between corresponding items are quite similar (e.g., HOT DOG/NUTRIENT MOLECULE, PASSED ALONG /DIFFUSED, EATEN:STOLEN/ASSIMILATED-OUTSIDE-CENTER, HUNGRY/DEPRIVED). In this case the similarity is no accident, crowds and cells are in many repects physically similar systems. That, too, could be communcated by constucting an analogical correspondence between the thematic patterns we use to define and describe them.

Analogies are most obviously a structural strategy in the case of explicit correspondences. We set up those correspondences according to fixed and familiar rhetorical structures (e.g.,"A is to B as C is to D" and "A is like C and B is like D" and also in many less formal ways). The relations of the parts of the Analogy structure help us build the correspondences between thematic patterns.

These are some of the most important of the structural strategies for thematic development. I want now to briefly mention two final strategies of another kind.

Metadiscourse

Metadiscourse is talk about talk. It is used in everyday speech whenever we comment on or explain what we are doing (including what we are saying), in addition to simply doing it. If we say, "I was only joking" or "this is a dumb conversation" or "what did you mean?" we are talking about our talk. In more formal activity structures, metadiscourse is most often used to mark the boundaries between parts of an activity: "Here endeth the Lesson" "Now let's move on to New Business," or in the episode from Chapter 1, "That's from the other class. We might as well use it for Review." Metadiscourse can of course also be used to identify and clarify semantic relations during thematic development. In fact, this seems to be relatively rare. The thematics of a subject tends to be taught as if all the teacher had to do was say it, not tell how to say it. Here are some exceptions.

Near the beginning of his discussion of "Solar Heating of the Earth," the teacher has written an Aim for the lesson on the blackboard

(LG-26-NOV). It contains the words "factors" and "terrestrial." He immediately says:

> And there are two words in this Aim that I think we better make sure we understand *first*, so we we can go *on* from there (. . .) What is a *factor*? What do you think the word *"factors"* means here? It can mean a *lot* of things, but in this *sense*?

The teacher is focusing on vocabulary here, but also on thematic *meanings*, because he specifies that he's asking what the word means in the immediate thematic context. After he gets a few answers, he says, "OK. In other words there are a lotta ways to describe it, but as long as we understand the key idea." He then gives his own definition and goes on to the other word.

In the lesson on "Longitudinal Waves," it is a student who uses meta-discourse to focus, not on a particular thematic item, but actually on a semantic relation (EL-20-NOV). He does so in order to be sure of just what sort of answer the teacher is looking for:

Teacher: What kind of wave motion is sound?
Student: It's a *wave* motion.
Teacher: What *kind* of wave motion?
Student: Vibration.
Teacher: What *kind* of vibration?
Eugene: Are you askin' which one of those four?
Teacher: Mm-*hmm*.
Eugene: Uh, long—long-i-tu-dinal wave.
Teacher: Eugene is correct.

Several students before Eugene have been unable to figure out what part of the thematic pattern from yesterday's lesson the teacher is asking about. They know that the teacher wants a "kind," a Classifer. They know that WAVE can be a Classifier of MOTION (first answer), that VIBRATION is some sort of synonym or hyponym of WAVE MOTION (second answer), but Eugene guesses that the teacher is asking about the hyponyms of WAVE, rather than of MOTION. He uses meta-discourse to ask if the teacher wants one of the four kinds of waves listed the day before. Once he has identified the semantic relation, he picks the correct Classifier (LONGITUDINAL). His difficulty in pronouncing it indicates just how new and relatively unfamiliar it is to him, but he has "homed in" on it by first checking out which semantic relation was involved.

Finally, in the "Giant Cell" lesson, a student is trying to clear up a particular point about the relation of cell size to the cell's efficiency. He says:

Student: When a cell divides, it gets smaller, right? So wouldn't—
it would not function as well as the perfect size? Now
you're saying *that's* the perfect size, OK?
Teacher: No. I'm *not* saying this is the perfect size. What I'm
saying is the cell could *never* reach a size this big.
Student: No-o-o. I'm just *proving*, you know. Assume that you've got
the ideal size.
Teacher: OK, let's assume there's an ideal size for a cell.
Student: That's the ideal size. Now split it in half. (. . .)

There is a diagram of a cell on the board. It has been referred to as a giant cell, impossibly inefficient, but that was a while ago. Now the student wants to use it to make a point. He says "Now you're saying *that's* the perfect size, OK?" to begin a hypothetical argument. He is speaking colloquially. A more formal equivalent would have been, "Now let's suppose that *that's* the perfect size, OK?" The teacher mistakes this Hypothetical Assumption for a direct Claim that the teacher thinks it *is* the perfect cell. So he denies the Claim. But the teacher has mistaken the Rhetorical Structure the student is trying to use. So the student uses metadiscourse ("I'm just *proving*, you know") to signal that he is trying to *prove* something (as in Geometry), that is, to use the structure of Hypothetical Argument. Now he uses the more formal language, "Assume that . . ." and the teacher catches on.

By talking about his talk and identifying the kind of argument he is trying to make, the student can now use the functional relations of its parts to build a thematic pattern. He is combining metadiscourse with a structural strategy.

Global Strategies

Most of the strategies for communicating the thematics of a subject that we have discussed have been *local* strategies. They are based on the relations of things said only a moment apart from one another. There are also more *global* strategies that rely on building up relations between things said all through a text or lesson.

We have noted that Repetition and Variation can carry over from one part of a lesson to another, and even from one day to another, as can all the strategies based on intertextual comparisons. We have also mentioned the occurrence of a *thematic nexus*, a point where several different strands of the thematics are all brought together and interconnected. Those separate strands, or themes, are pieces of the overall thematic pattern that may have been first introduced quite some time ago in the lesson, or in a previous lesson. Local strategies connect up these separate thematic strands at particular points, weaving the strands together across the whole of the lesson into an overall, or global thematic pattern. Global strategies determine which themes are sounded first and how and when they are brought together with each of the others, in a particular order, to complete the pattern.

In Chapter 2 we saw that one theme in the "Light-Heat Debate" episode, the notion that GROUND—ABSORBS—LIGHT (line 17 in the transcript of LG-26–NOV), had been borrowed by the student from a discussion about five minutes earlier in the lesson, and that discussion reintroduced this theme from the previous week's work. The student creates his own thematic nexus during the Debate, connecting this theme to the other themes of the Debate topic. In the "Longitudinal Waves" lesson, the connection between sound and longitudinal waves that Eugene first made in the lesson at about 1:15 p.m. is the key to answering another question at 1:35 p.m., and to several in between.

Further examples of the global analysis of "theme-weaving" in lessons can be found in separate articles on these lessons (see Lemke, in press-b,-c). You can actually analyze a lesson as you would a musical symphony, with various themes being introduced, connected to others, then disappearing for a time, being reintroduced, shifting from one "voice" to another, to form a harmonious global pattern. Not just lessons, but most forms of communication and cooperative (and even competitive) social activity are like this.

This concludes our general survey of thematic development techniques.

REASONING AS A WAY OF USING LANGUAGE

Early on in this chapter, I argued briefly that what we mean by "conceptual systems" in science and other subjects can best be understood by looking at how we "talk" (and write) them. That is, the systems of related meanings that constitute a scientific theory are learned and used primarily through language and correspond to a thematic pattern of thematic items (key terms, or "concept words") and their semantic relations to one another. That argument left a number of things unsaid. Some I will leave for a fuller discussion in Chapter 8, but there are a few that are worth talking about here.

We have been taught to associate the term "concept" with the term "thinking" and to speak of the use of concepts as a "mental" process.

As I argued earlier in the chapter, it is not very helpful to try to analyze the use of concepts in terms of the physiology of the brain and body in interaction with the environment: not at our present state of knowledge in the neurosciences, and never, unless we can associate physiological events with their *meanings*. Neither is it very useful to try to analyze the use of concepts as "mental" processes, since we know nothing about these processes except what we infer from observations of how people talk, write, and generally act.

Unless we prefer to believe that concepts or meanings have an existence independent of their being made and remade by the social use of language, pictures, and other other systems of signs, we may as well cut out the "middleman" of *mental* concepts, and simply analyze conceptual systems in terms of the thematic patterns of language use and other forms of meaningful human action. For a fuller critique of mentalism and cognitive theories of concept use, see Lemke (1988a, 1989a).

This change in perspective has important implications for what we are accustomed to calling "logical thinking." If the use of logic is not a "mental" process but a *linguistic* one (and more generally a *semiotic* one, see below and Chapter 8), then how can it be described and taught? Let's take "reasoning" as a term that means both a way of talking something through and a way of using logic. Reasoning then is not to be considered in any sense a "mental" process (though of course we do use our *brain* and other systems of our body when reasoning). Reasoning is primarily a way of talking, including a way of writing and a way of talking to ourselves ("inner speech"). We learn it by talking to other members of our community, we practice it by talking to others, and we use it in talking to them, in talking to ourselves, and in writing and other forms of more complex activity (e.g., problem-solving, experimenting).

What makes reasoning *logical* is that it follows certain rhetorical and genre structure *patterns*. That is, it is logical because it lays out an argument in a particular way, e.g., Major Premise, Minor Premise, Conclusion. Being logical, as every course in Logic teaches, has nothing to do with being right. It is simply a matter of following specific patterns of argument from premises to conclusions. The simplest of these patterns belong to the mode of organization of language which I have called rhetorical structures. The larger and more complex patterns, for example, those of a Lab Report or a Scientific Research Article, are genre structures. Anyone can be taught how to put together these structures: what their parts are, what the function of each part is in the whole, what order the parts come in, how the meaning of each part relates to the others. Reasoning is combining the use of a thematic pattern with the use of a rhetorical or genre structure pattern. One supplies the content, the other supplies the form of organization of the argument.

Talking science, in the fullest sense, always combines a thematic pattern of semantic relationships with a structural pattern for organizing how we will express (i.e., construct) them.

Students need to be taught both the thematics of science *and* the genres of science. In the narrow sense, those genres are the accepted patterns of organization of scientific description, argument, and writing. Each one combines various rhetorical structure patterns found in many different subjects (e.g., syllogisms, analogies, definitions) in a way that is characteristic of science as a specialized discipline.

There is a scientific way to describe a flower in botany that is different from how a flower is described in any other context. A Lab Report or Scientific Paper has certain well-defined parts, put together in a particular order, each with its own functions and relations to the others (that is, they are *genres*). A proof in Geometry is a genre, and so is a sonnet in poetry. A classroom activity structure like Triadic Dialogue is also a sort of genre, a genre of action, and so is a Classroom Lesson as a whole. (Some genres have very rigid rules; others are more flexible.) For more discussion of the importance of teaching genres in science and other subjects, see Lemke (1988a).

Reasoning as a total activity is, of course, more than just a way of using language. It is usually part of some problem-solving activity, or some problem-posing activity. We use thematic patterns, which are built from the semantic relationships that language enables us to construct, but we also use visual images, diagrams and formulas, body movements and postures, writing and manual skills. In the laboratory, we work with apparatus in complex ways at the same time we talk ourselves through the steps of what we are doing, to make sense of them, their relations and results. Language is only one resource of our community for making meaning. We also have the resources of depiction, movement, and action. Whether we picture "to ourselves" or on paper, we construct relationships of meaning between images and their parts that may or may not have equivalents in the semantics of language.

Talking science is not the totality of *doing* science. But very little science gets done, or could get done, without the semantic resources of language, and particularly the thematic patterns and genre structures specific to science. A more complete theory of "doing science," that *includes* "talking science," requires that we use a more general theory of how all kinds of action can make meanings. That theory is called Social Semiotics and is described in Chapter 8, but you will find that most of the points made there have already been made in these first four chapters, for the special case of making meaning relationships with language. Most of the basic principles are the same. Language (semantics, thematics, structures) may not be the whole of the means by which we do science, but it is the most important, the best understood, and the model for understanding the rest. (Even mathematics operates in science as a specialized form of language.)

VALUES AND TRUTH

The subtitle of this book is *Language, Learning, and Values*. In each of the first three chapters we have considered both the educational and the wider social implications of our analysis of the language of classroom science. For the most part we have tried to look critically at the ways in which science is commonly taught. Among other problems, we have identified:

- the lack of practice students get in using scientific language for themselves,
- the advantage our methods of teaching give to students with the right kind of middle-class language skills,
- the way classroom activity structures control students' behavior and enforce rules whose deeper implications we may not agree with,
- the ways social class and gender or racial biases can influence our interpretation of students' abilities, based on how they communicate in class.

In each case we have raised issues of basic social values and the social interests of different groups. Given the way things are done, which groups benefit most and which benefit least? How *should* things be, according to our own value systems, and why? What value-choices do we need to make in our daily practice as teachers, educators, and researchers? And what implications do the different choices have for us and for others?

In *this* chapter we have developed in more detail some new ways of talking about the language and teaching of science. The questions that they raise for me are not so much questions about *how* we teach science, about methods and techniques, as they are about the *intellectual status* we claim for what we teach. There are, of course, many practical implications of what we have said in this chapter about the strategies of thematic development used in the classroom. They will be spelled out in detail in Chapter 7. But the way of talking about science that proves so useful in analyzing classroom dialogue has some profound implications for the question of whether we should be teaching science as "objective truth" or not.

By the "intellectual status" of science, I mean whether it is taught as something that is simply "true," that has to be accepted and believed because it describes the way things are, or whether it is taught as one way of talking about the world among many others. I do not mean simply that we should teach that there are rival scientific theories and that any particular theory is tentative until it becomes established (and even afterwards). I am talking about the intellectual status we claim for science in relation to common sense, to poetry, to art, to religion and to all the fundamentally different ways of talking about the world that there are, have been, and can be.

How *does* a scientific theory become "established"? By being proven "true"? By defeating its rivals? By outpredicting other theories? By convincing the elite of the scientific community, or the vast majority of scientists? By getting itself enshrined in the school curriculum and the textbooks? By being taught in universities?

Historically, a new theory always begins as *somebody's* way of talking about a topic or problem. They argue for their theory, or someone else does, and convince others. A faction appear that lobbies for the theory in many ways: by research papers, by experimental tests of predictions, by talks at scientific meetings, by writing books and textbooks, by teaching students, and so on. In the end, a *community* of people, and, most influentially, the most powerful people within that community, determine which theories get published most, used most, taught most.

Science, like every other field of human activity, has its share of fads and fashions, biases and prejudices, crusaders and conservatives, feuds and politics. They influence what theories become "established" in the short-term and the intermediate-term. In the long-term, who knows? No theory is ever proven true. No specific theory, historically, has lasted forever (or even longer than 250 years or so), and the odds are that the science of the year 2500 will not be much like ours at all, if indeed they still have a distinguishable kind of activity that could be called "science" then.

What, after all, *is* a scientific theory? It is a way of talking about a subject using a particular thematic pattern. That does *not* make it a description of the way the world really *is*. Scientists can, and science teachers, I believe, *should* be "agnostics" on the question of whether ultimately there is a way the world *is*. Probably there are many ways the world "is," that is, many ways in which we can make sense of it, many ways in which it can have meaning for us as human beings and as members of various communities at different times in history. Not just this scientific theory or that one, but all of science presents only one way of making sense of the world, one way of making it *mean* for us.

Historically, science has had to fight to become an accepted and influential way of talking about the world. It has had to fight to get published; it has had to fight to get into the school curriculum. In many places today it is still fighting to get into the early grades. It has had to fight religion and it has had to fight common sense. One result of all this struggle has been that science has painted itself as a better, a superior way of talking about the world compared to its rivals. It has even claimed to be, and often presented itself intentionally or unintentionally as, a "truer" or even *the true* way of talking about the world. In science classrooms, except for rare occasions, this is the way science is taught and presented. Not as a way of talking about the world, but as *the way* the world is.

I would not be bringing this point up here if I only wanted to argue that we should emphasize the tentative character of scientific theories when we teach them, or if I wanted to argue for a kind of democratic equality of science, art, politics, religion, common sense, and so on in the curriculum.

I do not believe that these different ways of talking about the world are simply equal voices in a kind of "one-man, one-vote" intellectual parliament. We began this section by recalling the issues of value-choices and group interests. Who benefits most from a view of science as "objective truth"? Or from the view that it is superior to common sense or other discourses about the world? Or from the view that you have to be smarter than other people to understand science? Who benefits least? What are the value-choices to be made in deciding how we will present science?

This has already been a very long chapter. The issues I have raised here about the relations of science, social values, and social interests grow out of a view of science as a way of talking (and a way of doing that incorporates that way of talking) in a community. It is time to take up these questions in their own right. In the next chapter we look at episodes from science classrooms where we can frame these issues in terms of the ways in which teachers and students talk science.

EXPLORING FURTHER

In this chapter we have mainly been concerned with how content knowledge is communicated and jointly constructed between teachers and students. Further discussion of some of these issues will be found in Edwards and Mercer's *Common knowledge: The development of understanding in the classroom* (1987), in Heap's careful analysis in "Discourse in the Production of Classroom Knowledge: Reading Lessons" (1985), and in various chapters in Emihovich's *Locating Learning* (1989).

The methods of thematic analysis are described in more detail in my article "Thematic Analysis: Systems, Structures, and Strategies" (1983) and illustrated also in "Strategic Deployment of Speech and Action: A Sociosemiotic Analysis" (1987). These methods have much in common with the techniques of cohesion analysis developed in Hasan's "Coherence and Cohesive Harmony" (1984) and also described in Halliday and Hasan's *Language, Context, and Text* (1985). Both techniques are based on Michael Halliday's analysis of the semantics of English grammar (*An Introduction to Functional Grammar*, 1985).

chapter 5

Teaching Against the Mystique of Science

Science teaching today too often contributes to the "mystique" of science. We do not just teach science, we also communicate, often without realizing it, a set of harmful attitudes about science. It's understandable that science teachers want students to like science, to appreciate its achievements, and even to admire scientists past and present. Teachers in all subjects try to build positive attitudes. But in science we also tend to reinforce a special mystique of science, a set of harmful myths that favor the interests of a small elite. That elite does not include science teachers, or even most scientists. It is a *technocratic* elite: managers who try to control decisions by appealing to "the findings of experts."

What are these myths about the nature of science? And how do they strengthen the growing power of technocrats in our society? Science teaching often succeeds only too well in convincing students that science is inherently so much more complex and difficult that other subjects that most students will never really understand science. As more and more decisions that affect us all involve scientific and technical issues, this attitude encourages us to defer to what managers tell us "the experts" say we have to do.

Science teaching also tends to pit science against common sense and undermine students' confidence in their own judgment. Those who do understand science are made to seem geniuses in comparison with the average student, who feels frustration at not being able to understand. The "experts" come to seem superhuman, possessed of a perfect, objective knowledge that makes ordinary judgments and opinions irrelevant. Contrary to its spirit and its history, science is being made to legitimize rule by an undemocractic elite of technocratic managers. If we have confidence that most students can become scientifically literate citizens, capable of making informed judgments about issues of policy to which scientific findings are relevant, then we need to learn how to teach *against* this "mystique" of science.

How does science teaching alienate so many students from science? How does it happen that so many students come away from their contact with science in school feeling that science is not for them, that it is too impersonal and inhuman for their tastes, or that they simply "don't have a head for science"? One way this happens, I believe, is through the way we talk science. The language of classroom science sets up a pervasive and false opposition between a world of objective, authoritative, impersonal, humorless scientific fact and the ordinary, personal world of human uncertainties, judgments, values, and interests. It is the second world in which we are all comfortably (or uncomfortably) at home, and science, like all other human endeavor, is a part of that world. It is not something that lies outside it or should be set in opposition to it, but many of the unwritten rules about how we are supposed to talk science make it seem that way.

In this chapter I first want to make explicit some of these unwritten rules or *norms* of talking science that alienate many students from science, making it more difficult for teachers to communicate with them effectively. Then I want to look at some examples of how the twin myths of science's infallibility and its opposition to common sense are reinforced in the classroom. Finally, I will discuss how these teaching practices represent interests and values many of us will want to work against.

THE ONE RIGHT WAY TO TALK SCIENCE

Every specialized kind of human activity, every subject area and field, has its own special language. The language of science is special not just because of its thematic content, or because of its customary written and spoken genres and activity structures, but also because of its special "style." The style of scientific language is created partly by grammar, partly by choice of words, partly by its use of idioms and metaphors, and largely by its avoidance of many stylistic devices that are freely used in other kinds of language.

Many people have noticed, for example, that scientific language has a preference in its grammar for using the passive voice (e.g., "the earth was uplifted" not "pressure lifted the earth up"; or "what element is being represented" not "what element are we representing"). One effect of this is that people tend to disappear from science as actors or agents. Experiments "are conducted," elements "are represented"; you don't have to say that somebody conducted them or represented them. Very often, if it does occur to anybody to ask themselves *who* did or does these things, the answer is "scientists," and not "us" or *me*. Scientific language, especially in writing, also has a grammatical preference for using abstract nouns derived from verbs instead of the verbs themselves. Verbs tend to have subjects, often people; nouns don't (cf. "the representation of a 2s orbital" vs. "how we represent a 2s orbital").

These are subtle features of scientific style. Their cumulative effect very often is to project science as a simple description of the way the world is, rather than as a human social activity, an effort to make sense of the world. Statements about the way atoms are or the earth is tend to be less interesting to many students than statements about who did what to come up with these unfamiliar ideas. But there are some much more obvious features of scientific style that limit students' interest in and understanding of science. They consist of the many "taboos" in scientific language: the many means of engaging interest, helping an audience identify with what is said, humanizing a subject and making it more easily comprehensible that are *not allowed* in science. These *Don'ts* are of course complemented by many *Dos*; altogether I will call these rules of scientific style its *stylistic norms*.

One way to identify the norms of scientific style, of course, is to survey a large body of scientific writing and talk and compare it with the language used in other fields. Even if we were to do this, however, we would not have direct evidence that students were aware of these norms, or that they responded differently to classroom language that did or did not follow the norms. Fortunately, from time to time in science classes students comment directly on "how scientific" something sounds. Teachers also do this, and from such comments on both sides, it is possible to identify the norms that apply to science language in the classroom.

After I present the most important of the norms students and teachers actually comment on, I will discuss evidence that students do in fact respond differently to language that does and does not follow these rules. In fact, as we shall see, students tend to pay more attention to what teachers are saying when their teachers *break* these rules.

At the beginning of the lesson on the Giant Cell (JR-29-OCT), the teacher asks the class if they have seen a movie on TV called *The Blob*, about a giant cell that eats people. A discussion is just beginning which will eventually lead to the main question of the lesson: whether cells can in fact keep on growing to gigantic size. Some students are cracking jokes, and one, obviously unhappy at all this, yells out: "Why can't he explain *science* in a scientific way!" There is no direct response to this; the teacher just continues the discussion, but soon it does begin to sound more normal, more "scientific" again. What is it, however, that is so *abnormal* about discussing science fiction in a science class? Why is it so rare that we hear references to TV, movies (and in this case, the movie's star, Steve McQueen) in science class? Why aren't these, according to the student, "scientific" ways of talking science?

In the lesson on Chemical Periodicity (DRS-27-NOV) there are several instances in which students react to teacher's violations of the stylistic norms of scientific language. When discussing the shape of a P-orbital in going over the homework, the shape has been described first as a figure-8, then as an (infinity) ∞-symbol. A student reminds the teacher that the orbital's shape is three-dimensional, and the teacher agrees that yes, "It's fat. It's, uh, fat and skinny." No sooner has he said this than a student pipes up, "That's nice and scientific." The teacher says (ironically?), "Yes, it is nice and scientific," and goes on to the next question.

The use of colloquial language here violates a norm of scientific style, even though what was said seems no less clumsy than "figure-8 sideways" as a description, and was probably more revealing for many students than either "infinity symbol" or even the term "three-dimensional." During this discussion a few students had described the shape by gesture; but the teacher made it clear that an acceptable answer had to be in *words*.

Later in the same lesson, the class is discussing a difference between the order in which orbitals are listed by the teacher and the order listed on the printed charts they have been given. The teacher tries to explain why the chart has a different order by saying:

> On the chart it—because the chart was put together by a *printer*, who likes to go in numerical order. If it was put together by a chemist, or if it was put together by *nature*, it would go *this* way.

A student immediately responds, "Mother Nature, huh?" A few other students laugh at this comment, which the teacher ignores. The teacher's remark, which meant that "in nature" the orbitals come in this order according to their energies, was seen by the student as a violation of the rule against Personification in scientific language. Something similar happens when the teacher uses a metaphor and talks about an electron coming to town, looking for the cheapest hotel, and going into the lowest energy orbital (see Metaphor, Chapter 4).

As a final example, at one point in this same lesson, a student has asked about electron pairs and the teacher, trying to get the class' attention (they have been working on a problem individually at their seats), says, "When we discuss bonding, it'll be important to know they're in pairs, because they like to have these opposite spins." The reaction is swift. A student calls out, "They *like* to?" Again the teacher is being chided for Personification, though these students know perfectly well that *like to* here is a more humanizing, slightly humorous metaphor for *tend to*.

In all these cases, and in many more throughout the science lessons, we find students directly or indirectly commenting on teachers' deviations from how they expect scientific language to sound. And we also find teachers insisting that students conform to these rules as well. Let me give a brief summary of the norms of scientific language as they are indicated by this kind of teacher and student behavior in the science classroom.

Scientific language that is *correct* and *serious* so far as teachers and students are concerned must follow these stylistic norms:

1. Be as *verbally explicit* and *universal* as possible. This means that verbal, rather than gestural or other nonverbal signs are required, and that implicit forms of grammar (e.g., use of pronouns of any kind, or ellipsis) are not fully acceptable. Teachers do not accept statements like: "It reflects it" or "One left in each" as complete answers. Statements also need to be expressed in the form of propositions that seem to have universal validity (e.g., using the indefinite present tense) and make no reference to the here and now, to accidental features of the immediate classroom situation, or to specific people, time, and places. This kind of language is sometimes called "abstract" or "decontextualized" though both these descriptions are misleading. In more precise linguistic terms, minor clauses, ellipsis, and all indexical forms (deictics, shifters) are avoided. The effect is to make "proper" scientific statements seem to talk only about an unchanging universal realm, rather like Plato's world of Pure Ideas, cut off from the here and now, and from human action.

2. *Avoid colloquial* forms of language and use, even in speech, forms closer to those of *written* language. Certain words mark language as colloquial (e.g., *like, you know, gonna, gotta*, etc.), as does use of first and second person (especially, *I, you, we*).

3. Use *technical terms* in place of colloquial synonyms or paraphrases, including specialized usage of words that also have colloquial meanings, and spoken symbols (e.g., "H_2O" or "2P").

4. *Avoid personification* and use of specifically or usually *human attributes* or qualities (e.g., "fat and skinny"), human agents or actors (as grammatical subjects or objects), and human types of action or process (as verbs, e.g., "like to have").

5. *Avoid metaphoric and figurative language*, especially those using emotional, colorful, or value-laden words, hyperboles and exaggeration, irony, and *humorous* or comic expressions.

6. *Be serious* and dignified in all expression of scientific content. *Avoid sensationalism.*

7. *Avoid personalities* and reference to individual human beings and their actions, including (for the most part) historical figures and events. Scientific language tends to *ignore history* if possible. When it does refer to history it clearly separates it from science content.

8. *Avoid reference to fiction or fantasy.*

9. *Use causal forms of explanation and avoid narrative and dramatic accounts.* This rules out the use of stories for description or explanation, not just fictional stories, but any form of discussion that uses the story-

form of narrative. Similarly forbidden are dramatic forms, including dialogue, the development of suspense or mystery, the element of surprise, dramatic action, and so on.

These rules are a recipe for dull, alienating language. They mainly serve to create a strong contrast between the language of human experience and the language of science. This is a contrast that we are taught to associate with the "objectivity" of science vs. the "subjectivity" of experience. It artificially and misleadingly makes students and the public imagine that science stands somehow outside of the world of human experience, rather than being a specialized part of it.

Working scientists, historians of science, sociologists who study scientific research, and common sense all tell us that science is a very human activity. It involves human actors and judgments, rivalries and antagonisms, mysteries and surprises, the creative use of metaphor and analogy. It is fallible, often uncertain, and sometimes creatively ambiguous. There is no way that the *products* of science (theories, techniques, textbooks) can legitimately disclaim the heritage of these undoubted features of the *process* of science. But the language of science seems to do so, to contrast science with human experience, to set the sciences in opposition to the humanities, to exempt science from social processes and real human activity, to oppose its language to the colloquial language of common sense. From this comes much of the "mystique" of science and the *mystification* of science.

These stylistic norms of science also impede the communication of the thematic content of science to students, as every good science teacher knows. Imagine journalists or popular writers trying to follow these rules. The norms of scientific language veto most of the techniques that all good communicators know are necessary for engaging the interest of an audience, helping them to identify with a point of view, and getting a point across to them effectively. Because of this, all good science teachers find it necessary to break the rules and violate these stylistic norms, humanizing science as they communicate it. We have seen, however, from the students' own reactions at points where a teacher does this, that the norms themselves are well established. Students may even feel that they are being talked down to if a teacher breaks these rules, or that what they are being taught is somehow not "genuine science."

COLLOQUIAL LANGUAGE AND STUDENT ATTENTION

What happens when teachers break the rules? Occasionally, as we have seen, students remind teachers, in good humor or with some resentment, that they are not talking science in the official, humorless, dehumanizing way we are all accustomed to. But it also happens, quite systematically, that students take these moments when the language of science is less alienating, more colloquial, and more accessible, to pay closer attention to the lesson.

It is not easy, of course, to observe when students are paying more or less attention to the teacher and the lesson. But it is possible to gauge this approximately from a number of visible signs. There are moments in every class when fewer students are looking at the teacher or the board, or writing in their notebooks, and when more students are talking to their neighbors, staring out the window, or reading a comic book. Teachers are usually too busy teaching to have the leisure to observe the details of the ebb and flow of students' engagement with each moment of a lesson. Nevertheless, teachers are aware of the drift in attention of a class to and away from the lesson. There are moments when, like a performer, you know that you really "have them," and there are times when you feel that you are "losing them."

In a classroom research study I conducted for the National Science Foundation (Lemke, 1983b, pp. 284–290 and Appendix 1), two trained observers kept track moment by moment of the numbers of students who were or were not "communicatively engaged" with the lesson according to a number of specific criteria such as those I've just described. This was done in such a way that it was possible to correlate the degree of engagement of the class at any given time with the language of the lesson at that point. We found a very high degree of quantitative agreement between the observers, and we double-checked this by comparing our observation notes with videotapes of classes. The figures are certainly reliable to within 10% accuracy.

This is not as surprising as it may seem, nor is it any great testimony to our research techniques. It just happens that human behavior in groups is very regular. You don't have to keep track of 25–35 individual students; when two or three students "tune out" of the lesson, the odds are good that within a few moments so will others. When something draws students' attention back again, it affects many students almost simultaneously. These ups and downs in communicative engagement are *group phenomena* and so are relatively easy to observe. In addition, there are certain basic levels of engagement in a class, a sort of normal level (70–80%), a low level (30–40%), and a high level (90–95%), and at any given moment the class seems to be at or on its way to one of these relatively stable levels. This also makes the task of the observer much easier.

In order to compare levels of communicative engagement when the language of the lesson follows vs. when it breaks the stylistic rules, it is also necessary to identify bits of the lessons that can be considered "rule-breaking" in relation to the norms I have listed. Fortunately for the research, and for students, teachers do break the rules fairly often. Even so, in lessons selected for a relatively high frequency of rule-breaking, at most 15–20% of the science talk deviated from the established stylistic norms of scientific language. A more representative sample would undoubtedly show even less norm-violating science talk. However, what was found to be the case is that in fully 89% of these instances of more colloquial, more humanized ways of talking science, the enagagement of the class with what was being said increased significantly (up to the high level of engagement for that class).

For a truly systematic comparison, a careful estimate was made of the fraction of the time that engagement was high or rising-to-high when the science talk was its usual formal, dull self. Engagement can be high or rising for reasons other than the style of scientific talk. It tends to rise when students have to copy important material from the blackboard or when the teacher introduces a new topic question. Taking all this into account, a conservative estimate is that when the science talk is "normal" stylistically, there is at most a 20–25% chance of finding high engagement with what is being said (compared to the 89% for rule-breaking talk).

This means that we can be quite confident in saying that *students are three to four times as likely to be highly attentive to "humanized" science talk as they would be to "normal" science talk in the classroom.* (For details see Lemke, 1983b, Chapter 5.)

We should not really be surprised by this, though it is nice to have an estimate of just how much difference the style of the science talk makes. Just as students pay more attention to the lesson when they know that something very important is being said or written at the board, so they pay special attention as well at those moments when the teacher is speaking a language that is more familiar and accessible. I believe that much of the time most students do not really follow the full meaning of what is being said to them in science class. The "windows of opportunity" (identified by students' own responses to them), when they are more likely to be able to catch on to what is being talked about, are the moments when what is being said is more interesting, more familiar, more colloquial, and more human. These are the moments when the mystique of science is set aside.

In order to make this point more concretely, let me end this section with a sampler of the kind of language that breaks the rules, humanizes science learning, and signals to students that the doorway to science may be open for a moment:

So to allow the ions that're present to move, we use *pickled rope*. [KF-15–APR, introducing a "salt bridge"]

Student: People would start to stink! . . .
Teacher: The people in the *middle* would be dying from the smell. [JR-29–OCT, analogy of crowd to giant cell]

That's water vapor, in my *breath*. [LG-26–NOV, describing condensation after exhaling on the board]

Student: To us it's counterclockwise, but to you it's clockwise.
Teacher: *Relativity*. That's how Einstein made his fortune! [DRS-27–NOV]

Today there's a rally on Wall Street to stop nuclear reactors. [JR-29–OCT, motivating the crowd analogy]

Except we didn't figure out what this word *terrestrial* means. Except all of you who watch *Star Trek* and *Planet of the Lost Chicken*, and all of those terrific programs must know what that means already. Monica? [LG-26–NOV]

SCIENCE AS AUTHORITATIVE AND DIFFICULT

The mystique of science is more than a matter of style. The stylistic norms of the language of science reinforce two sets of beliefs about science that serve the interests of a technocratic elite.

The first of these we can call the ideology of the *objective truth* of science. Students are taught that there are *facts*, plain and simple and not to be argued with. These facts are said to be true because they are based on observation or experimental evidence. They are generally presented without any discussion of their dependence on theories, the reasons why some particular investigators chose to make certain observations rather than others, or do certain experiments rather than others. They are taken out of the context of science as a human social activity that is subject to biases, interests, and prejudices of individuals, groups, and periods of history.

The facts of science (and in practice nearly everything in the science curriculum is presented as established, permanent, incontrovertible fact) are given an aura of total objectivity which no statements made by people at particular times and places can ever possibly deserve. But a belief in the objectivity and certainty of science is very useful to anyone in power who wants to use science as a justification for imposing the policy decisions they favor. Science is presented as *authoritative*, and from there it is a small step to its becoming authoritarian.

The second set of beliefs we can call the ideology of the *special truth* of science. Students are taught, often very subtly, that science is opposed to common sense, that it is a special truth available only to experts and mainly incomprehensible to the layman. "Scientists" are talked of as a breed apart, possessing not just some specialized skills and knowledge available to anyone, but having special talents and exceptional intellects which the average student does not and never will have. Science is presented as being a *difficult* subject. When students fail to master it, they are encouraged to believe that it is their own fault: They are just not smart enough to be scientists.

No one points out that science is taught only in very restricted ways. The restrictions tend to insure that only people whose backgrounds have led them to already talk a bit more like science books do, to already learn in a particular style and at a particular pace, to already have an interest in a certain way of looking at the world and certain topics and problems, will have much chance of doing well at science.

It is not surprising that those who succeed in science tend to be like those who define the "appropriate" way to talk science: male rather than female, white rather than black, middle- and upper-middle class, native English-speakers, standard dialect speakers, committed to the values of North European middle-class culture (emotional control, orderliness, rationalism, achievement, punctuality, social hierarchy, etc.) No one points out that science has been done very effectively by other sorts of people in other kinds of cultures, or that science might look a little different in its models and emphases if its recent history had come at a time when other cultures had been politically dominant in the world and in a position to command more of its resources (say Italy, or China, or India).

Science is not limited to one culture, one dialect of English, or one style of communication. Science teaching today is.

There is nothing "special" about the truth of science. It is just one specialized offshoot of common sense. It can be mastered by any normal human being. The experiences of everyday life are a rich intellectual resource that is highly relevant to the study of science. Nor is science intrinsically more difficult than any other subject. It cannot be. Every subject consists of certain conventionalized ways of talking, reasoning, and acting. All equally are learned by participation in a community that practices them. We know today, for example, that all the languages of the world are equally difficult, equally complex. Any normal child growing up in a community that speaks one of them can learn it. So too with all the cultural practices and specialized "languages" of a society, including science. If some foreign languages are more diffi-cult for you to learn than others, that is mainly because they are less like the language you already know, or the experiences they represent are less familiar.

Science has its own distinctive genres, its thematic formations, its practical skills, its specialized modes of reasoning or calculating. In their forms they are no more intellectually complex or difficult than those of any other subject. They are only less familiar, less like what we are already used to.

If some students do badly in science, it is not because science is so difficult or because they are so dumb. It is because the way in which science is presented to them seems too unfamiliar, or too unlike what they have been taught to find interesting and valuable. If the teaching of science is so arranged as to make it seem otherwise, that too favors the interests of those who find it convenient that the mass of people leave science in the hands of a small elite. People are taught that they must defer to "the experts" in all these matters, even if they don't trust them.

I don't want teachers to be blamed for all this. It is not just science teachers, but *everybody* who has been taught to believe that science possesses an objective and special sort of truth and that only the most intelligent people can really understand it. Science teachers are not members of the technocratic elite that benefits from this mystique of science. Most scientists are not members of it either. It consists of much more powerful groups in our society who make policy decisions for large institutions (mainly corporations and government departments) and justify their decisions by appealing to technical expertise in "man-agement science" and innumerable specialized fields (economics, en-vironmental chemistry, reactor physics, weapons research, medicine, psychology, and so forth).

The new technocrats do not understand science as a scientist does. They pick and choose from among "results" and "findings," promoting these as facts. They fund and influence the kinds of research that are done to produce these facts. And they develop policies that serve their own interests, justifying them by telling us what "the facts" (not them!) require us to do. In this way they bypass democratic debate over issues. There is no discussion of values or of the real interests of various sec-tors of society that have a stake in the outcome. The technocrats "inter-pret" the experts for us, having convinced us that the experts are "ob-jective" and that we cannot interpret them for ourselves. (See Lemke, in press-a, for a fuller discussion of the relation of technocratic and tech-nical discourse, with examples drawn from the politics of educational research.)

Propagating this mystique of science, then, produces the antithesis of what science education claims to stand for. The language of science teachers, textbooks, and tests are the instruments through which this happens. Let's take a closer look at some examples of that language at work in the classroom.

THE IDEOLOGY OF EVIDENCE AND AUTHORITY

Take a look at the episode "Facts and Theory" (and see Appendix, lesson SC-20-MAR). This is part of the Earth Science lesson about the earth's crust having been uplifted (see Chapter 4). The episode takes the form of a typical Teacher-Student Debate (cf. Chapter 2). It begins with the teacher summarizing a previous discussion by reading the official Answer (to a previous topic Question), which he has just written on the board. This Answer statement is Challenged by two students, Charley and Vito. The teacher responds with a "Yes, but. . ." defense of his statement, and then a third student, Scott, partially shifts the issue of the Debate away from the truth of the teacher's statement to its scientific status as "fact" or "just theory." The Debate continues until about line 24, when the teacher cuts it off by appealing to an authoritative Law of Science, in this case the geological principle of Uniformitarianism (that past geological events are to be explained by the same processes that still occur today).

What is interesting for our discussion in this chapter is not the thematics of the geology, or the structure and strategies of the Debate, but the beliefs and attitudes about science itself that come out in this episode. Here, for a moment, a part of the mystique of science becomes highly visible: the authority of science's claim to objective, "factual" truth.

In lines 9 and 10 the teacher is showing scientific caution. He uses terms like *possible* and *believe* rather than *is* and *know*. In a subtle way, the very emphasis on cautious statement in scientific language helps prepare the way for the *certitude* of those things that are asserted in absolute terms (cf. Halliday, 1985a, pp. 85–89, 332–341 on the semantics of "modality"). Scott and Vito translate this cautious assertion into the use of the term "theory," meaning by it something like *hypothesis* or *interpretation*. The teacher, however, will not let that pass. He asserts that this is not just a matter of his or anyone's opinion, that it is *fact*, plain and simple (lines 13–14).

Now with leisure and hindsight we might be critical of this teacher's dogmatic insistence on this point, but the language of scientific discussion which he and the students both use here is quite common in science and science teaching, and that is what I want us to analyze. In the first place there is the very distinction, agreed to by both teacher and stu-

Table 5.1.   Facts and Theories [From Lesson SC-20-MAR]

1	Teacher:	Now let's try and understand this Answer that I gave
2		you here. It says "Marine fossils are found in
3		mountains of high elevation; this suggests that the
4		crust has been uplifted." It means the earth is pushed
5		up, OK? The earth is pushed up. That's what we mean
6		by uplifting.
7	Charley:	Couldn't the water go down?
8	Vito:	Yeah!
9	Teacher:	It's possible that the water level has gone down, but
10		we believe that the earth has been uplifted.
11	Scott:	It's just a theory though.
12	Vito:	It's always a theory.
13	Teacher:	This, this is fact. This is fact, OK? This is not a
14		theory.
15	Vito:	It's fact?
16	Scott:	Wait a minute, it can't be a fact. There's no proof
17		that the earth was raised up, unless they took
18		measurements.
19	Teacher:	They—measurements have been taken.
20	Scott:	Measurements have been taken?
21	Teacher:	Right now, OK? Now I'm gonna try 'n explain you some-
22		thing else.
23	Robert:	How can you prove that that's a fact?
24	Teacher:	I'm gonna try and tell you what happens. Just a
25		second, Scott. Just listen carefully. Somebody by the
26		name of James Hutton came out with a theory of
27		Uniformitarianism. Does anyone know what that means?
		[IN THE OMITTED LINES TEACHER REJECTS THREE ANSWERS]
28	Teacher:	OK. What Monica is trying to say, in one sentence is,
29		what James Hutton tried to prove was: The Present is
30		the key to the Past. OK? We look at things, things
31		that are happening today, happened exactly the same in
32		the past. [Teacher repeats this.] So the present is
33		the key to the past. So by looking, by looking at
34		geologic formations, we can tell, if things were
35		uplifted, uplifted, or things subsided. OK, just by
36		looking at them. And that's how, that's how there's
37		ways, in which they prove, that things were uplifted,
38		how can they tell they were uplifted. Alright, let's
39		go on to our Question.

dents between *fact* and *theory*. The students, and most of us, use *theory* to mean something tentative, fallible, and subject to the foibles of those who propose it. *Fact* here is clearly being semantically contrasted with theory (cf. Chapter 4 and Appendix C). It is being made to seem certain and objective, not a matter for debate the way we might debate alternative theories.

In lines 16–18, Scott makes the initial connection between *facts* and *measurements*. The connection is by way of a notion of "proof." It seems that a theory is no longer a theory when we have "measurements," i.e. data, observations. At the end of the Debate (lines 30–38), the teacher tries to clinch his argument by basing his conclusions on "just looking," i.e. again on observations. A detailed analysis (Lemke, 1983b, pp. 266–268) of the semantics here shows that across the lesson as a whole *suggests, possible,* and *believe* join with *theory* to maintain a systematic contrast with *fact, proof, measurements,* and later *looking.* The basic contrast is one of uncertainty and arguability vs. certainty and unarguability. You may have noticed that in a lot of scientific discussions, and perhaps especially in classroom and policy debates, what things are taken to be facts and what are only theories varies a lot depending on the purposes of the speaker.

The authority of science derives, we are told, from "evidence and logical argument" rather than from the power relations between people or groups in a society. However, unless we are going to personify Science, we are entitled to suspect that it is always some *persons* who wield authority, and that they do so for their own interests. The rhetoric of "evidence and proof" presumes that evidence itself simply exists, is found simply "by looking." It conveniently ignores that *people* always have to *decide* that something will count as evidence for something else. The notion of *proof* presumes that one particular kind of logic and argument embodies "necessary truths" rather than that such forms of argument are simply specialized genres, used by particular groups for certain purposes. Very often those purposes extend beyond the construction of useful explanations to include winning arguments and imposing your views on other people.

Our best protection against the authoritarian use of the notion of "facts" is a critical view of how (and why, and by whom) such statements are made. The belief that there are absolute facts creates the power for someone to say what the facts are. It is always some one, or some group, that in practice does say what the facts are (and what the correct rules of proof are, what legitimately counts as evidence and good argument and what does not). This power is inevitably abused. Its foundation is a belief in absolute facts that we can do very well without.

Every statement of "fact" is a statement that it is useful for some purpose to act as if something were true. Theories and models and hypotheses are just that: statements useful for some purposes. We do not forget that they are likely to have limitations, that there are always possible alternatives to them, and that people have their own reasons, good and bad, for favoring one over another. Science and society are both safer if they remember that a "fact" is just an assertion that is not currently being challenged. The history of science alone should be enough to teach us that "facts" die like everything else.

Science teaching, and science itself, are also incredibly antihistorical in their treatment of "facts" and theories. Apart from lionizing a few scientists of earlier generations (almost all European, male, and depicted as middle-aged or older no matter at what age they did their best work), and all scientists by implication, science ignores or scorns history. Science teaching conveniently ignores the wrecks and ruins of major theories, and "facts," of past generations. It clings to a theory of continuous upward progress, long ago rejected by modern historians.

It is extremely inconsistent to say that modern science supersedes the science of the past and also that it builds directly upon it. A great deal of the science of every generation has been rejected a few generations later, and there is no reason to suppose that the science of our own generation will be an exception. Science's myth of its own past remembers only the bits that still fit today's theories and conveniently forgets the many more that don't. This selective amnesia ignores the problem that scientists of the past had no way of knowing which parts of the science of their day would be approved by ours and which would not. And neither do we know what the future will think of our science, which bits will be kept and which forgotten. Science's mythical history is rather like an amateur genealogy that only includes the ancestors we are proud of; it would hardly do as an analysis of our total genetic inheritance, and it gives a pretty misleading idea of what to expect from our descendants.

History ought to teach humility, but genuine humility is not part of the mystique of science, and genuine history is excluded from science teaching.

Let's conclude this section by looking at the way the teacher in this episode uses the ideology of fact and theory to buttress his authority and that of the scientific mystique. In lines 24–27, the teacher uses the standard ploy for winning a classroom debate by appealing to an authoritative principle of science. He introduces it as "a theory of Uniformitarianism." After trying unsuccessfully to get the class to define this word, he sums up the principle as "what James Hutton tried to prove." The words *theory* and *tried* here are in tension with *what happens* (line 24) and *prove* (line 29).

At line 30 he makes the transition from theory/principle to its application in this lesson. From here on we return to the rhetoric of evidence and proof, with "by looking" taking the place thematically of the students' earlier "measurements" as the basis for proving something to be a fact. From line 34 to line 37, there is also a shift from *we* to *they* ("we can tell" to "they prove") as the ones who establish what is proven, what is fact. The first *we* could have included the students, or meant the teacher and other scientists. *They* clearly means "scientists," "experts." *We* could have been coopting; *they* is more nearly coercive in this context.

The teacher has exercised the authority to determine what principle is relevant here and then used it *deductively* to support the myth that science distinguishes facts from hypotheses by making observations. This framework of beliefs about facts, theories, observations, and proof is shared by both the teacher and the students. The students have in fact learned it from their prior education in science (where else?) This framework, this central myth about science, is reinforced by the debate, and even strengthened by an argument that formally contradicts it (the teacher has "proved" a fact from a theory, Uniformitarianism). In the long run I don't think it matters whether the teacher's argument was a good one or a bad one here. What matters is that the authority of science, the power to say which things are absolute facts and objective truths, is reconfirmed.

UNDERMINING COMMON SENSE: THE SPECIAL TRUTH OF SCIENCE

There is a second, complementary ideology fostered by the mystique of science: that the truth of science is a special one, contrary to common sense and accessible only to experts. The language of science, and especially that of science teaching and popularizations of science, has a habit of running down common sense, denying the relevance of common experience in understanding "real" science, and undermining students' confidence in their own background and judgment. This emphasis on the antagonism between science and common sense tends to undercut opposition to "expert" opinion and judgments, again paving the way for technocratic domination of public policy.

It is sometimes true that the scientific way of talking about something runs contrary to tradition or to a narrow definition of common sense. But the scientific point of view is most often a highly specialized one, adapted to the peculiar events of the laboratory and of very "uncommon" situations (stellar interiors, molecular collisions, cell division, etc.). Science is most often an *extension* of common sense, not an esoteric alternative to it.

Certainly *learning* science is easier when science teaching builds on students' backgrounds and teaches them to use their common sense and extend its patterns of reasoning to new problems. Learning science is only made more difficult when science is treated as a sort of secret knowledge, understood only by scientists, that students must simply trust because they cannot trust common sense or their own reasoning and experience. Yet the denial of common sense and the undermining of students' confidence in their own experience is pervasive in science teaching.

As an example, consider part of an episode from the lesson on Longitudinal Waves (see also Transcript EL-20-NOV). The teacher here is reviewing and reenacting a simple demonstration of how a wave-pulse appears to travel down a long coiled spring (a "Slinky"). He bunches the coils together at one end, lets them go, and the bunching moves down the spring toward the other end, which is fastened down. From the beginning he emphasizes observation of specific events in time and space: *as you saw in here* (line 1), *now notice* (lines 4, 11). When he asks (lines 14–15), "Which way does the *spring* move?" the students reply that it is not moving. His response, however, is that it *is* moving (line 18), and he repeats his question about which way it moves. This happens despite his having just said very clearly, and even with the same emphasis on the word *spring* (lines 4–7), that the spring does *not* move.

Table 5.2. How the Spring Moves [From Lesson EL-20-NOV]

1	Teacher:	Now. If you compress a spring, as you saw in here,
2		what we did, last week, what we did, before yesterday.
3		If you compress a spring, a pulse goes down that
4		spring. [Demonstrates] Now notice that the spring
5		does not move, from me to the door, say, if I have it
6		attached to the door. The spring is between me and the
7		door. But something does move, if I push that spring,
8		something does move between me and the door. What
9		moves, William?
10	William:	A wave.
11	Teacher:	Alright. A pulse does move. Now notice that the wave
12		motion goes to the right, from me to the door, if I
13		push it in that direction. So the wave motion is
14		toward the door. [Writes on board] Which way does the
15		spring move? Paul?
16	Paul:	The opposite.
17	Student:	It's not moving.
18	Teacher:	But it is. If you recall that spring, it did wiggle.
19		Which way does the spring move?
20	Student:	The same way.
21	Teacher:	If it didn't move, there would be no wave traveling.

The implication here is that students can answer "just by looking." From our previous discussion of fact and theory, we recognize this emphasis on the observational, empirical basis for the claimed authority of science. But observation is supposed to be objective, to be there for anyone to see just as the scientist does. In this episode we have a very clear example of why this just isn't so. The students have been told that the spring does not move, that a pulse or wave moves. That is what they see: a stationary spring, fastened down, lying on the demonstration table, and the appparent motion of the bunched coils of the spring, the wave-pulse. Now suddenly they are expected to "see" the spring as *moving* and even tell, by observation, which way it is moving.

One student guesses a direction, but the rest of the students are calling out that it is not moving. We get another guess, and in line 21 the teacher goes so far as to say that it is *because* the spring moves that the wave-pulse travels. In lines 4–7, he has said that the spring doesn't move, "but" the wave-pulse does. Neither the semantics of action (what's happening), nor the semantics of logic (the relation between actions) is still the same. The students are left confused by this. The relevance of their common observational experience is left in doubt.

The teacher, following the thematics of science, is claiming here an authority of *interpretation* to say what the relevant facts are. That authority is made to supersede ordinary observation. What the "facts" are here depends on your thematics. The spring is both moving and not moving, but in two different senses. It is not moving in one sense that the wave-pulse is moving: It is not "traveling" (cf. line 21). But it *is* moving in another sense, "wiggling" (line 18), that has a causal relation to the traveling motion of the wave. The basic distinction of two kinds of motion, traveling and wiggling (translational and oscillatory), is essential to seeing these things the way the scientist and teacher do.

The students do not see things this way, or more precisely, they do not make sense of what they see in these terms. What the eye "sees" has little enough to do with science or learning. It is the sense we make of what we see, the meaning for us of what we see, that matters. That meaning is always an interpretation of what we perceive, a construction of its sense in relation to something else. Usually we construct these relations according to some thematic pattern of semantic relationships that we have learned. As we saw in Chapter 2, when teacher and students use different patterns to do this, they consistently misunderstand one another.

For the purposes of this chapter, however, what matters this time is not so much just the thematic discrepancy between teacher and students, but the fact that this discrepancy is used to undermine common sense. It is made to seem that the students should be able to answer these questions "just by looking." In fact, they must learn to see as the teacher sees, to look for what he looks for, to see as relevant what he does, and to make sense of what they see according to a particular thematic pattern.

In the next minutes the teacher and students go back and forth about 10 times until a student finally gives an acceptable answer (that the spring wiggles "both ways"). By that time the class considers itself lucky to have gotten to an acceptable answer by *any* means. They have learned that the right answer cannot be found by applying common sense to ordinary observation. Nor do they have any idea how or why science chooses to see things as it does here. Their confidence in themselves is thoroughly undermined by all this.

A few minutes later in this same lesson (see continuation of transcript EL-20-NOV), we find an example of another common way in which the mystique of science upholds itself by undercutting students' confidence. Our first example illustrated how students are made to feel stupid and mistrust even ordinary observations, when all they are really lacking is the extension of common sense to a specialized, scientific way of talking about something. In this second case, a student is made to feel "innocently" stupid because, after all, he couldn't even be expected to understand about telephones. The teacher has asked for examples of longitudinal waves. The answer he is looking for, because it has already been discussed, is *sound*. This student assumes that he wants a new and different example and takes a chance on *telephone* transmissions. The teacher's reply (lines 30–33) seems sincere at the same time that it is condescending and patronizing: "Uh sorry about that. . .," "I know you might think . . .," and "You might not believe this, but . . .."

The result again is to contrast science with what the students could possibly be expected to know from common experience. In fact, the teacher could have made a more positive response, pointing out the ways in which telephone communication *is* like a wave (wave-pulse transmission on a co-axial cable, use of microwaves, etc.) and in fact like the kind of waves he will be discussing later in the lesson, transverse waves. What he emphasizes, however, is the point of greatest difference between common understanding and scientific description: the average speed of an electron in a wire carrying electric current.

He illustrates this point at great length by a clever analogy, then asks students for another try at an example of a longitudinal wave. This time the answer is waves at the beach. His response to that does mention transverse waves, but only to point out that water waves are not of either of the two kinds (longitudinal and transverse) to be discussed, rather "It's a different kind of thing." Again it has been taken out of the realm of common experience, its relevance to a discussion of waves

Table 5.3.   A Telephone Call? [From EL-20-NOV]

22	Teacher:	What's an example of a longitudinal wave?
23	Mike:	Uh, a telephone call?
24	Teacher:	Say that out loud.
25	Mike:	When you call someone on the telephone.
26	Student:	Good God! [Students laughing]
27	Teacher:	What is it that goes through the wire when you call
28		somebody?
29	Student:	Electricity.
30	Teacher:	OK, now—that, uh, is not a longitudinal wave. Uh,
31		sorry about that. It's uh—I know you might think
32		that the electricity goes from my house to yours. It
33		really doesn't. The electricity goes back and forth.
34		Uh—you might not believe this, but the individual
35		electrons in a wire travel slower than you can walk.

effectively denied. Finally the students go back to sound as their only example.

These instances are not peculiar to this teacher, nor is he doing a poor job by the prevailing standards of science teaching. Science teaching routinely creates a radical disjunction between science and common sense, routinely sets aside students' own associations, arguments, and even observations. It routinely alienates students from science, undermines their self-confidence, and proclaims a special and superior truth to be taken on trust, or on authority.

Certainly, this is not what most science teachers want to do. Many try very hard to build connections between students' experiences and the topics of the curriculum. In doing so, however, they frequently have to break the norms of "really scientific" ways of talking. As the examples in this chapter show, the mystique of science can be reinforced in very subtle ways, despite teachers' best intentions. The problem lies with what science teachers themselves are taught, or not taught, about the nature of science and its relations to common sense. They too have mainly been taught to accept the mystique of science and many of its myths about itself.

EDUCATION VS. ELITISM

Why does this mystique of science exist in our society? Whose interests does it serve to maintain that science provides absolute, objective truths whose proofs are accessible only to experts who are much smarter than the average person? I have already suggested that it is not just scientists themselves who benefit from this image. Those I have called "technocrats," professional managers and decision makers who justify their own preferences with selective interpretations of "the facts" and "expert knowledge," benefit far more and are far more dangerous to society. They are dangerous because they disguise their own privileged interests as objective public and institutional policy. They tell us that something must be done because the facts require it. The facts, they say, are provided by the experts, the scientists, and no one who is not a qualified expert has the right to dispute them. In this way, narrow interests are made to seem objective necessities, and policy debate excludes most of the people whose lives will be affected by a decision. That is dangerous. A complex society is headed for disaster when its basic decisions are made solely within the frame of reference of a small elite.

When there is policy debate these days, it usually turns out to be a debate over what the facts are, a debate between rival groups of experts. It is rarely a debate over *values*, over *choices*, between *alternatives*. Rarely does public debate, or debate within institutions (schools, universities, churches, corporations, governmental departments) openly recognize that different social groups have conflicting *interests*. No matter what we may agree that the "facts" are in a given situation, our different interests and values will lead us to prefer different choices of alternative policies and actions. The dangerous technocratic sleight-of-hand is to bypass all genuine debate about policy choices and impose a single course of action that seems to have the "objective" support of expert opinion. The technocrats love to tell us how things *have* to be, as if that were not exactly the way *they* decided they wanted them to be, or as if it were not inevitably *their* interests that such policies would favor.

The mystique of science is an essential tool for technocratic rule. Through it we are all taught that science, as the paradigm of all expert knowledge, has an objective, superior, and special truth that only the superintelligent few can understand. Science education, like it or not, does a great job in foisting these myths on most of us.

The alternative to a society in which decisions are made in their own interests by technocratic managers, and sullenly deferred to by an increasingly resentful population (including most of us), is a society in which a scientifically literate public can make informed policy judgments. The technocrats foster the belief that this is impossible, that the average person will never be able to understand science well enough to participate in decisions in a technological society or a complex institution. What they mean is that the average person, any person (including themselves) will never be a specialized expert in all the fields relevant to a decision.

But, of course, neither are they, and it is not the economists, systems programmers, or scientists who make such decisions anyway. The decisions are never dictated by the facts, by expert knowledge. They are made on the basis of values and interests, and we all have those. The managers themselves are only scientifically literate (often not very much so), and their degree of literacy, the degree needed to participate in real decision making, is certainly available to most of us. Science teaching can do the job.

If we are to effectively teach against the mystique of science, we are going to have to stop making it seem that science is intrinsically a harder subject than any other. We are going to have to present science not as an arcane mystery that only the superintelligent can understand, but as one specialized way of talking about the world. We will need to present science not as the one best and truest view of the world, but as one view among many, each needing the others. We must teach students that scientific conclusions are always fallible human judgments, not absolute facts, and that science as a whole is a messy, human business, not a perfect method for discovering absolute truth. We are going to have to give students practice at using science, together with an appreciation of differences in social values and interests, to make decisions about real issues. Otherwise, as educators, we may still be well paid to turn out technicians who can compete with the Japanese, but we may not sleep very well at night.

In Chapter 7 I provide some specific recommendations for science teaching, and for teaching in general, based on the arguments of this chapter and the preceding ones. Before that, however, consider briefly how much of what I have been saying about talking science should also apply to the other subjects in the curriculum.

EXPLORING FURTHER

In this chapter we have returned to many of the important issues of the social nature and social implications of our ways of teaching and learning. We have been using an approach that is both linguistic and sociological. Important sociolinguistic perspectives relevant to the concerns of this chapter can be found in Edwards' *Language in Culture and Class: The Sociology of Language and Education* (1976), Stubbs' *Language and Literacy: The Sociolinguistics of Reading and Writing* (1980), and Cook-Gumperz' *The Social Construction of Literacy* (1986).

Gilmore and Glatthorn's *Children in and Out of School* (1982) and Shirley Heath's *Ways with Words* (1983) both describe some of the important relations between the culture and language of the home and the school, as do David Bloome's own chapters in the volumes he has edited (Bloome 1987, 1989).

Some of the themes of this chapter are also developed in two of my own papers, "Social Semiotics and Science Education" (1987) and "Genres, Semantics, and Classroom Education" (1988).

chapter 6

How Different Is Science?

This book is mainly about talking *science*, but many of the points I have tried to make would seem to apply to the teaching of other subjects as well. Just how different is science teaching from the teaching of other academic subjects? What is the role of language in education across the curriculum? How much of what has been said in this book applies specifically to science, and how much would apply equally to other subjects?

I think that the mystique of science discussed in Chapter 5 tends to prejudice our answers to these questions. Science often presents itself as a radically different way of looking at the world, and as teaching a special body of knowledge unlike any other. Worst of all, I think, the mystique of science favors the rather superstitious view that science requires a special kind of "thinking" different from that of any other subject. If all this were so, then we might expect the teaching of science to be very different from the teaching of other subjects. A study of science teaching, such as the one on which this book is based (Lemke, 1983b), might not have much relevance for the teaching of anything else.

But the basic theme of this book, and the principal conclusion of my own studies of classroom science teaching, has been that the mastery of science is mainly a matter of learning how to *talk* science. This means that there is no special form of "thinking" required in science. Science requires only the same language-using skills employed in talking about anything. Yes, science, like every subject has its own specialized thematics, but as we have seen in Chapter 4, the conceptual relations of different topics in science are put together with the same basic semantic relations that we use in every subject (see, for example, the list in Appendix C). Those semantic relations, all of them, can be found in any long conversation or piece of writing. It is not in principle any more difficult to learn to talk science than to learn to talk the language of any other specialized subject.

Talking science requires more than mastering a thematic pattern of conceptual terms and their semantic relationships, of course. It also requires that we learn to use the *genres* of science: the conventional formats for organizing scientific reasoning, talking, and writing, large and small (e.g., syllogisms, hypothetical arguments, lab reports, etc.). Many of these are not special to science either. The smaller ones (see Rhetorical Structures in Chapter 4), which are the building blocks for the larger ones, tend to be found in all subjects. Only the topics to which we apply them differ.

What is different about talking science, then, is mainly the topical content of its thematics and the formats of its longer, more complex and specialized genres. The generalizations of physics, say, regarded as statements in language, and the specialized formats for scientific reasoning and writing (such as lab notes and research reports), are different. But they are no more than specialized formats, no more than statements, and no harder in principle to learn than any other statements or formats.

Finally, *doing* science, as we have said before, is more than simply talking science. We talk science as part of some larger activity, such as solving a problem, conducting an investigation, making a policy decision. Those activities involve nonverbal actions as well as talk. They require us to integrate reasoning, talking, and writing with other forms of action such as using scientific apparatus or a computer, and making observations and measurements.

Most other academic subjects do not involve the range of unfamiliar and specialized nonverbal activities that science does, and this is a genuine difference. But the teaching of science does not heavily emphasize these activities, because students spend only a small proportion of their time in laboratory work in most science courses. Certainly the test grades by which we judge science achievement do not require these other nonverbal skills to any great degree. In this sense, science teaching is perhaps less different from that of other subjects than it should be.

Why is it then, if science is fundamentally no more difficult than other subjects, that it seems so much more difficult to most students? There are many reasons, some of which have already been discussed in earlier chapters and most of which I will summarize in Chapter 7, but in the context of the argument I'm making here, one of the most important is probably that the subject matter of science is made to seem very alien to students' ordinary experience. It is very hard to master a thematic pattern and make correct statements about something, if you have little or no direct experience of it. The content of science as it is defined in the traditional curriculum is as much disconnected as possible from students' experience. The experience of the laboratory cannot bridge that gap, and I rather doubt that very many students learn science better in the lab than they do in the classroom.

Science is made to seem difficult because its curriculum emphasizes topics and approaches to topics that are too far outside students' experiences, needs, and interests to be easily learned. Science teachers are always looking for new Motivations and Demonstrations, new ways to make science real, immediate, and interesting to students. Why is this so hard? Because the science curriculum begins from the needs of practicing research scientists; it organizes, presents, and teaches science from their extremely specialized viewpoint. It does not bring science to the student; it insists that the student come to it, and most students never get there. The mystique of science conveniently blames this partly on the laziness and stupidity of everyone who ever found science difficult or boring, and partly on the mythical "inherent conceptual difficulty" of the subject.

I will return to issues of science curriculum and science teaching in the next chapter, but for now we need to continue to look at the similarities and differences between science and other subjects.

FUNDAMENTAL SIMILARITIES AMONG SUBJECTS

Like science, every subject can be regarded as a special way of talking about some set of topics. We all recognize that there is a "language" of economics, of history, of literature, grammar, mathematics, and music. These languages are all, of course, *parts* of English. They use the same grammatical and semantic resources, but they use them in different ways, for different purposes. When these languages (referred to in linguistics as the *registers* of English) are used to talk about particular topics, we can identify and map out the thematics of the topic as it is constructed in that subject. Mastery of any of these subjects depends critically on mastering its language. Just as in science, the language of economics or grammar or mathematics is more than a matter of special vocabulary: It is a matter of the ways these special words are used *together*, the semantic relations we construct among them when we use them.

Like science, again, every school subject also has its own special genres, or formats of reasoning, speaking, and writing. English has sonnets, short stories, and persuasive essays; mathematics has geometry proofs and mixture problems; history has chronologies and comparisons. We all have, or used to have, book reports and project reports. And too many of us still have multiple-choice tests, a very specialized (and entirely artificial) educational genre.

In every subject, students have to learn to master the interconnected use of particular terms and their semantic relations of meaning (thematic patterns). In every subject teachers and students will often find themselves talking about the same subject, using the same or similar words, but making and assuming completely different patterns of meaning (cf. Chapter 2). In every subject, students have to learn by listening to, and occasionally practicing, the teacher's language of the subject. In every subject, they must learn to talk, write, and reason according to the formats and genres of the subject, some of which are shared with other subjects, and some of which are not.

In most subjects, teaching tends to use the same basic communication strategies, the same ways of demonstrating, by talking, what the thematics of the subject are. The thematic strategies listed in Appendix D (and discussed in Chapter 4) will be found in the teaching of every subject. It is likely that some subjects use some of these strategies more than others, and that there may be some which are more common in other subjects but so rare in science that I have not listed them.

Much the same goes for the activity structures of classroom learning across subjects. Triadic Dialogue is used in nearly every subject, and so are most of the activity structures listed in Appendix A (discussed in Chapter 3). Some subjects may use some of these more than others, and the proportions are certainly different, say between science and English classes.

In view of all these fundamental similarities, it seems likely that most of what I have said about talking science and teaching science will apply, with minor changes, to other academic subjects as well. But there certainly are also differences, and while we know much less in detail about these, it's worth raising some important questions about them.

SOME POTENTIALLY IMPORTANT DIFFERENCES

In my own research, I have not tried to systematically analyze the role of language in the teaching of subjects other than science. In fact, there is a great need for research by others to do just this, especially in the middle grades and in secondary education, where we emphasize mastery of specialized subjects. I have, however, had the opportunity to make some comparisons. In my original research project, I included two social studies lessons (on the Reconstruction period in American History). Since that time I have taught graduate-level courses to many new and experienced teachers in all subject areas, and many of their research projects have included transcripts of classroom language, together with analyses of the use of the language in the teaching of their subjects. Here are some observations drawn from this experience, and from many personal visits to classes in various subjects over the years, mainly in junior and senior high schools.

Science in the laboratory *is* different. But it is as much different from science in the classroom as it is from the teaching of other subjects. In the laboratory, students talk science to each other to guide themselves through prescribed experimental procedures, to decide what to do when something seems to have gone wrong, and to write up notes on what they have done. They talk science with their teacher when he or she comes around to see how they are doing, asking a question when they have initiated the contact, or answering one when the teacher has. This is often a lively use of the language of science, integrated with nonverbal activity. Unfortunately, too often, students don't seem to have enough command of the language they need to be able to figure out what's really going on in lab while it's happening. At best, some of them reconstruct it later. This is why I am skeptical about how much science students actually learn from lab work itself, though of course lab work is necessary and valuable as one part of a good science curriculum.

There are not many parallels to science laboratory work in the teaching of other core academic subjects. Some mathematics curricula include practical activities, and there are now many kinds of simulations on computer for various subjects. We know very little yet about how language is used around the computer; it may have some similarities to the science lab, but I suspect that it will really be essentially different.

Not all science is "lab science"; there is still a tradition of "field science" as well, and in biology and the earth sciences, and in urban and environmental studies, there is plenty of science talk on field trips. Again, we know very little about how this kind of talk differs from that of the classroom, or that of the laboratory. Other subjects may not have labs, but all do (or should) have field trips. Any opportunity for students to make a firsthand connection between an academic subject and a real-world context can be valuable, and there are not nearly enough opportunities like this in most curricula.

But these are all "extramural" activities, carried on outside the regular classroom if not outside the school building. Within the classroom, science and the other subjects look and are taught much more alike. Still, there are differences. Science classes often include Demonstrations of a sort not usually found in English, history, or mathematics classes. Many physical and chemical processes, and many biological organisms and specimens, can be exhibited directly in the classroom. The analyses of the use of language, of thematic and rhetorical strategies, of stylistic norms, and so on that I have done for science, however, do not show anything very unusual happening during Demonstrations as compared with other science classroom activities. The Demonstration is a simply a pretext for discussion, usually for Triadic Dialogue, not unlike the reading of a passage in an English or History class, or the solution on the board of a sample problem in Mathematics.

What *is* sometimes different is the use of language in studio art and music, physical education, home economics, or technical education classes. In these subjects, there is usually more going on than just talk. They may have similarities to the science laboratory, especially when students are working on projects in small groups with the teacher as a roving supervisor. Often, in these subjects, the teacher's language is that of directives, explaining in detail how to perform some nonverbal action or master some skill. This, of course, happens in the science classroom, too (e.g., teaching the use of the microscope, measuring techniques, etc.), but much less so.

In all these "practical" subjects, of course, there is also a "theoretical" component, but there is a basic difference in approach between science, mathematics, english, social studies (and even art history or music appreciation) on the one hand, and studio art and music, physical education, and other subjects oriented more to nonverbal skills and techniques. And there are corresponding differences in their uses of language. Students who are reasonably good at (if not equally interested in) the more theoretical, verbal subjects may lose many of their academic advantages when they enter these other classes. This happens in part because they are no longer simply learning another set of verbal skills: new thematic patterns, new genres, new stylistic norms. Now they have to master really very different kinds of nonverbal performances. It is basketball, or playing the violin, that requires a really distinctive kind of "thinking," not science.

There is another major sort of difference, within the verbal "academic" subjects, from the use of language that I have described for science. The language of science teaching is "expository" or "analytical" most of the time. It is used to express relationships of classification, taxonomy, and logical connection among abstract, or generalized, terms and processes. The language of other subjects, notably literature and history, tends to be more "narrative" in character. It is used to express relationships of time, place, manner, and action among specific, real or fictional, persons and events. The science teacher will tell you that light and heat are two forms of energy. The history teacher will tell you that the Democratic and Republican party leaders in Congress reached a specific compromise concerning the end of Reconstruction. The English teacher will establish that Hamlet had ambivalent feelings toward Gertrude. This is not to say that there is no abstract or theoretical knowledge in the history and English curricula, but only that the language of these subjects seems to be used more to deal with specific and concrete relations than is the language of theoretical science. We certainly could use some good studies of talking English and talking history to find out more about these similarities and differences.

Mathematics is often considered the subject most similar to science, and commonly students either do well in both or poorly in both. The uses of language are in many ways quite similar in these subjects, for both deal mainly with abstract generalizations and logical relationships. This is so whether the science topic is directly making use of mathematical ideas, as it often is in physics and chemistry, or not, as is more often true in biology or the earth sciences.

What is different about mathematics, however, is that it is far more focused on the mastery of skills and techniques than is the science curriculum. In science you are mainly supposed to learn what is so, but in mathematics you are mainly learning how to do. One of the major differences in approach within mathematics concerns the balance between practical skills and theoretical knowledge, but there is generally more practical skill taught in any math curriculum than you will find in most science curricula. For some science activities, such as problem-solving in chemistry or physics, the use of language may turn out to be almost identical to what is normal in math classes.

This is perhaps also the right place to point out that from a linguistic point of view, mathematics itself, that is the use of mathematical expressions, is *part* of language, not something different from or alternative to language. You can, quite literally, talk mathematics, either by reading the symbols, or by converting them into conventional words and phrases of the language (register) of mathematical English. Most mathematical expression is a form of *written* language, and mathematics makes use of its own specialized written genres, such as the Proof. Much the same is true of "computer code," that is, programs written in a computer language. The exact relationships between mathematics, computer languages, and the whole of a language like English in which they can be embedded (or into which they can be translated) is another important area in need of further study. Many students have trouble translating between mathematical symbols, mathematical English sentences, and ordinary English.

I have at times made an analogy between teaching science and teaching a foreign language. The analogy is suggestive, but very inexact. Learning to talk science is like learning a foreign language in that both require us to learn to translate back and forth between two very different systems of expression. In our case these are Scientific English and Colloquial English. It is not just the vocabulary of Scientific English that is foreign to many students. While it doesn't use any grammar you can't also find elsewhere in English, it does tend to follow the patterns of *written* English rather than those of speech. It also has its many "idioms" (elements of the thematics), and its norms of style. Its grammar may not be unique, but it tends to use grammar differently (see

Chapter 4) to express things. Teaching science as if it were a foreign language reminds us of all these differences, and encourages us to discuss them explicitly with students.

Actually, learning to talk science is very different from learning to talk French. When we learn a foreign language, we are usually just learning to translate *familiar* thematic patterns, ways of speaking about *familiar* topics, from the vocabulary and grammar of one language to that of another. The thematic relationships remain the same; their expression in words changes. Only at a very advanced level, if ever, do we learn the semantic distinctions, stylistic norms, and subtle differences between genres in different languages (or, more properly, in different cultures).

In learning to talk science, it is the resources of grammar that remain essentially familiar, while the thematic patterns are new and unfamiliar to us. It is very easy for a scientist or mathematician to learn to translate an article in their specialty from French to English (even if their French is quite poor otherwise), because they basically know how to express the thematics of the subject in English already. It is much harder to master a new thematic pattern, especially one that refers to a subject with which you have little direct experience, as is so often the case in science for many students. It is actually, therefore, rather unlikely that the teaching of science and of foreign languages will have much more in common than science and other academic subjects. The tasks are too different.

IDEOLOGY ACROSS THE CURRICULUM

Science is not the only subject which communicates social attitudes along with knowledge and skills. In Chapter 5, we saw examples of how both the stylistic conventions of scientific language and the attitudes toward science and common sense that are communicated in the classroom can sustain a harmful "mystique" of science. The more precise word for a set of attitudes and beliefs that favors the privileges and interests of one group in society at the expense of others is *ideology*. In Chapter 5, we identified two core elements of the technocratic ideology of science: that it can produce absolutely factual, objective truths, and that the scientific basis for such truths can only be truly understood by a superintelligent elite.

These two beliefs are harmful because they distort the nature of science as a human activity and they alienate many students from science, creating a false impression of a coldly impersonal, inhuman subject. But they are even more harmful in the long run because they permit a small elite of technocratic managers to make (in their own interests) decisions that affect the lives of others, justifying their policy choices by the authority of "expert knowledge."

It's not likely that science is the only subject that communicates an ideological message along with its curriculum content. To the extent that modern curriculum in social studies includes "technical" subjects like economics or sociology, I would expect its classroom language to also support the same technocratic ideology I have described for science. But, traditionally, social studies has dealt more with history and with the customs of other nations and cultures.

We all know that at least the American history curriculum tends to paint a ridiculously rosy and patriotic portrait of America's past. Students scarcely get any view of their country's past mistakes from which they might learn something useful for the future. Is the average citizen really expected to make decisions about this country's future? If so, maybe American history should tell them about such things as the long history of our mistakes in Latin America, or about the long period in our history when troops were regularly called out to shoot at workers on strike.

All through our history there have been critical perspectives on the decisions made by the powerful in America. Yet the "official history" as taught in school ignores all that and teaches a sort of Establishment view of our history, as if all those decisions were right or necessary. It does not so much create patriotic pride as deny students the knowledge needed to judge the decisions and correct the mistakes of the past. True patriotism, after all, is the desire to make our country better, at home and in its relations with the rest of the world.

It would be interesting to see how the language of the history classroom supports the interests of, if not the modern technocrats, at least the traditional Establishment elite of wealth and political power in our country. It would also be interesting to know, looking perhaps at changes in history textbooks, if the newer technocratic myth, that the decisions made in our history were always the ones that "the facts" forced on us, is gaining ground there too. How often do the books, or the teachers, help students analyze the conflicts of values and interests, and the relative power of different groups, that in fact led to actual decisions? And how often are students told of important events in our history that today no one is very proud of? How often are students given information that might lead them to condemn the decisions of the past, much less seek to change the policies of the present?

Is there an ideology hidden in the English curriculum, too? A set of attitudes and beliefs that promotes the interests of a powerful elite at the expense of the rest of us? Insofar as the English curriculum is a literature curriculum, there are certainly questions that can be raised about the selection of what is to be read, and of what is to be taught as being good, or great literature. If this were only a matter of taste, there might not be much chance of finding a harmful ideology lurking here somewhere. But perhaps we are entitled to wonder why there is such a traditional emphasis in the English curriculum on 19th century, Victorian British and American literature. I remember being taught, essentially, that great literature was an English novel about well-drawn middle-class characters who lived in big houses with servants and anguished over moral dilemmas with philosophical overtones. What are the *value systems* embodied in this tradition of what literature should be? Whose *interests* do those values reflect? What do students read in school that might give them the chance to consider alternative value systems from the ones with which the wives and daughters of 19th century British bourgeois bankers felt comfortable?

Why is there so little ethnic literature in the curriculum? So little, or no working-class literature? So little contemporary literature? So little non-European literature? So little literature that appeals to the interests of the average student? And so much *safe* literature?

The traditional answer is that the literature that is taught is the best quality literature, that it teaches our Anglo-American tradition, and that it is "age-appropriate." Is literary quality to be judged by the standards of only one group in society (middle-aged, upper middle-class Anglo-philes)? How many of *us*, how many students today in America have any real family or cultural connection with 19th century England (or even with the backgrounds of Americans writing in that century?) Is the English curriculum another *history* curriculum? And if so, who's history is it teaching? Not that of today's new immigrants, or of those of us, undoubtedly a majority in America, who are the descendants of Jews, Italians, Africans, Irish, Poles, Russians, or Chinese who came here late in the 19th century or after. The American literary heritage is *world literature*. In whose interest is it to maintain the much narrower myth of a British literary tradition, a bourgeois literature? I believe there certainly are significant ideologies at work in the English curriculum.

There is, or should be, most of us would agree, more to the language arts curriculum than just literature study, whatever the literature to be studied. Students need practice at oral and written communication skills; they need to be able to read and write not just literary English, but scientific English, journalistic English, and so on. In recent years people have been saying, with great justification I think, that these skills need to be taught "across the curriculum" and not just in classes taught by teachers trained mainly in the history of American and British literature. But science teachers are not trained in how to teach language arts skills in science, and neither are history teachers, mathematics teachers, or those of most other subjects. An emphasis on science teaching as teaching students how to talk science, and write science, and reason with scientific language, should lead us to train science teachers more fully in the language arts (see Chapter 7)—similarly with teaching students how to talk economics, talk history, talk literature, talk mathematics, and so on. But this still leaves us with one more major ideological issue concering language in the curriculum.

The English curriculum, more than any other subject's, maintains an ideology about language itself. This ideology is, once again, a set of attitudes and beliefs, this time about language, that favors the interests of one group in society over all others. The belief, basically, is that there is "Good English" and "Bad English." The English curriculum convinces most students that they do not and never will speak or write really "good" English, even if they are native-born Americans who have spoken nothing but English all their lives. This achievement of the English curriculum compares closely with that of the science curriculum in convincing most students that they will never really understand science. In these achievements these two curricula are outstandingly successful; for many students, however, these harmful attitudes are about all they will get from the curriculum.

"Bad English" is the English of the majority of Americans; it is the language of the people of our country. It might more precisely be called Diversified English because it embraces, as our country does, a rich diversity of cultural and language traditions. It includes all the many dialects of the American language: urban and rural, Afro-American and Hispano-American, upper-middle and lower-middle class, all the ethnic dialect traditions, and all the new immigrant dialect traditions. It is the richest language in the world, and because it unites so many dialect traditions, it is becoming (together with the Englishes of other parts of the world) the future World Language. This is what is called "Bad English."

"Good English" on the other hand is spoken and written by very few people. More precisely, it is called Standardized English, meaning that some small group of people want to impose it as the standard of "good" English on everyone else. Linguistically, it is basically the dialect of urban, upper-middle class, university-educated speakers whose families have either lost or given up their original ethnic or regional dialect traditions. For most of its speakers it is a formally *learned* dialect, especially in its written forms. Very few people grow up speaking this dialect; but those who do tend to come from relatively prosperous backgrounds, do well in school, and have better opportunities to make money and wield power in our society. "Good" English is good for a small minority. Calling it Standard English, and making it the only path to success, denies equality of opportunity, and adds to the burdens of those not to the "manner" born.

The ideology about language that is perpetuated in the curriculum maintains the myth that Narrow English (as I will call the purportedly "good" dialect) is necessary for effective communication and that it is "better English" than the other dialects. These are harmful beliefs. We could just as easily promote Diversified English in the curriculum. I believe that the reason we do not has nothing to do with effective communication. It has to do with maintaining the advantages of one group in society over others.

Perhaps the most difficult of the core subjects of the academic curriculum to analyze for its possible ideological messages is mathematics. I suspect that, at least superficially, it does help reinforce the technocratic mystique. Certainly most students do not believe that they really understand math, whether they can answer test questions or not. The New Math of the 1960s tried to insure that they would understand what they were doing at least some of the time, but it only succeeded, it seems, in making mathematics teaching more abstract and theoretical than students, or parents, were willing to put up with.

The central problem of mathematics education is probably the contradiction between its view of itself and everyone's else view of it. Mathematics educators see their subject from the viewpoint of professional, research mathematicians (much as science educators are taught the research scientist's view of science, see Chapter 5). That viewpoint is essentially "artistic": Mathematics is a creative art form, a sort of exploration of the possibilities of various abstract worlds. The knowledge of mathematics consists of two parts: a practical knowledge of how to perform various manipulations of quantitative and logical relationships, and a theoretical knowledge of how those relationships fit together to form an overall system within which the manipulations make sense. It is only the first part that most people have any conceivable use for, but it is only the second part that enables you to understand why mathematical procedures work.

What science and social science, medicine, agriculture, and industry want from mathematics are the practical arts of problem solving. What mathematicians want us to learn are the elegant systems that make the methods of solution work. Most people who use mathematics, even research scientists, statisticians, actuaries, and systems programmers know very little of what is called "abstract mathematics" or "pure mathematics," that is, the theoretical part. They get along very well without it because their uses of mathematics take place within well-known mathematical models, and their motivations for performing manipulations are not pure mathematical ones but physical, chemical, or statistical reasons. Asked why they performed a particular operation, they will give you a scientific answer, not a mathematical one. Only those who seek the deepest understanding of why the models work, or who want to change the models themselves in fundamental ways (like the pioneers of quantum physics or the new "chaos" theories) need pure mathematics. Even many of them get by with rather little. For most of us mathematics is a tool to be used without understanding why it works, as we use most of our modern technology with only a vague understanding of how it does its tricks.

The technical mystique is certainly reinforced by impressing on math students that they do not really know what they are doing, and then occasionally trying to explain the abstract basis for something, which only seems to insure that they give up completely and accept mathematics on faith. I suspect that students challenge teachers over subject matter least often in mathematics. Good math teachers try to encourage students to see that there may be more than one way to get a result, but they rarely have the luxury of discussing with students *why* any of the methods works to begin with.

For nearly all students, abstract theoretical mathematics will remain a luxury, not a necessity, in their educations. While it should certainly be available to those students who want to study it, perhaps we should be honest with all students about the role of mathematics as a "tool" subject and the real reasons why they don't understand how it works. As things stand now, teaching abstract mathematics outside the context of familiar, concrete applications is an extreme form of one of the errors of science teaching discussed in Chapter 5. It makes unfamiliar thematic patterns all the harder for students to learn, and the students are then labeled as stupid when they fail to learn them. It is the shame of mathematics education that it produces such an extreme reaction in students that the syndrome has been given the name of "math anxiety." Many students actually get sick to their stomachs at the mere thought of trying to do math. Not even science pushes its ideology quite that far.

I hope that I have been able in this chapter to establish at least a *prima facie* case that science is not fundamentally all that different from other subjects. All subjects teach a specialized language, with specific thematic patterns, specific genres and rhetorical structures, and their own stylistic norms and harmful ideological messages. In the case of science, I have been able in the preceeding chapters to be fairly specific about what these are. I hope that in not too many years, we will have the same kind of detailed research about the teaching of the rest of the curriculum. In the next chapter I try to draw together and elaborate on what I have said throughout the book about how we can better teach students to talk science. Perhaps this chapter will provide some inspiration for those who may want to consider how the recommendations to be made in Chapter 7 might apply to other subjects as well.

EXPLORING FURTHER

The role of language strategies in the teaching of subject-matter content across the curriculum is discussed in research reports by Jo-Ann Crandall (*ESL through content-area instruction: Mathematics, science, social studies*, 1987), C. J. Thaiss (*Learning better, learning more: In the home and across the curriculum*, 1983), and K.S. Berry ("Using Oral Language to Learn in a Grade 5 Classroom," 1983, available through many libraries as an ERIC Education Document ED 234378). Each of these deals with science, mathematics, and social studies or humanities subjects.

James Heap has done a careful analysis of language and social interaction in small groups writing with a computer (*Collaboration in word processing*, 1986), and there is a study of meta-language in social studies texts by Crismore ("Meta-discourse: What it is and how it is used in school and non-school social studies texts", ERIC ED 229720). A number of specialist studies appear in the Emihovich collection (*Locating Learning*, 1989), including Campbell's work on mathematics education and my own chapter on science.

There are a number of other studies of the role of language in the teaching of mathematics, of which three studies in a recent special issue of the journal *For the Learning of Mathematics* (Vol.8, No.1, February, 1988) by David Pimm ("Mathematical Metaphor"), John Fauvel ("Cartesian and Euclidean Rhetoric"), and Martha Burton ("A Linguistic Basis for Student Difficulties with Algebra") are representative.

chapter 7
Changing the Way We Teach

In each chapter of this book I have tried to demonstrate the importance of teaching students how to talk science. Teaching them to use the specialized language of science in speaking, writing, and reasoning is essential to every goal of science education. For some students, to some degree, we already succeed in doing this, whether we talk about science teaching in these terms or not. But for many more students we do not succeed very well, and we know that all our students should be able to master the use of science to a greater degree than they do. In this chapter I want to make a number of explicit recommendations for improving science teaching.

Throughout the book I have tried to make connections between the ways we use language in classrooms and larger issues of social values and social interests. I certainly don't want to tell you now that a few "technical" changes in teaching methods, based on research findings, will solve the problems of education.

The problems of education are rooted in the problems of our society. They are not simply technical problems. They do not have technical solutions. They are problems of fundamental conflicts of interests and values between different groups in society, and their solutions require us to openly discuss those conflicts and make some compromises with our own values, and even against our own interests, to accomodate those of others. Research alone should never be the basis for recommending changes in educational policy or method. Recommendations always involve value choices. Research only helps us to understand what our choices are and what the consequences of making different choices may be.

Although we cannot separate educational problems from more general social problems, neither can we afford to wait for somebody else to solve those larger problems before we do anything to help students learn more effectively. If everyone, in every institution of society, waited for social change, we would all wait forever. Change begins when people decide to do things differently. Each change spreads in unpredictable ways, leading to other changes. If those changes go against powerful social interests, they will meet with resistance. But if the changes are in our interests, or those of our students, we will fight back against obstacles placed in our way. "Technical solutions" to educational problems are attractive because they seem painless. No important social change in history has ever come without pain to somebody.

167

And changes in education, perhaps especially changes in educational access to the power of science and technology, are certainly important.

I want to begin with the simplest and most direct changes to improve students' mastery of the content and forms of science. Then I will move on to more controversial recommendations to change basic attitudes and emphases in science education. I will mainly be talking about teaching methods and about attitudes toward science and learning that have important social consequences. I will have much less to say about the topics of the science curriculum, though I do believe that the selection and priorities of topics in most science subjects need changing, too. Whatever topics in science are really most useful for students, we still have to face the basic questions of how to help them learn and what view of science they should come away with. Here, then, are a number of general and specific recommendations for you to consider. They are divided for convenience into four major groups.

TEACHING STUDENTS TO TALK SCIENCE

Give Students More Practice Talking Science

The one single change in science teaching that should do more than any other to improve students' ability to use the language of science is to give them more practice actually using it. Students must be given opportunities to speak at greater length (in monologue and dialogue), and to write more, about science topics. The single greatest obstacle to this at present is the dominance of Triadic Dialogue.

Teachers should use question-and-answer dialogue less than they do now and organize more class time for student questions, student individual and group reports, true dialogue, cross-discussion, and small-group work. Students should do more science writing during class, always following oral discussion of topics.

Triadic dialogue is an activity structure whose greatest virtue is that it gives the teacher almost total control of classroom dialogue and social interaction. It tends to lead to brief answers from students and lack of student initiative in using scientific language. It is a form that is overused in most classrooms because of a mistaken belief that it encourages maximum student participation. The level of participation it achieves is illusory: high on quantity, low on quality. The many other activity structures described in Chapter 3, from Student Debate to True Dialogue and Cross-Discussion, are probably all superior to Triadic Dialogue for purposes of general discussion and review.

Teachers should make every effort to find activities that encourage students to ask the teacher questions, rather than the other way around.
Triadic Dialogue should mainly be used to lead students in inquiry and investigation, or through complex chains of reasoning. But it should not be used as the principal means for introducing new thematic content. Science is not a catechism.

Teachers should encourage students to talk to one another during class about science topics and should be as tolerant as possible of quiet side-conversations. Laboratory time should be ample and used as an opportunity for informal science talk as well as practical work.
Learning is an essentially social process. Talking to one another, in small-group work or even in side-conversations, gives students an opportunity to talk science in a different way, free of some of the pressures of talking science with the teacher. Much more small-group conversation is tolerated in the lab than the classroom, but this is a function of our expectations, which may need to be changed to allow more side-talk in the classroom, so long as it is also "science talk" (see Chapter 3 on "Side-talk").

Teach Students How To Combine Science Terms in Complex Sentences

Given extra time to talk science, how should students be talking? Essentially they should be practicing the use of one particular thematic pattern of semantic relationships among scientific terms. That does not mean drawing thematic pattern diagrams. It means combining first two and then three or more key thematic items together in a single sentence. In the beginning these will be simple sentences, but they will need to become grammatically more complex in order for several semantic relations to be expressed in one sentence. Eventually single sentences will become awkward and students will be using sequences of sentences and, when writing, paragraphs.

Students should engage in activities that will require them to first practice combining science terms in longer grammatical sentences, and then describe, compare, or discuss real objects or events using the science terms in a flexible way appropriate to the situation. Following this, they should use the terms in writing sentences and paragraphs deriving directly from the oral discussion (e.g., a summary of it, the main points, questions they have, how they would explain it to someone who wasn't there, etc.)
All this requires some special work by the teacher, not simply to set

up these situations and tasks, but to teach the students explicitly how to use scientific language. This needs to be done in several ways:

Teachers should model scientific language by explaining to students how they themselves are combining terms together in sentences. They should stop to point out special idioms and phrases (e.g., use of prepositions), forms of grammar (e.g., passive voice, noun forms of verbs), and especially to identify the semantic relations of terms and various ways of expressing the same relationship in different words. Teachers should always explicitly identify when two expressions have the same meaning and when they have different or contrasting meanings.

In present practice (as we have seen in Chapters 1, 2, and 4), teachers tend to leave much of the semantics and grammar of scientific language completely implicit. Students are expected to figure all this out for themselves. That is too much to expect of students who have to deal with topics and thematic content that are so distant from common experience. Teachers need to get in the habit of using Metadiscourse (talk about how we are talking). They should also be familiar with at least the simplest kinds of semantic relations (Appendix C), so that they will know how to explain relations of meaning among scientific terms in a clear and systematic way. This is not to say that students have to learn semantic terminology (though it's not a bad idea), but every science teacher will recognize that students do need to understand these basic sorts of relationships between concepts (e.g., classifiers, whole/part, member/category, etc.). But they also need to be told how to acceptably put these relations into words in science.

Students should be required to be able to say anything in science in more than one way, and be taught how to do so.

In teaching science, or any subject, we do not want students to simply parrot back the *words* we have said. We want them to be able to construct the essential *meanings* in their own words, and in slightly different words as the situation may require. Fixed words are useless. Wordings must change flexibly to meet the needs of the argument, problem, use or application of the moment. If you can't say something in more than one way, you have only memorized it. You can only *use* it flexibly, if you can get past a set of words to a *meaning*. That means saying the meaning without that same set of words.

Discuss Students' Commonsense Theories on Each Topic

The most important conclusion of Chapter 2, reinforced in Chapters 4 and 5, was that both teachers and students need to see the similarities and differences between commonsense ways of talking about a topic and the ways science talks about it. When students have their own thematics, they will often misinterpret what the teacher says, and disagree with it for bad as well as good reasons.

Teachers should ensure that students' own ideas about each topic are discussed, so that alternative views of the subject are "on the table" for everyone. Teachers should show respect for commonsense views and alternative religious or cultural views, while presenting the view of science and the reasons for that view.

Teachers need to know students' alternative views, even if they embody misconceptions, as much as they need to teach the view of science on each topic. Never assume that students have no views on a subject. Very often they have the means to construct such a view even while the topic is being presented, and they may well produce a view that disagrees with the teacher's. Alternative views have their reasons, too, and teachers should be as concerned with understanding them as with presenting the case for science. It is not always necessary for students to give up alternative views. They can have both and use both, for the same or different purposes. Science education only needs to ensure that they learn the view of science, not that they prefer it to all others, or give up any other views. Science need not be a jealous God.

Teach Students the Minor and Major Genres of Science Writing

Most of the emphasis in this book has been on the spoken language of science as used in the classroom, but the written language of science is the form in which students must read about and often make use of their science. Moreover, the spoken language of science is much closer to the formal language of writing than it is to ordinary colloquial spoken language. In learning to talk science, students need to learn the grammar and forms of organization used in scientific writing. The "minor genres" of science are the shorter, simpler forms like descriptions, comparisons, definitions, and syllogisms. They have much in common with the corresponding genres (which I have also called rhetorical structures in Chapter 4) in other subjects. The "major genres" of science, like the lab report, are usually longer, more complex, and more specialized to the work of science.

Students should be taught in great detail, with many models and examples, the parts, order, and meaning relations among parts of the major and minor genres of science. They should also be taught how to write each part, down to the specifics of appropriate sentence construction.

By now science teachers are used to the ideas of reading and writing "across the curriculum." We know that our students need this practice. What we need to remember, however, is that this is still part of teaching *science*. No English teacher is going to be able to teach students how to write a lab report, or even how to write a proper description of a flower or a molecule. We should introduce students to more genres of science writing and give them more practice writing science. It will pay off in their ability to read science, to reason with science, and to use science later in life.

All testing in science should include questions requiring full-sentence and paragraph-length written answers.

We all know that tests send students the clearest message about what is important to learn. Multiple-choice tests do *not* test students' ability to get beyond memorized words to *meanings*. Only tests that require them to flexibly assemble words for themselves can indicate useful mastery of the language of the topic and its concepts. Even problem-solving items should be accompanied either by full work in symbols, or (better) by a written description of the method of solution.

Testing is the last stage. Before that, of course, students should have had ample writing practice in class, for homework, and on quizzes or separate assignments.

BRIDGING BETWEEN COLLOQUIAL AND SCIENTIFIC LANGUAGE

Have Students Translate Back and Forth Between Scientific and Colloquial Statements or Questions

The language of science is not part of students' native language. It is a foreign "register" (specialized subset of a language) within English, and it sounds foreign and uncomfortable to most students until they have practiced using it for a long time. Students understand best what is explained to them in the language they use themselves, ordinary colloquial English. When students are encouraged to discuss their own commonsense views on a topic, they will mostly be using colloquial language. In the classroom today, students mainly answer teachers' questions using as much colloquial and as little scientific English as they can get away with. For most of their education in science, most students will need to learn "bilingually" in both colloquial and scientific English.

Teachers should express all semantic relations among terms, and all conceptual relationships for each topic, in ordinary colloquial language as well as in scientific language, insofar as possible, and clearly signal when they are using each.

Students will begin to grasp semantic and conceptual relationships in colloquial language first. Then they will substitute scientific, technical terms for colloquial words. Only much later will they be able to speak "pure science." Along the way their version of scientific language will be an "interlanguage," a sort of *hybrid* of colloquial and technical registers. The teacher will need to use these different varieties of language as well, and keep them straight for the students. In order for this to work, and in order to increase students' fluency and flexibility in using the foreign register of science when dealing with topics that are initially equally unfamiliar, they need practice in translation as well.

Students should regularly have oral, and occasionally written, practice in class in restating scientific expressions in their own colloquial words, and also in translating colloquial arguments into formal scientific language.

Translation practice needs to go both ways: scientific to colloquial, and colloquial to scientific. The second will, of course, be harder and take longer to master. Written practice will mainly be translating into formal scientific register, but the reverse should be done sometimes as well. Teachers should regularly translate their own statements during the lesson as they go, or call on students to do so.

Discuss Formal Scientific Style and Use Informal, Humanizing Language in Teaching Scientific Thematics

Closely related to the problem of translation is the problem of getting around the stylistic norms of the formal written and spoken language of science. Students need to know what these norms are so that they can use them when they need to, but the teaching of science and classroom discussion cannot be limited in this way.

Teachers should explicitly discuss with students the fact that scientific language tends to use certain forms of grammar and argumentation, emphasize abstract principles rather than human actions, and avoid humor, fantasy, and many kinds of metaphor.

It is likely that many students already do catch on to these features of scientific style, but many more do not, and most probably do not understand why scientific language is like this and what the advantages *and disadvantages* of this style are. Students need to know that scientific language does *not* give a complete picture of what science is like, or what scientists do. They need to understand that in order to learn science and appreciate it as a human activity, they, the teacher, and scientists themselves, break these rules all the time, except in formal lectures and writing. They need to understand that it is all right to talk about science in other ways, and that the formal scientific style is not the whole of science. It is used for a few special purposes, mainly to summarize the results of what scientists do, but it does not reflect how science really gets done.

Teachers should use all the stylistic and rhetorical means available to communicate science to students, including narrative and dramatic presentations; humor, irony, and metaphor; fiction and fantasy; reference to actual scientific activities, disputes, and persons; personal anecdotes and historical examples.

In Chapter 5, I have discussed in some detail the many kinds of alternatives to the usual style of scientific language. Teachers should make extensive use of these and inform students that these alternatives are important tools for communicating science more effectively.

Students should be encouraged to use alternative stylistic forms in speaking and writing science, whenever they do not have to use the language of science formally. They should be taught when formal language is needed and when alternatives may be used.

If students are to remain free of the restrictive conventions of formal scientific language, and if they are to understand and appreciate (rather than criticize) teachers' use of stylistic alternatives in teaching, they need to learn to use the alternatives themselves. Students should occasionally write fictional or fantasy narratives using scientific principles, construct scientific jokes or satires, read and write about historical events in science, write colloquial explanations of phenomena for younger students and parents, and so on. They also need to know when to stick to formal scientific style (on tests, in problem-solving and complex reasoning, in lab reports, etc.), and why.

TEACHING ABOUT SCIENCE AND SCIENTIFIC METHOD

Describe the Actual Relation between Observation and Theory

The antiquated version of the "scientific method" that is still being taught today is both highly dubious as a realistic description of how science actually works in practice and educationally harmful. Students should not be taught that there is such a thing as "proof" in science, that any theory is ever proven true by observations, that observations provide us with absolute facts independent of human judgment and interpretation, or that theories are built from such facts. Neither theories nor observations are "true" or "false."

Theories are complex ways of talking about phenomena that are constantly modified to be more useful, but which are never proven and almost never disproven, either. They are used when they seem useful, modified again and again until they have become in effect new theories, and sometimes are simply allowed to fall into disuse because they answer questions no one wants to ask anymore, or because a new theory seems more useful or more interesting.

Observations are always descriptions in the language of some theory. The observer decides what to look for on the basis of a theory, decides how to look for it, again using the theory, and decides when he has found it, again using criteria of theory. Perhaps the theory is not yet written down anywhere, or even systematically worked out. It may even be simply a commonsense theory. But it is always there, and it can always be described by a thematic pattern in language (including the specialized languages of mathematics and other symbols). Sometimes a theory is added to or modified in the course of trying to give a better description of some observation, and if others find the modification useful, it will continue to be used and become a part of the theory.

Teachers should help students to understand the interdependence of theory and observation, to be critical of claims of absolute fact or proof in science, and to recognize that alternative theories can coexist, each used for different purposes or by different people.

Science teachers have a special responsibility to study the nature of science as a discipline, how it works, how it is described by sociologists, historians, and philosophers from different points of view (functionalists, Marxists, internalists, externalists, positivists, social constructivists, etc.). Science education cannot just be about learning science: Its foundation must be learning about the nature of science as a human activity.

Describe Science as a Fallible, Human Social Activity

It is dangerous to society to have students leave school believing that science is a perfect means to absolute, objective truths, discovered by people of superhuman intelligence. Apart from the danger that scientific "findings" could be used to justify wrong social policies, an impersonal, inhuman view of science alienates many students from the subject. If we are to encourage students of all kinds to take an interest in science, and use it for their own purposes, we need to show it as it really is.

Teachers should emphasize the human side of science: real activities by real human beings, both today and in specific periods of history. Personal characteristics of scientists, with which students can identify, should be emphasized rather than making scientists seem superhuman or alien.

Emphasize that Science is just another Way of Talking about the World, No More Difficult than any Other

It is extremely important that science teachers stop telling students that science is more difficult than it is. Science is *unfamiliar*, but it is not intrinsically more intellectually demanding than any other subject. Science is a different way of talking about the world, but it still uses the same basic semantic and logical relations that every other use of language does. Even when it uses mathematics, this basic similarity still holds true.

Teachers should help students understand that science is a way of talking about familiar and unfamiliar experiences that enables us to relate them to each other in new ways. It does not require any special talents or above-average intelligence to learn this way of talking.

It is also important that we place science in proper perspective. Too often science education seems to lobby for science as the one "true" way of talking about the world. Historically, science has had to fight religious, literary, and political ways of talking about the world for its intellectual place. There are still many conflicts among these and other basic ways of making sense of the world and our life in it, but the job of education is to see to it that students can use all of these perspectives, not to convince them of the absolute superiority of any one of them.

Students should be taught that science is one basic way of talking about the world among many others, and is important and useful, but not that it is the best, truest, or even a complete and sufficient point of view. Its strengths and limitations and its relations to literature, politics, and religion should be openly discussed.

HELPING ALL STUDENTS USE SCIENCE IN THEIR OWN INTERESTS

Adapt Teaching and Testing to Students' Language and Culture

Many of the techniques we now use to communicate the thematic content of science depend on extremely subtle linguistic cues. A change from singular to plural, active voice to passive voice, even a difference in a single preposition can change the meaning of a statement or its logical relation to something else. It is very common for the key meaning of a sentence to depend on a change in stress or emphasis on a single word. Difficult as this may be for most students to follow, it is doubly difficult for students who are not native speakers of English, and for students whose native dialect is not that used by teachers. This often means that not only foreign-born students, but students from families that speak Black dialect or any dialect that differs significantly from the standardized one will be at even more of a disadvantage in the classroom than previously suspected. Alternative dialects are generally more common among working class and poorer families than among the upper-middle class in the United States.

The forms of argument used in science, such as assuming something is true in order to show that it is not, can also be highly unfamiliar to students from backgrounds where language is not used in the way it is in middle and upper-middle class families. To some extent, my second recommendation should help to ensure an equal opportunity for students from different language backgrounds, but being explicit about wordings and meanings is not enough.

Teachers should learn and use some of the language patterns of alternative dialects and languages other than English when teaching science to classes with large numbers of students who speak them.

I do not mean that we must teach science in Black Dialect or in Spanish or Chinese, although it should be much easier for students to learn science at least partly in their usual dialect, and then translate the thematics of any topic into standardized English later. I do mean that just as teachers need to learn the alternative views (thematics) their students may hold on a subject in order to teach the scientific view effectively, so they also need to know something about how their students' dialect or language differs from their own.

Teachers should give the benefit of the doubt to students who express scientific propositions in unfamiliar ways and enlist the aid of other students in translating them into more familiar forms.

We saw in Chapter 2 how easy it can be to dismiss a student's argument without really understanding it. This is especially so when the student uses unfamiliar language, an alternative dialect, or unfamiliar forms of expressing logical relations. Other students in the class may understand the point better than you do.

What is true of language differences is also true of cultural differences and social class differences in attitudes and values. Many students do not share teachers' predominantly middle-class, North European values about individual effort and achievement, attention to detail, the separation of reason from emotion, respect for authority, following instructions exactly, and so on. They also may not identify with science if it is presented as the monopoly of people do share these values.

Teachers should actively portray science as an activity open to people of every gender, race, ethnic and social background and potentially compatible with whatever cultural and social values their students hold. We should not imply that to do science you have to identify with white, middle-aged, middle-class, North European males and their interests and values.

I realize that some parts of this Recommendation will be more controversial than most of the previous ones. All the Recommendations are based, not simply on research and judgment, but also on value-choices and interests. I believe that in some cases teachers ought to put the interests of their students ahead of their own interests, and this often means going somewhat against the prevailing values of your own social group. I do not think there is any way to make this easy.

Methods of testing and grading in science should not penalize students for use of alternative dialects or forms of organization and argument, except where the use of formal scientific language is specifically required for good reasons.

By this I mean that we ought to allow for a wider range of spelling, vocabulary, grammar, punctuation, style, and organization of arguments and answers (including, for example, narratives). So long as we can recognize the underlying thematic pattern to be the same as the familiar scientific one, we should clearly distinguish when we are testing for science content, in whatever form expressed, and when we are specifically testing for use of standardized English or for specific forms of argument or genres.

Testing today combines both content and form of expression and creates an artificial advantage for students from privileged backgrounds. Of course, we should still teach and test for mastery of the formal language of science and its genres of argument and writing. But we should also give students the message that alternative forms of expression which are more comfortable and familiar to them do not invalidate thematically correct answers. I also believe that partial credit should be given for incorrect answers for which "good reasons" are given by the student, though it can be difficult for teachers to judge these impartially.

Acknowledge and Work to Resolve Conflicts of Interest Between the Curriculum and Students' Values

I do not believe that teachers should always defend the established curriculum. Teachers have a professional obligation to criticize the curriculum and work to change it in the interests of their students. A teacher's credibility and effectiveness can be seriously damaged if students see the teacher only as a representative of a curriculum that they do not respect.

The present curriculum is *not*, in my opinion, a very good one from the viewpoint of most students. At best, it represents a safe set of topics and priorities for preparing students for advanced work in science. It is mostly dull, alienating, and irrelevant to the uses to which most students might actually put an education in science. It is the result of finding the lowest common denominator of agreement among science researchers, and fettered by historical traditions long out of date besides. It is not a curriculum that reflects student interests (in either sense of the word), teachers' cumulative experience and advice, or any systematic study of the life-value of its content. As a student, I was bored to death by much of what is in the standard science curriculum. In later life, I have often missed not having learned many other things that would actually have been useful, but were not in the science curriculum.

Teachers should offer students choices concerning the topics to be covered in the curriculum and the time to be spent on each. Classes should discuss the potential usefulness of proposed topics in a realistic way. Where necessary, teachers and students together should change the established curriculum for good reason.

I believe that as part of these discussions, teachers and students should consider the social, economic, and political issues at stake in the curriculum. Teachers should inform themselves about the history of the science curriculum and why it has the form it does, and critically analyze the interests it represents.

Many of the Recommendations I have made, including those in this group, obviously add many layers of discussion to each science topic actually taught. I believe that these are necessary and desirable for the reasons given here and elsewhere in this book. But I also recognize that if many of these Recommendations are followed, it will not be possible to teach nearly as many topics each year as are now "covered." Hopefully, however, the result will be that we can do more than just "cover" a syllabus: We can actually teach science in a way that students can make real use of. Even beyond the consequences of changing our priorities in this way, we need to acknowledge the great diversity in rates of learning among students with different initial backgrounds (linguistic, cultural, social, and scientific). This diversity in rates results not so much from inherent differences in speeds of learning, but from circumstantial differences in relevant knowledge and learning styles.

Students should not be forced to "cover" topics in science at a rate greater than they can truly master them. The number of topics in most courses should be reduced by about 30–50%, and some students should be allowed up to twice the amount of time now available to complete a given number of topics. Students should be allowed the option of taking two semesters to complete the study of topics which others choose to complete in one semester. Much of the additional time should be used to fill-in needed background for learning science topics.

Science education should not be held hostage to the tyrany of the calendar, inappropriate notions of uniformity in mass education, or technocratic illusions about "educational productivity."

Give Students Practice Using Science to Decide Policy Issues According to their Own Values And Interests

The primary goal of science education should not be to prepare all students to undertake advanced study in science. It should be to prepare students to use science in making value-based policy choices directly affecting their own interests. This primary goal should automatically ensure the kind of mastery of scientific language, thematic content, and reasoning that would enable any student who wishes to do advanced study to quickly learn the additional content needed to do so. The present emphasis in science teaching gives students no practice at all in using science as citizens.

Science teachers should devote a substantial amount of class time to discussions of policy questions of importance to students, helping students practice combining scientific language, thematic content, and reasoning with value-choices and analysis of their own interests.

These are my recommendations. They are based on the research and arguments presented in the preceeding chapters, but they are also based on my own values and convictions. I hope that you will share most of these values, and that you will want to try putting many of these recommendations into practice. I know that some teachers will not agree with some of the value-choices I have made here, but I hope that no one will dismiss any of these recommendations as being politically or practically unrealistic. I know that everything recommended here is possible because, somewhere, someone is already doing it. Everything here is part of the repertory of actual ways of teaching science. This list brings together the teaching practices that I believe can make the most difference for our students—for *all* our students. These recommendations would, I believe, improve science teaching for even our most successful students, but they are most needed to bring the chance of success in science to everyone.

In many ways this is the end of my argument and the end of this book. But every argument I have made in every chapter has been constructed with the aid of a new and powerful theory of how human beings communicate and make *meanings*. While I have been using this theory, known as *social semiotics*, all along, I have mainly been interested in what the theory could *do*, not in telling what it says. I have saved a complete overview of the theory itself for last. In Chapter 8, *I* talk science: a new, social science.

Making Meaning: The Principles of Social Semiotics

In the last 10 years, students of social behavior have begun to construct a new theoretical synthesis. It provides a radically different way of looking at how human beings make sense of and to one another: how we make *meaning*. This new theory is still incomplete, but I believe that it is the foundation on which the social science of the future will be built. Because it is so new, and still unfinished, it doesn't yet have a commonly accepted name. Following the lead of the social linguist Michael Halliday and others, I will call it *social semiotics* (Halliday, 1978; Lemke, 1984, 1987a, 1987b, 1989a; Threadgold, in press).

THE GENEALOGY OF SOCIAL SEMIOTICS

Social semiotics is a synthesis of several modern approaches to the study of social meaning and social action. One of them, obviously, is *semiotics* itself: the study of our social resources for communicating meanings. Historically, semiotics (also called *semiology*) was invented as part of the effort to find a scientific basis for linguistics (de Saussure, 1915; Bakhtin-Voloshinov, 1929; Hjelmslev, 1943). Semiotics is the study of all systems of signs and symbols (including gestures, pictures, even hairstyles) and how we use them to communicate meanings. Linguistics covers the one special case of language and so is part of semiotics.

The name *social* semiotics is meant to distinguish the new synthetic theory from more traditional approaches to semiotics (e.g., Peirce, 1908/1958; Eco, 1976), which we can call *formal* semiotics. Formal semiotics is mainly interested in the systematic study of the systems of signs themselves. Social semiotics includes formal semiotics and goes on to ask how people use signs to construct the life of a community.

Social semiotics is not new in trying to unite the study of human behavior, especially meaning-making behavior (talking, writing, reasoning, drawing, gesturing, etc.), with the study of society. There is a long tradition of doing this in cultural anthropology and ethnography. While many anthropologists and ethnographers have taken the role of language too much for granted, they have still made great contributions to the study of symbols and symbolic actions. One of the founders of modern anthropology, Bronislav Malinowski (1923, 1935), also for-mulated several of the principles of social linguistics incorporated in modern social semiotic theory. And social semiotics also builds directly on the work of the modern anthropologist, Gregory Bateson (1972).

Linguistics itself has often been concerned with language as a tool of social action, especially in the European traditions of functional linguis-tics (Propp, 1928; Bakhtin-Voloshinov, 1929; Bakhtin, 1935, 1953; Jak-obson, 1971; and many members of the Prague School, see Garvin, 1964). A branch of this tradition took root in the United States and influenced early American anthropology to investigate the relations of language and culture among Native Americans (Sapir, 1921; Boas, 1922; Whorf, 1956). Another branch of functional linguistics flourished in England (Firth, 1957) and led to the work of Michael Halliday (e.g., 1961, 1975, 1978, 1985a), whose theory of linguistic meaning is gener-alized by social semiotics into a theory of meaningful social action.

There is one essential piece still missing from this synthesis: a theory of society as a whole. Cultural anthropology has usually been more interested in describing the similarities and differences between so-cieties than in explaining them in the way that physics tries to explain material processes. Traditionally this job has fallen to sociology, but it too has found it easier to describe and compare than to explain. Recently a minor branch of sociology, known as ethnomethodology, picked up the ethnographers' interest in everyday life, and looked at processes of social action in our own society (Goffman, 1959, 1974, 1981; Garfinkel, 1967; Garfinkel & Sacks, 1971). This approach, too, is incorporated in social semiotics, but it still lacks any theory of society in the large. It is still only a *microsociology*; what we need is *macrosociol-ogy*.

The problem with most general theories of society is that they are written from the point of view of the dominant groups in the society. They tend to be elaborate rhetorics that really only repeat commonly accepted rationalizations for the way things are. There is, of course, one famous exception: Marx's political sociology.

In the United States, mainstream sociology has largely ignored Marx's social theory because of its political implications. But in Europe, Asia, Latin America, and even Canada important parts of Marx's theory have been reworked and incorporated into a number of different mod-ern social theories. Most of these theories have a few basic principles in common, however different they may be from Marx's original theory of over a century ago, or from each other (cf. Gramsci, 1935; Althusser, 1971; Habermas, 1972; Bourdieu, 1972). The basic theory today can be called *critical sociology* because it explains social processes without assuming that the way they are is the way they have to be, or the way they ought to be. Social semiotics modifies critical sociology considerably in the process of joining it to other essential elements of the synthesis, hopefully improving it in the process.

There are two other pieces in the puzzle that are worth mentioning here. Ethnomethodology is the application in social science of some philosophical approaches known collectively as *phenomenology* (Husserl, 1960, 1965; Schutz, 1932; Merleau-Ponty, 1945). These perspectives also make important contributions to social semiotics' view of the relation of social action to the human individual (the so-called "problem of the subject" cf. Lemke, 1988c). Finally, social semiotics makes use of the insights of Michel Foucault (1969, 1976), the French historian and social theorist, who has analyzed the relations between how we talk about the world and how we act and are acted upon in it. He connects discourse and the technologies of action and control to the larger patterns of belief and power in society.

All these approaches to the study of language, symbol, symbolic action, and human culture have influenced and been influenced by a major philosophical change in Western culture itself. The great battle between theology and science from the Renaissance to the Enlightenment had led philosophers to try to reconcile Idealist theories, which held that Truths existed in an absolute sense (like God), with Materialist theories, for which only Things existed absolutely. Eventually concern with these *metaphysical* issues gave way to interest in *epistemological* questions: how can people *know*, or find out, what truths or things really exist? In science, these became the familiar questions of scientific method. The dominant belief for most of the 18th and 19th centuries was that we discover absolute *truths* by systematically studying *things* and by making theories that correspond to our observations.

This answer, however, has not held up very well in the 20th century. In science, and in all other fields, it seems, we do not so much "discover truths" as we *construct meanings*. We devise useful ways of talking about things and processes, and useful systems of technical action (e.g., measurements, technologies). We construct systems of meanings by using language, mathematics, diagrams, and techniques. They are our social *tools*, and they differ from one social community to another. This is the view of Social Constructionism in philosophy (cf. Wittgenstein, 1949; Rorty, 1979), and it is also the view of social semiotics.

I want now to give a systematic overview of the principles of social semiotics. A complete version would take another whole book, so this outline will have to leave out many of the details. They can be found in the various books and articles in the References that are cited in this chapter. Social semiotics presents a way of looking at human behavior and human society that makes a lot of sense once you get used to it. But it has a way of talking about these subjects that can seem a little strange at first. Having read the rest of this book, however, you should find that much of what I will be saying in this last chapter will sound at least a little familiar.

ACTION, CONTEXT, AND MEANING

Social semiotics is basically a theory of how people make meaning. It asks how we make sense of and to one another and how we make sense of the world. It concerns itself with everything people do that is socially meaningful in a community: talking, writing, drawing pictures and diagrams, gesturing, dancing, dressing, sculpting, building—in effect, everything. But it looks at everything from a particular point of view. Social semiotics tries to answer these questions:

- How does does the performance of any particular socially meaningful action make sense to the members of a community?
- How do people interpret it?
- What are its parts and how are they related to each other?
- What alternatives could have been done in its place, and how would their meanings have differed?
- When do people make this particular meaning? Engage in this particular action?
- How does the meaning change in different circumstances or contexts? How do people feel about the action and its meaning?
- What larger social patterns does the action belong to?
- How does it tend to recreate or change the basic patterns of the society?

The basic assumption of social semiotics is that meanings are *made*. This is a change in the semantics of the term *meaning*. It is misleading to say, as people often do, that something *has* meaning, as if the meaning was somehow built-in. A word, or a diagram, or a gesture does not *have meaning*. A meaning has to be *made* for it, by someone, according to some set of conventions for making sense of words, diagrams, or gestures.

Different people make different meanings for the same word, the same diagram, the same gesture. The same person may make different meanings for something at different times, depending on circumstances and past experience. The most important differences are differences in the conventions for how to make a meaning in a particular context. People from different communities, including different groups within one larger community, tend to have different ways of making meaning. We can only make sense of and to one another to the extent that we share the same ways of making meanings. We must belong to the same, similar, or overlapping communities to do this. To the extent that we do share meanings, we have become members of the same social group, at least partially.

We do not, of course, just make sense of, or for, words and gestures. We make sense *with* words and gestures, that is, we use them to make socially recognizable meanings, to perform socially meaningful actions. We use them to communicate information, to make requests and offers, to praise and blame, to insult, joke, and pray. The *ways* in which we use them are characteristic of the communities we belong to.

We do not use just words and gestures in this way, we also use lines and spaces (in diagrams), notes and rests (in music), mathematical symbols (in formulas), steps (in dance), fabrics and colors (in dressing), supports and spaces (in architecture), moves and plays (in games), and every other form of symbol and action. We speak meaningfully, draw meaningfully, compose and choreograph meaningfully, dress and move meaningfully, build and play meaningfully by deploying the resources our community gives us (words, lines, notes, steps, moves), according to patterns that make sense to others in our community. We use those same patterns to make sense of the actions of others.

Every community has its own meaning-making (i.e. semiotic) *practices*. These are the ways in which its members perform actions that are meaningful in the community. They are patterns of action that are repeated many times. Everything you do that makes sense of, or with, a word, an object, or an action follows one of the semiotic practices of your community. It *is* a semiotic practice of your community (or a combination of semiotic practices). Semiotic practices are actions that make sense in a community. The form of action may be speech, gesture, drawing, building, or even washing the dishes. Semiotic practices are the fundamental elements of social semiotic theory.

What makes an action a semiotic practice? This is another way of asking how an action becomes meaningful in a community, how we make sense of an action (or event). Social semiotics begins with an answer to this basic question. Fundamentally, every action is made meaningful by placing it in some larger context. In fact, we place every action or event in many contexts in order to make it meaningful. The meaning we make for an action or event consists of the relations we construct between it and its contexts. Making meaning *is* the process of connecting things to contexts. We make actions and events meaningful by *contextualizing* them. The most important of all semiotic practices are these *contextualizing practices*. Social semiotics analyzes the kinds of contexts in which we place things, and the kinds of relationships we construct between them and these contexts.

Consider, for example, the meaning of a word said by someone. Take the word "scientific" used by the student who complained about his teacher, saying, "Why can't he explain *science* in a scientific way?" (see Chapter 5). What are the contexts we connect that word to in order to make it mean something? First of all, there is the context of the whole utterance: What words preceded and followed it? Then there is the context of the situation in which it was said: Who said it to whom? What was the event or activity that was going on at the time? What were the relations of the participants to each other? There are also the wider contexts of the community: Under what circumstances is that word ordinarily used in this community? What alternative words might have been used in its place? Is use of the word in this way typical of a particular social group?

What we can say about contextualizing a word holds just as well for a gesture, a diagram, or any action. Social semiotics identifies and names these different sorts of contexts. The wholes in which any action (or thing, event, word) is placed as a part are its *syntagmatic* contexts. The most common sorts of syntagmatic contexts are sequences of actions that are themselves built up of shorter sequences and in turn belong to longer sequences.

The activity structures of the classroom, like Triadic Dialogue, are syntagmatic contexts of this kind. A word is taken to be part of a Teacher Question, or a Student Answer, as well as part of a (complete or incomplete) sentence. Sentences and paragraphs in writing, moves and exchanges in dialogue, plays and innings in baseball are all larger contexts of this kind. There are also syntagmatic contexts in spatial arrangement that are not necessarily sequential: details and figures in a painting, place settings and table arrangements in dining, and so on. Ultimately, however, all semiotic structures can be analyzed as activity structures, because they are all the product of semiotic practices, the results of sequences of social actions (writing, drawing, painting, arranging a dinner table, etc.).

In addition to syntagmatic contexts, there are also *paradigmatic* contexts. These are the contexts of "what might have been." They consist of other words, or actions, that might have taken the place of the one that occured, in the same syntagmatic context. In the same sentence, what other words could have been used? At the same point in the game, what other plays might have been made? For the same detail in the painting, what other colors could have been used? What matters here is the relation in meaning of what was to what could have been. How would we make sense of something differently if a word or color had been different?

Finally, there are what I can call *indexical* contexts. These are social contexts that are usually associated in some way with an action in a particular community. The action and the context "index" or point to one another with a certain degree of probability. For example, there are some actions which index or point to the teacher as the person who is performing them (e.g., Admonitions, Evaluations), and others which are more usually associated with students (e.g., Calling Out, Requests for the Pass). The meaning of an action does depend on *who* performs the action, who speaks the words or makes the gesture. It depends, specifically, on the *type* of person: teacher or student, doctor or patient, lawyer or client, policeman or suspect, parent or child, and so on. Most actions *can* be done by anyone, but the meaning will be very different if it is done by someone of the "wrong" type.

What the right type of person to say or do something is, or what the right situation or circumstances are to do it, depends in turn on wider social contexts. They index and are indexed by one another. If parents and children speak as equals at the dinner table, we are more likely (in America, in the 1980s) to be in a liberal middle-class home than in a conservative, working-class one.

Who speaks how to whom, when, points to social group, to culture, to historical period. And *vice versa*. What, after all, does it mean to be middle-class, except that you do certain things and say certain things in certain ways under particular conditions? Indexical definitions of social context and the social meaning of actions apply not just to social group, class, and period. They apply as well to gender, nationality, ethnic group, occupation, age, and all significant social categories—to all the ways in which we divide society according to differenes in patterns of behavior.

Notice, by the way, that what matters in indexical contextualization is the *pattern* of actions, the systematic relations of actions to each other and to categories or other sorts of "context." Young and old, male and female, rich and poor, Black and White, artist and scientist do not behave completely differently in our society. They perform many of the same actions, but they perform them in slightly different contexts, with differences in background and circumstances, and so with different social meanings. They read, write, reason, labor, and play according to different patterns. These patterns of action of different social groups within a single society are not just different: They have systematic rela-tionships to one another. We will come back to these issues a little later (e.g., see the discussion of "heteroglossia" and "heteropraxia" below).

There is one very important special case of indexical contextualiza-tion: thematic contexts. Everything we say can be made sense of by hearing it in relation to other things we have heard on other occasions that use the same thematic pattern. And just as different social groups behave differently in similar circumstances, their members also identify themselves (i.e. index their social group) by how they talk differently about a subject. Scientists and artists, teachers and students, managers and workers talk about many subjects in characteristically different ways. They construct (or reconstruct) in their speech, writing, and reasoning the different thematic patterns that index their social group.

Contextualization is a very powerful notion. From it a complete theory of meaning and social relations can be built, if we take into account that it is actually the pattern of *probabilities* that an action will index and be indexed by some social category or type of context which distinguishes (and relates) one social group or community from (and to) another. A social group can be indexed by what actions index what contexts in that group. As you can see, this can get pretty complicated, but the mathematical theory of redundancy provides a way to keep straight what is indexing or contextualizing what. The complex patterns of relationships that result can be called "metaredundancies" or "metacontextualizations" (see Lemke, 1984, pp. 33–44).

PRACTICES, PROCESSES, AND COMMUNITIES

An action that makes a socially recognizable meaning in a community is a semiotic practice. We need to look at these meaning-making practices in two ways. First, they are actions which make sense in the community. Second, they include the actions by which we make sense of other actions (and, by analogy, make sense also of events and things). As we have just seen, a social group or community can be defined indexically by the typical (probable) patterns of action of different types of people under different circumstances in that community. In this sense, a community is not composed of people per se, but of people *acting*. It is made up, not of individual biological organisms, but of interconnected life-processes. It is the patterns of those processes that define a community and tell us how it is similar to and different from other communities, how it keeps itself going, and perhaps even how it may change in the future.

An action, if it is socially meaningful in a community, can be talked about as a semiotic practice. In those terms it has semiotic relations to other practices in the community, relations of indexing and being indexed, contextualizing and being contextualized. It has syntagmatic relations to the larger wholes in which it is placed, and paradigmatic relations to the alternatives that could have stood in its place. But an action can also be talked about as a material, physical (and usually biological and ecological) process, as well. As such, it has other sorts of relationships to other actions: relationships of exchange of matter, energy, and information (entropy).

A community is not just a system of semiotic practices: it is also a dynamic, physical, biological system. To survive it must regulate itself internally and interact externally. It needs to cycle matter and energy through itself: It needs food and resources, and it needs to get rid of wastes. It also needs to maintain a relatively stable, useful environment, and to be prepared to change and adapt to that environment when it cannot control it. Most such systems also develop from immature to mature forms, reproduce imperfectly, and evolve (Lemke, 1984, pp. 27–30, 104–112; and Lemke, in preparation).

A social community, therefore, is both a dynamic, open material system of physical and biological processes, and it is a dynamic, open semiotic system of meaningful actions and meaning-making practices. Every semiotic practice is simultaneously a material process. And every material process we know is assigned a social meaning by how we talk about it and how we act with respect to it. Because social practices are also social processes, they have material relations to one another that may not already be recognized in the social system of meanings. This makes social change both possible and inevitable (see below).

In social semiotics "things" are not fundamental. An object or entity of any kind is always analyzed as a social construction, that is, as the product of social practices/material processes that make it something meaningful in a community. When you see a pencil, your perception combines biological processes and semiotic practices to "see" something that you have been taught to regard as an object, with size, shape, color, and a name, a description, a value, and a set of typical uses. Your community endows the object with meaning, and every meaningful thing you do with the object is guided by its meanings in your community.

This applies to people as well. An individual *biological organism* is socially constructed in much the same way that any other object is, but in our society we combine (and often confuse) this notion of an organism with the very different notion of *social individual*. Social individuals are known, recognized, and identified by how they act. In the case of people, this also has a lot to do with how they look. An individual is assigned a biological sex and a social gender (and, as in the case of transsexuals, these two don't have to be the same). How do we tell that a person is male or female? Masculine or feminine? Straight or gay? Handsome or ugly? We do it by employing specific semiotic practices of our community, whether they are scientific ones or commonsense ones.

Our community also has its specific ways of connecting the individual at one moment in time to "the same" individual earlier or later. We apply particular criteria to construct this social continuity of personalities, just as we do to construct the temporal continuity of organisms and other objects. In our own community, for instance, we insist on an exact "one body, one person" correspondence and regard multiple personalities in a single body as abnormal, even if each of the personalities is normal by itself. We do not construct personal continuity from generation to generation (cf. reborn spirits, reincarnation), and we are divided over whether to construct any continuity of individuality at all beyond the moment of death. Other cultures disagree with us on these matters and on many of the details of constructing the social meaning of persons, places, and things. (See Lemke, 1988c.)

We construct social "subjects" as well as social "objects." Subjects act and live; they make meaning. And yet they are also made meaningful. Social semiotics has a long way yet to go in analyzing such things as human emotion and the social construction of personality and individuality. There is more to an individual than the sum of all the social groups and social categories he or she can be assigned to in a community. But the larger social patterns of the community tend to depend more on what social role or type an individual represents than on their uniqueness, because those patterns are patterns of relationships among groups and categories. The patterns are themselves social constructions, but they are not made up by individuals. They are the result of history, of many individual actions that have tended to recreate and change these patterns over long periods of time.

SOCIAL SEMIOTICS VS. MENTALISM

Where in all this grand picture is the "mind"? Somehow it hasn't seemed necessary to use this word, or others that go with it, like *intention, cognition, thought*. The language of *mentalism*, which is basic to the recent revival of cognitive psychology, assumes that there is an autonomous domain of phenomena between the biological and the social. I do not believe that this is so, and social semiotics rejects mentalism completely.

After a long decline, mentalism was revived just a few decades ago because of the failure of behaviorist psychology to explain how people learned and used language (Chomsky, 1959). It was then rapidly generalized, under the name *cognitive science*, to include computer models of many forms of semiotic activity: problem solving, writing, learning behavior, and so on. Much of the research that has been done in these areas is extremely valuable, but the basic theoretical language used remains hampered by the limitations of mentalism.

Mentalism ignores both the biological and the social, but the problems it addresses are precisely the problems of the *relations* of the biological *to* the social. Cognitive science originally sought a close relationship with neurobiology, but it has long since gone its own way instead. Mentalist models treat cognitive processes as isolated phenomena that happen within a single mind isolated from others, as mental processes isolated from social processes.

Mentalism hides from social reality behind an assumption of universality: that all human minds work in the same way. But the work that cognitive science seeks to describe is the work of engaging in semiotic practices, and those practices are crucially different in different cultures and different social groups. Most cognitive science research describes a small number of social practices of middle and upper-middle class Americans. In many cases, apart from its use of the language of mentalism (which it does not actually need), it does this very well. There is no reason it should not, since the data of cognitive science is not "mental" data at all: It is data in the form of language and social behavior, records and descriptions of semiotic practices.

But by ignoring the social, mentalism hides, not just from the reality of social differences, but from the problem of social *values*. Cognitive science is fond of identifying "expert" ways of solving problems, writing, reading, learning, and so on. It then describes these and implies that everyone should learn to re-program themselves to do things in these "expert" ways (or else rely on computers that do). These are the narrow values of technocrats and efficiency experts. They take the preferences of one small but powerful group in society (white, male, upper-middle class, with North European cultural values) and project them as intrinsically superior. Since cognitive science acts as if all minds basically worked the same way, it is saying that the way this one group does things is the way the Mind, all minds, work best. They have safely insulated their "science" from cultural diversity and social conflicts of values and interests.

Mentalism also largely ignores linguistics and semiotics, despite the fact that it was revived by a well-known American linguist (Chomsky, 1959). Most cognitivist accounts of language use pay little or no attention to the semantics of functional linguistics, but try instead to invent an autonomous cognitive logic (*lingua mentis*, the language of the mind). But what we call "thought" is itself constructed through the medium of language and other semiotic resources (depiction, action structures), and the semantics of natural language, far richer than any cognitive logic, is all that's needed to account for what people do with language. I have put "thought" in quotation marks, because, so far as social semiotics is concerned, there is no separate phenomenon to bear this name. What we call thinking is simply material processes which enact the meaning-making practices of a community: the use of language and other semiotic resources. This is not to say that there are not individual differences in what we say or write or reason: most texts and many actions are unique, but every meaningful text and action largely conforms to recognizable social patterns.

Social semiotics identifies those patterns and analyzes individual behavior in relation to them. Mentalism does not have a theoretical language for doing this, though in practice, given the nature of its data and methods of analysis, much cognitive research does describe parts of these patterns very well, even though it misunderstands and misidentifies their social nature. For more detailed critiques of mentalism, see Geertz (1983, Chapter 7), Lemke (1989a), and Thibault (In press, Chapter 2).

SEMIOTIC RESOURCES AND FORMATIONS

Semiotics describes social action in terms of semiotic resources and semiotic formations. A semiotic *resource system*, such as language, is a system of *possible* ways of meaning. Information about it tells us what one *can* say in the language, and how to say it. In general, a semiotic resource system matches the kinds of meanings you can make (semantic functions) with the actions (such as words) needed to make those meanings in a particular community. This is a generalization of Halliday's model of language as "meaning potential," a semantic resource (Halliday, 1978).

A semiotic *formation*, on the other hand, is an *actual* pattern of meaningful action, using semiotic resources, that is repeatedly performed and recognized in a community. Activity structures and thematic patterns (more properly called *thematic formations*) are examples of semiotic formations. A community deploys its semiotic resources in certain habitual ways, and these are its semiotic formations. A formation is a sort of "institutionalized" way of talking, or gesturing, or behaving. Semiotic resource systems tell us what you *can* meaningfully do or say in a community; semiotic formations describe what repeated *does* get done and said.

Resource systems and formations are interdependent. Ultimately, a resource system, like the English language, is an abstraction from the uses of English in a community. Those regular, repeatable, habitual uses are formations (or parts of formations). When the formations change in systematic ways in relation to one another, the language resources have changed, too. But semiotic resources, because they are defined at a higher level of abstraction than formations, change very slowly. New thematic formations in science or politics can appear very quickly, but the grammar and semantics of English changes much more slowly.

There are many different resource systems in addition to language. There is the system of Depiction: the conventions of drawing, painting, diagrams, and so on (cf. O'Toole, in press). As a resource system, Depiction defines what can be pictured and how, what options are available to us. Pictorial *formations* include typical kinds of depiction: bar graphs, outline drawings, stick-figures, portraits, still lifes. Gesture and movement give us further semiotic resources, and common gesture-routines (shaking hands, waving good-bye) and movement patterns (sauntering, jogging, waltzing) are examples of formations that deploy these resources.

There are, of course, many more semiotic resource systems: Music (van Leeuwen, in press), Architecture (Preziosi, 1983), Dress and Grooming (Barthes, 1983), Cooking and Dining (Douglas, 1984), and so on. Each has its own typical formations: sonatas and concertos, villas and skyscrapers, tuxedos and sarongs, roasts and puddings. The most general semiotic resource system is that of social action itself, and its formations are the activity structures of a community, from factoring polynomials to washing the dishes, from writing sonnets to playing a game of tennis.

Social actions, including speaking particular words or writing them, do not make meaning simply by repeating the patterns of common semiotic formations in a community. As we have seen, they also make meaning (or we make meaning of and with them) by how they are used in a particular situation. It matters *when* we say or do something, *where* we do, and with or to *whom* (i.e., what type of person). You can dance, and if you follow the conventions of dancing for your time and place, others will recognize that that is what you are doing (and not having a fit, for example). If you enact a recognizable formation, they may see that you are waltzing. But the meaning of your waltzing then and there will depend on the situation: Is there audible music or not? are you dancing alone or with a partner? Is there a dance floor? are you in a place and situation where dancing is normal? Are you dancing with someone of your own or the oppposite sex? Is your partner unusually young, or old? Is your partner related to you socially in a way that makes the dancing specially significant? Is this kind of dancing normal for your social group?

A record of social action, whether it is a piece of writing, a transcription of a tape recording, a film or video, or just an account of some events, is a *semiotic text*. The actual events constitute a *semiotic performance*, and any material artifact that results can be called a *semiotic production*. When there is no particular reason to use these distinctions, and especially when the resource system of language plays an important role, I will just use the word *text* to refer to the actual, concrete, particular enactment of some semiotic practices, or a record or product of the performance. Semiotic texts are the basic data of social semiotics. They are the stuff of lived social life, so far as it is available for systematic study.

When we engage in a semiotic performance, that is, when we do any meaningful social action, we deploy semiotic resources *strategically*. We can never stray too far from some recognizable pattern of our community (semiotic formation), or our actions will become meaningless for others. But within those broad limits, we have considerable freedom to make an enormous variety of subtly different meanings through what we do and how we do it. That is why we need to take so many different sorts of contexts into account in analyzing how a particular "text" of actions means what it does. And we can never forget that it means different things (or nothing) to those whose social meaning-making practices are significantly different from our own.

In analyzing any action-text, including a purely verbal one, there are two perspectives we need to use. One is the *dynamic* perspective. This is the point of view of someone witnessing the events as they were actually happening. At each point in the sequence of action (or words), we have a different sense of what is being meant or done *now*, what things mean up to this present point, and what is likely to happen next. When the next action occurs, all that could change: What we thought just happened could, retrospectively, have turned out to be or mean something quite different than it seemed to as it happened. It is even possible that our whole sense of what was going on up to that point might have to be revised. And certainly our expectations about what may happen next can be radically changed. In real life the unexpected happens. It art and literature it often does, too.

There is a second perspective which is also important: the *synoptic* perspective. This is the viewpoint of someone who stands outside of time, after the whole sequence of actions has taken place, with the complete text of what happened in hand. This is the usual perspective of researchers, and it is quite useful, but it must be complemented by the usual perspective of participants, the dynamic perspective. We need to see how *strategically* (and tactically?) the events unfolded; not just how things turned out in the end. This is especially true when there are surprises, or when the events unfold over a fairly long period of time.

From now on I am mostly going to talk about semiotic formations, rather than semiotic resource systems. But first I want to identify the general semiotic functions that all semiotic resource systems provide the means to do. These are again generalizations from Halliday's model of the most basic semantic functions of language (which he calls its *metafunctions*; see Halliday, 1978, especially Chapter 2).

First, a semiotic resource system enables us to make *representations*. Basically this means that we can perform one action to represent the meaning of another. This is possible because contextualizing practices associate one action with another, allowing them to index each other. In representation, an action constructed with the semiotic resources of one system indexes the meaning of an action usually constructed with another. We can index the act of climbing a tree with a sentence, with a picture, with mime, with music, and possibly with other resource systems as well. In most communities, language is probably the most versatile semiotic system in this respect (cf. the *ideational* or *experiential* function in Halliday). Other semiotic systems tend to be specialized to represent only some kinds of actions (or objects, events, processes).

The second, closely related function is the ability to make *relations* or connections between actions, objects, events, processes. There are many kinds of relations obviously: spatial, temporal, sequential, structural, causal, behavioral, possessive, attributive, equative, conjunctive, disjunctive; relations of means, manner, condition, similarity, and so on. (Cf. Halliday's *logical* function.)

The third and fourth functions are also closely related (cf. Halliday's *interpersonal* function, with its distinction between Mood and Modality; Halliday, 1985a, pp. 68–94, 332–346). On the one hand there is the ability to *interact*, to constitute a dialogue, either explicit (represented) or implicit: to make a move to which there are possible responses, and to convey meaning through the relation of move and response that goes beyond what either can mean alone. And then there is the ability to establish an *orientation* towards one's action and its meaning, a point of view: favorable or unfavorable, serious or joking, literal or metaphoric, committed or uncommitted, tentative or definite, and so forth. Of these, probably the most important for social analysis is *evaluative orientation*. There are a great number of ways in which we indicate whether we approve or disapprove of things, associate ourselves with them or dissociate ourselves from them.

Finally there is the *organizational* function. A semiotic resource system must provide the means to bind together actions into coherent wholes, to fashion activity structures and other types of formations, and to distinguish between actions randomly strung together and those that are organized according to a pattern into a larger whole. (Cf. the discussion of the *textual* function and of textual cohesion in Halliday & Hasan, 1976).

ACTIVITY STRUCTURES, GENRES, AND THEMATIC FORMATIONS

An *activity structure* is a socially recognizable sequence of actions. Actually, it is a little more abstract than that. The action sequence itself is the result of enacting an activity structure. The same activity structure can be realized in many ways, by many actual sequences of actions. Think of all the sequences of actions that can constitute a lesson, or even an exchange in Triadic Dialogue. What all these sequences have in common is their activity structure. It is a structure in the sense that it has parts, each a functionally defined action *type* (e.g., Teacher Question, Student Challenge), and that these functional elements have specific relationships to one another (e.g., Teacher Evaluation to Student Answer), including restrictions on the order in which they can meaningfully occur.

An activity structure must also be *completable*, in the sense that you can get to the end of the structure and have a sense of closure to the activity. Activity structures are repeatable in a community, and most of them are repeated frequently, even though any particular action sequence may never be exactly repeated again. That is why is it useful to define activity structures in this abstract way.

In addition to the activity structures of the classroom (Do Now's, Going-Over-Homework, Student-Teacher Debates, Admonition Sequences, etc.), there are recognizable activity structures in every aspect of human life. Every routine and ritual, every activity for which we can specify rules or procedures, every activity that is endlessly repeated with minor variations can be described as an activity structure. Large, complex activity structures can be analyzed as being composed of smaller, simpler ones. Dining-in-a-Restaurant is a major activity structure, and within it we could identify Getting-the-Check as a smaller one. Washing-the-Dishes (hopefully not in the restaurant) is an activity structure, and so are Going-to-the-Movies, Making-a-Phone-Call, Writing-a-Letter, Painting-a-Portrait, Taking-a-Photo, Buying-Stamps, Telling-a-Story, Changing-Diapers, Mowing-the-Lawn, Doing-your-Taxes, Washing-a-Car, Measuring-Blood-Pressure, and so on.

Activity structures can be everyday or special. Many of them in our society are technical, learned and performed by specialists: medical lab procedures (even when automated), scientific measuring techniques, astronomical observations, drawing weather maps, compiling economic statistics, cataloguing new books in a library, fitting new pipes, taking inventory, writing an annual report. Some of these involve the use of language or mathematics; others deploy only other sorts of semiotic resources (including the basic resource of meaningful action itself).

Some human activities may not be regular enough, not similar enough from one performance to another, to be described as activity structures: writing a book, taking a vacation, committing a murder. On the other hand, there are undoubtedly more specialized versions of such activities that are structured in a more or less repeatable way. Part of the job of social and cultural analysis is to identify the regularities in human action.

An activity structure can be interrupted and resumed later; it need not be enacted continuously from start to finish (except in special cases where continuity is an essential relation between its elements). This is possible because the basic relationship between elements in an activity structure is usually *not* simply that one comes (immediately) after the other. The relationship is functional. An Answer can come long after its Question and still be recognized as the Answer to the Question.

A synonym for activity structure might be "action genre," by analogy with the terms "speech genre" (Bakhtin, 1953) and *genre* itself, which usually refers to a written genre. The notion of genre is a useful one when it is understood in relation to activity structure. Originally, a *genre* meant a literary genre: short story, one-act play, epic poem, sonnet, limerick, novel. It referred to certain standard types of literary product that were repeatedly produced in European society. The notion is sometimes extended to other arts: The genres of painting include still-lifes and crucifixions, those of music include concertos and sonatas. But a sonnet or a sonata is not an activity structure. The activity of Writing-a-Sonnet or Composing-a-Sonata, however, is. A sonnet is a semiotic production resulting from a performance of the activity structure of Writing-a-Sonnet. The sonnet is also a semiotic text, a sort of indirect and transformed record of the activity of writing (it is usually highly edited, not an accurate record of the actual writing process).

This interpretation of the traditional notion of genre does not always work. A novel is probably not the product of a definable activity structure because writing novels does not seem to result in the degree of similarity in functional structure from one novel to another that is found in other genres like limericks or haiku. Some kinds of novels (formula mysteries, for example) may be specialized and regular enough that writing them is describable as an activity structure. The Novel is not a genre in social semiotics, and Writing-a-Novel is not an activity structure. It is a recognizable activity *type*, however, because there are semiotic practices in our community by which we can usually decide whether somebody is "writing a novel" or not. Similarly, the Novel is a semiotic text-type because we can decide whether something counts as a novel or not.

Speech genres tend to be less literary and more typical of everyday life. They are also usually integral parts of activity structures that deploy other sorts of action in addition to speech. Formal, extemporaneous speaking is somewhat out of style today, but Toasts and Eulogies, spontaneous Limericks, and even Playing the Dozens in Black English are obvious examples. So, less formally, is the language of buying and selling (Ventola, 1987), or the language of the classroom, or the courtroom (e.g., Walter, 1988). It is not clear whether Casual Conversation is truly an activity structure, or just a recognizable activity type (Eggins & Slade, 1987).

It is particularly important to be clear that activity structures are not rigid formulas for speaking, writing, or doing. Only a very few sorts of ritualized or automatic activities are performed in a mechanical way. Because activity structures are defined at a relatively high level of abstraction from actual performances, they leave a lot of room for dynamic variability (and creativity) in their enactment. To write a sonnet is not usually a mechanical process, but however the parts of the sonnet are produced, they do conform to certain regularities (or else the result is not a sonnet). An activity structure always gives a predominantly *synoptic* view of human action: it tells what the dynamic performance amounted to in the end, not how it was produced.

We can make a more dynamic account of human action by looking at the moment-to-moment strategies and options within a performance, but the categories we use in doing so are always synoptic ones. This "slippage" between the dynamics of performance and the synoptic perspective of functional analysis is an aspect of the more fundamental incommensurability of analysis in terms of material processes and analysis in terms of semiotic practices. This slippage makes it possible for semiotic systems to change (Lemke, 1984, pp. 143–146).

Probably the most important and neglected kinds of genres are non-literary written genres (Kress, 1982; Martin, 1985b; Lemke 1988a). From Book Reports to Book Reviews, Persuasive Essays to Editorials, Lab Reports to Research Papers, both as students and as mature writers we need to master many specialized activity structures for writing a variety of genres. Very few of us will write novels, plays, or short stories, but most careers and lives make use of the skills of writing these nonliterary genres. Those genres through which power is exercised in our society particularly need to be analyzed and taught. Synoptically, we need to know what the parts of each genre are, how they are functionally defined and recognized, what their functional relations are to each other, and what possible orderings they can meaningfully have. Dynamically, we need to know at least some of the ways in which each part can be realized, right down to the level of phrase- and sentence-types.

We all know that you can start a fable with "Once upon a time, there lived . . .." How many other ways can you start one, and still have the opening be recognized as probably the start of a fable? (Cf. Hasan, 1984b; Halliday & Hasan, 1985, pp. 63–69). How do you start a Book Report? Or a Legal Petition? They too have their rules and conventions and ought to be taught systematically in the curriculum.

The functional elements of a particular genre or activity structure are specific to that one genre or activity. A Teacher Question in Triadic Dialogue (where the teacher knows the answer) does not perform the same function as a Teacher Question in True Dialogue (where the teacher does not), even if we happen to give them the same name. On the other hand, the basic semantic relation of Question to Answer *is* the same in all forms of dialogue, although at a slightly more abstract level. The Question-Answer pattern, like the Problem-Solution, Cause-Consequence, or Generalization-Example patterns are widely used across many different genres and language-using activities. One can think of these as "mini-genres" that are used to fill the functional slots of the major genres. They are certainly structures in their own right, though typically they only have two or three functional elements of their own. It is useful, however, to recognize that they are more abstract than genres or activity structures proper, and that because of this fact, they can be used in different genres, while retaining their own basic structure. I call them *rhetorical structures* (cf. Mann & Thompson 1983, 1987).

A piece of written or spoken language, that is, a *text*, can be analyzed at three sequential levels: as the product of an activity structure which results in a definite sequence of functionally defined and related elements, as a sequence of rhetorical structures that realize these elements and relations, and as a structure of grammatical constructions and words that realize the elements of the rhetorical structures. The scheme of analysis looks something like this:

GENRE:

FUNCTIONAL ELEMENTS:

RHETORICAL STRUCTURES:

GRAMMATICAL CONSTRUCTIONS AND WORDS

THEMATIC FORMATIONS, DISCOURSE, AND TEXT

Analyzing the uses of language in a community in terms of activity structures, genres, and rhetorical formations helps us to identify *syntagmatic* contexts. Whatever is said or written is always a part of some functional element in an activity, and it will have syntagmatic relations to other elements in these larger wholes. A phrase in a Teacher Question is part of the whole question, part of the complete exchange (with relations to Preparation, Answer, Evaluation, and Elaboration), and part of the overall activity of the episode, the lesson, the unit, and the course.

In relation to these activity structures, we can also place the phrase in some of its *paradigmatic* contexts: What else might the teacher have done at this moment? How else could he or she have asked the question? But there are still other equally important contexts in which we place the phrase to make sense of its full meaning. The phrase may repeat the words used by the teacher or by a student at an earlier point in the lesson, or it may use the wording of a problem or discussion in the textbook. The wording may serve to remind students of something they learned earlier in the year, or even in a different course or outside school. It may even disturb students because it sounds too colloquial or "unscientific."

If the question was about a particular topic in science, then the odds are that there are only a few ways in which the teacher could have asked it. There are only a few, because all the meaningful ways of asking it have to use the same basic semantic relationships among key concepts or terms. The teacher can ask: "What kind of wave is sound?" or "Sound is what type of wave motion?" or "Is sound a longitudinal wave or a transverse wave?" However the question is asked, it has to express the semantic relationship of classification and it has to refer to what is to be classified (*sound*), and in what category the classification is to be made (*waves*). It also has to imply, or state, that there is more than one type (the Classifiers) to choose from. The question must fit this *thematic pattern* of semantic relationships. That pattern is a small piece of a semiotic formation, a recognizable way of talking about this topic in a particular community. Such a *thematic formation* is another important context for the meaning of the question, or any words used in phrasing it.

Thematic contextualization is the process of placing anything said or written in the context of some larger, familiar thematic pattern of semantic relationships. Because there is often more than one way to express the parts of a thematic pattern in words, the pattern itself has to be defined at a slightly more abstract level than that used to describe wordings. A scientific "concept" (unfortunately, a mentalist term) can always be expressed in different words: *sound* can be expressed as *sound, sound wave, acoustic vibration, pulse,* and so on at different points in the same text (or from one text to another). The element of a thematic pattern which can be expressed in all these ways is called a *thematic item* (to avoid mentalist terms like *concept* or *idea*). The web of semantic relationships among different thematic items form the thematic pattern or *thematic formation* of the topic.

We can use words to construct the semantic relationships of a thematic formation in many different ways, even using very different genres or activity structures in doing so (e.g., poems, essays, debates). Thematic formations are what all the different texts that talk about the same topic in the same ways (semantically) have in common.

The thematic meaning of a word or phrase is the meaning we make for it by placing it in the context of a particular thematic formation. If we are talking about money, *bank* and *deposit* will probably be contextualized by their semantic relations to *cashier* and *withdrawal* in one particular thematic formation. If we are talking about a river, we will construct meanings for them according to a different pattern that relates them to *current* and *sediment.* Saying the words *bank* or *deposit* are merely ways of using language to make meanings; the meaning depends on the thematic pattern. A meaning is made by our thematic contextualization of a word, by *which* pattern we place it in. In many cases, we can place it in more than one pattern. What is true of a word, is true also of phrases, clauses, sentences, and even whole texts.

While it is basically true that thematic formation, genre structure, and particular choice of wording are all in principle independent of one another, in practice these different features of a text index one another and the community in which they are used. We do not see the thematics of science constructed in the genres of poetry as often as we see them in the genres of the textbook or research paper. We do not hear the word choice "pickled rope" as often as we do "salt bridge" or "conduction pathway," when the genre is a textbook and the thematics is that of chemistry. If we do find it, the activity structure is more likely to be informal talk about science than formal writing.

The stylistic norms of science, discussed in Chapter 5, are social conventions (metaredundancy relations, as in Lemke, 1984, pp. 33–44), that link thematics, genre, and wording to make some combinations more likely than others in a particular community. Those patterns of combinations in turn index the community itself, distinguishing one social group from another.

A particular, recognizable combination of thematics, genre, and stylistic choices of rhetorical strategies and word-choices can be called a *discourse formation*. The actual texts of such a formation make up a very specific *text-type*. The discourse formation is an important indexical context for the meaning of every part of every text of its text-type. Every Shakespearean sonnet about love is a potentially relevant context for making sense of every other one. Every research article about the theory of superconductivity is potentially a relevant context in which to interpret every other one.

INTERTEXTUALITY AND TEXT SEMANTICS

Social semiotics begins with texts and other records of human behavior or products of human activity. It does not begin with activity structures, genres, or thematic formations. Semiotic formations are abstractions from texts: They are the common patterns shared by many similar texts. They describe how we make meaning by placing actions and words in some contexts rather than others, connecting them to certain other actions and certain other words. Every community or social group has its own characteristic ways of making meaning, its own ways of contextualizing and connecting, its own activity structures, genres, and thematic formations.

When we participate in an activity, read a text, or make sense of talk and other forms of socially meaningful action, we connect words or events up in familiar patterns. They may be words and events in the same text or action sequence, or they may be words and events from different texts or times. This is the principle of *general intertextuality* (Lemke, 1985a, in press-b): Everything makes sense only against the background of other things like it.

The *intertexts* of a text are all the other texts that we use to make sense of it. Some of them are texts that share the same thematic pattern (cothematic texts). Others belong to another element in the same activity structure (coactional texts), or have the same genre structure (cogeneric texts). A poem and a textbook passage, both about evolution, may be cothematic. A speech by a defense lawyer and the text of a letter entered in evidence in the same trial may not necessarily be cothematic, but they are coactional. Any two limericks are cogeneric.

The text-connecting practices of a community are an important part of its ways of making meaning. We can make meanings through the relations between two texts that cannot be made within any single text.

Real texts and sequences of actions are not pure, ideal types. They do not necessarily stick to one genre or one thematic formation. Many texts mix different thematic formations, often creatively. Some texts also mix different genres. Semiotic analysis is not a straightjacket, it is a systematic expression of how all of us make sense of texts and events, including the irreducible ambiguities and multiple meanings we find.

A real text will have many thematic strands, many thematic formations which it links together to make its arguments. At each point in a text, there will be one or a few thematic formations that will normally be used to interpret the text there. In addition to its generic or activity structure, a text is also organized by the ways in which these thematic formations run through the text. Like a piece of music, there are various themes that appear, disappear, return, are transformed and linked to other themes (see Lemke, 1988d, in press, b). This sort of thematic analysis of the meaning of a text is part of general *text semantics*.

Semiotic productions in general, of course, use resources other than (or in addition to) language. A thematic formation does not have to be expressed only through the medium of language. Very often when speaking we use gestures or objects around us, rather than words, to stand for thematic items or express relationships. In writing we can also use pictures for these purposes, and various multimedia productions (which will become more common with the use of computer systems) can express thematic formations through the deployment of many kinds of semiotic resources. For a discussion of *codeployment* of different semiotic resource systems, see Lemke (1987a).

Just as communities have specific ways of connecting texts to one another, thematically or actionally, so they also construct characteristic patterns of relationships among activity structures and thematic formations themselves. Some activity structures are considered to be rival ways of doing things, or are characteristic of social groups that may be in conflict with one another. Certain thematic formations are also set up as being opposed to one another, as being contradictory or representing conflicting ways of talking about a subject. In order to understand the importance of these relationships in analyzing the social practices of a community, there is one more aspect of semiotic formations we need to discuss.

So far we have talked mainly about how formations express three of the five fundamental semiotic functions: representation, relation, and organization. To the extent that we have emphasized the importance of *dialogue*, we have also touched on a fourth: interaction. But the fifth function, orientation, is the one that enables us to communicate our attitude or stance toward what we are saying or doing, and especially our *evaluation* of it: whether we value it positively or negatively. The resources of language and social action enable us to sneer and ridicule as well as admire and promote, to dissociate ourselves from an action or way of speaking as well as to take it for our own.

Everything we say, write, or do carries with it an evaluative orientation. It is "colored" by ways of saying or doing that indicate our attitude and stance toward what we do (Lemke, 1988b, 1989c, in press-a). We can speak or act with reluctance or enthusiasm, disapproval or endorsement. We can express our stance explicitly in so many words, or more subtly in tone, body language, facial expression, pacing, or choice of words. In a community where the attitudes of different groups can be taken for granted, we need only index a group by one of its views or characteristics to project its attitudes toward anything else.

When used in a text or discourse formation, a thematic formation is always given, in a particular community or social group, not only a set of *semantic* relations to other formations, but also a set of *value relations* (or *axiological relations*). Formations are regarded as good or bad, right or wrong, appropriate or inappropriate. This is part of the means by which they are made to oppose each other, complement each other, or directly ally with each other (Lemke, in press-b). Since social groups are indexed by (and identify closely with) the formations they use and their stances toward them, these kinds of relationships between different ways of speaking and acting play an important role in the social dynamics of a community. They form the community's systems of *heteroglossia* and *heteropraxia*. These notions are essential to the ways in which social semiotics analyzes a community.

HETEROGLOSSIA AND DISJUNCTION

One of the most important social facts about how people use language (and all the other systems of semiotic resources) is that people from different communities deploy these resources differently. Every different social group and category makes different meanings. They have different activity structures, different thematic formations, and different probabilities for which formations and activities will be used by whom and when (i.e. under what circumstances, in what contexts). Not just people from what we recognize as different countries or cultures, but people from different groups within a single social community, and even people who simply belong to significantly socially different categories in the community act and speak differently. People who differ in age, sex, social class, religion, occupation, and political views, for example, whether they form distinct communities or not, talk about many subjects differently and act differently in many situations.

From the way a person talks about a subject, especially if it is a controversial one (e.g., abortion, Gay rights, feminism, legalization of drugs, euthanasia, military spending, nuclear reactors and weapons, multinational corporations, etc.) you can tell a lot about the social groups and categories they belong to or have been influenced by. But even in much more everyday matters, like choice of newspaper or preference in clothing, people from different social groups behave differently and talk differently (Bourdieu, 1979/1984).

Different social groups and categories correspond to different patterns of combination of social practices. From those differences arise differences of interests and differences in values. Included in these differences are differences in tastes and preferences, differences in opinions and beliefs, and differences in propensities for actions of various kinds in various situations.

If we were to take any topic (e.g., see Lemke, 1988b on Gay rights) in any community, we could identify a certain relatively small number of basic ways of talking about that topic (i.e., different thematic formations). Nearly everything said or written by anybody could be analyzed as some combination of elements from these formations, and would vary systematically with social group and social interests. But in addition to this, we would find that each group also had its opinions of the views of the other groups.

For example, on the issue of Gay rights, there is the Moral Majority's view of homosexuality as "willful and sinful," calling the secular scientific view (that it is a normal sexual variation) "blasphemous," while civil libertarians opppose the Moral Majority's positions for violating the separation of church and state, and mainstream religious denominations denounce their methods of interpreting the Christian bible. Each social group has its own way of discussing the subject and its own stance toward the others. There are about a dozen different positions on this issue, and their innumerable combinations (Lemke, 1988b).

From any social position in the community, we can construct a picture of how the different possible viewpoints on an issue are talked of as being allied, opposed, complementary, and so on. This is the *system of heteroglossia* for that topic, from that social position, in that community. The term heteroglossia derives from the work of Bakhtin (1935, pp. 262–300), who first emphasized the importance of social differences in the use of language for analyzing society.

While heteroglossia (diversity of ways of speaking) covers the differences of thematic formations and the different value orientations of each group to those formations, we need a more general term to cover the similar sorts of differences in forms of social action other than just speaking. For this I use the term *heteropraxia* (diversity of ways of acting). A complete description of the system of heteropraxia (or even heteroglossia) for any community would be very complex indeed. But what these concepts give us is an important perspective: They remind us that not only do different social groups and categories speak and act differently, but that these differences form a *system*. That is, they are not just differences: They are differences that are systematically related to each other. The ways in which different groups speak about a subject, or tend to act, are part of the dynamics of their overall social relations to one another: their conflicts and alliances in matters of economic and political interests and power (Lemke, in press-c).

Within the system of heteroglossia, any two thematic formations which people regard as being more or less "about the same thing" (see Lemke, in press-b) have two different sorts of relations to one another. One kind, obviously is their thematic-semantic relations: how do they construct similar or different semantic relations among similar or different thematic items. The other kind is their *axiological* relations: What value orientations do they take toward each other? These two are closely interrelated because each social *discourse voice* (thematic-formation-plus-value-orientation, as spoken by a particular group) tends to reconstruct the thematics of each of the others in the process of approving or disapproving of them (cf. Lemke, 1988b, in press-a). It is thus discourse voices, rather than abstract thematic formations alone, which constitute the basic elements of a system of heteroglossia.

Discourse is a mode of social action. It is not just language, but language-in-use in a community. A discourse voice does not just speak in a particular way about a topic (thematics), even with a value orientation to other voices (axiological stance). It is always doing some social work in the community, it is always "up to something." Very often, as we have seen in Chapter 5, the use of a particular way of talking (e.g., using the stylistic norms of formal science, or promoting the technocratic view of scientific objectivity) tends to promote certain social interests at the expense of others, and help people from some social groups while hindering others, even when we are not aware of this, and even when we would not want to do it if we were aware. This phenomenon is often called the *ideological* use of language.

In social semiotics, an ideology is a discourse voice that systematically promotes the social interests of a privileged or powerful group while at the same time disguising the fact that it is doing so. It is important to note that a thematic formation is not necessarily in and of itself ideological. It is the way it is used in the community that determines its ideological force. The same thematic formation can often be used by several groups whose interests are in fundamental conflict.

SOCIAL SEMIOTICS AND SOCIAL CHANGE

The brief sketch of principles in this chapter has taken us from a theory of how people act meaningfully in a community to a model of the structure and conflicts among factions within that community. At the same time, social semiotics recognizes that communities change and that their dynamics depend on human actions seen both as semiotic practices and as material processes. The ultimate challenge for a social science based on the principles of social semiotics is to tell us what we can predict about the future of a community and what we cannot.

It is probably not possible for any individual or group to directly control the future of a social system. The processes which organize, sustain, and modify large, complex communities operate on a vastly different scale than do their parts, whether groups or individuals. Communities live on a different time scale than we do, and the processes which change them are processes operating between groups, between discourse voices, and most generally within and between systems of heteropraxia.

Communities also change because of rapid or gradual responses to slippages or mismatches between the complex systems of relations among their semiotic practices and the equally complex but very different systems of relations among the material processes which sustain them (and which include the semiotic practices themselves). Individuals and groups can no more control the future of a community in the long term than a cell or organ in our body can control our lives. One cancerous cell or defective organ can perhaps end our life, but no single mutant cell or specialized organ, even the brain, determines the overall course of human development and individual response to an environment which the organism itself partly controls.

The tools of social semiotics provide the means to refine our present, rather hazy models of social systems in the large. Even critical sociologies only give us a starting point. Notions like heteroglossia enable us to relate individual actions to wider social processes by way of intermediate constructs such as activity structures, thematic formations, and discourse voices. We can look at the ways in which the activity structures of a community converge differently in different types of individuals, creating and subdividing significant social categories. We can redefine and refine notions like social class, gender, and life stage. We can reconnect individual and groups interests with their systems of values and patterns of action. But, most importantly, we can now begin to analyze the dynamic relationships between two patterns: the pattern of social relations among actions viewed as semiotic practices and the pattern of biophysical interactions among those same actions viewed as material processes.

A community is simultaneously a social system and a dynamic, open biophysical system (Lemke, 1984, pp. 104–112; in press-c). As a material system, it belongs to a special and important class of systems: those which maintain their existence by continual dynamic interaction with their environments. Like open flames, hurricanes, biological cells, and independent organisms, communities have particular nonequilibrium thermodynamic properties that lead to internal self-regulation, exchange of matter, energy, and information among subsystems and with the environment, and a developmental pathway characteristic of their type or species. Along that pathway they undergo discontinuous changes in their internal organization, build up internal complexity, and export entropic disorder to their environments. They pass through successive stages of ascendance, maturity, and senescence in which they tend to respond differently to the challenges of a changing environment (cf. Salthe, 1985, in press).

Even more than this, communities are systems whose types can evolve, because the material base of their semiotic practices can preserve information, accomodate variability, and transmit information to future communities of the same or a successor type (Lemke, in preparation). In this way communities are very much like biological organisms, though in other respects they are a quite different kind of system. The community maintains itself, follows the developmental course specific to its type, undergoes at the same time an individuation unique to its history, and contributes to an evolutionary lineage of communities over longer periods of time.

A complete discussion of the developmental-evolutionary model of social change would require several more chapters or another book. Here it may be enough to point out that the developmental forces in the lifetime of a community, or even of one of its components, in affecting the dynamics of the material processes of the system, also play a role in the changes in our meaning-making practices: in the life-histories of activity structures, thematic formations, and discourse voices as social phenomena. By correctly defining the various constituent subsystems of a community, we can in principle distinguish predictable, type-specific developmental changes from individuating community-specific changes and inherently unpredictable evolutionary changes. Across various time scales and communities there will be a spectrum from (probabilistically) predictable to unpredictable responses to internal and external forces.

SOCIAL SEMIOTICS AND POLITICAL RESPONSIBILITY: MAKING TROUBLE

I want to conclude this chapter by projecting from the model of social systems sketched here a few conclusions about our own responsibility for social change. Social systems are neither objects nor machines, and we are inside and part of them, not outside and independent of them. We cannot deceive ourselves that we can guide and control them with the help of social science the same way we manipulate our conventional technologies on the basis of physical and biological science. We have a better chance of "managing" even the ecosystems of which we are also a part than we do our own social systems, though we would do better with ecosystems if we at least tried to imagine a viewpoint larger than that of our own interests. In the case of social systems, even our viewpoints are necessarily contained within the system: we *cannot* imagine a viewpoint outside our own system of heteroglossia (in trying to do so we merely enlarge that system, remaining inside it).

Every attempt to construct an overview of the whole of a social system, encompassing all the interests and differences represented within it, will always necessarily be constructed from the perspective of some single social position within the system, and therefore from the viewpoint of a particular set of social interests and values. Neither traditional liberal politics nor the newer technocratic ideology of rational management (see Lemke, in press-a) want to face this issue.

The traditional view is that we can rely on a political class (lawyers, politicians, their advisors) to represent among themselves the interests of social groups and categories to which they themselves do not belong and whose patterns of social practices (i.e., lifeways) they do not share. The newer technocratic position is that complex problems can be solved by expertise without considering conflicts of values and interests or the diversity of viewpoints in society. The traditional political class and the new technocrats claim to be representing, in the one case, everyone's interests, and in the other, a purely objective viewpoint, but in neither case do they admit that they must in the long run represent the only interests they can: their own.

No individual, group, or class, can represent—or even imagine—a complete, representative, or positionless view of the whole of a social system. In the case of the schools, no principal or administrator can claim to be able to make decisions that truly take into account the interests of teachers, students, parents, and the public in all their real diversity. Neither, for society as a whole, can politicians or even elected legislatures as presently constituted do so. And certainly no class of professional experts or managers, even educational researchers or social scientists, can legitimately claim to be able to make "objective" decisions.

Society itself, as a whole, is the only complete representation of the social system. Ideally, decisions should be made, after issues and interests are articulated by each social constituency in its own terms, by the whole of the community. Short of that, any representative system of decision making, whether in schools, corporations, or government bodies, needs to seek representation by members of diverse social categories, and means to articulate the interests of these constituencies.

Any such system of decision making would result in much more open conflict of views than now exists. In our present system of social ventriloquism, a relatively homogeneous few speak for a narrow range of their own interests in the name of all. This minimizes the appearance of conflict, but the reality of conflict remains. Denied a forum and political power, the full diversity of social interests, values, and viewpoints creates a dangerous social instability. This instability arises from the long-term contradictions between decisions which reflect the special interests of the decision makers and the full spectrum of actual social interests in the community.

Let us not romanticize the social upheavals and political revolutions which result. They are as cruel and devastating as any war; they bring about enormous real suffering, and they can wreck the complex and technologically vulnerable economic base of a modern society. Neither those who benefit from the status quo, nor those who seek to change it radically should be eager for a violent confrontation of conflicting social interests. Just as national wars are pointless for modern nations in the nuclear age, so are violent revolutions and civil wars too potentially devastating to consider in complex, technologically vulnerable societies. In both cases there would be little left for the victors to govern. Far better to institutionalize these conflicts, and all future conflicts of interest, in the political process itself and strain the political system to its limits, rather than destroy the social system itself.

I am speaking here of changes in institutions: in activity structures in politics and decision-making, in the range of discourse voices to be heard on every issue, and in the distribution of power among social groups and categories. These changes do not have to begin with the national government, and are not likely to. They can begin with individual institutions: schools, social organizations, businesses, advocacy groups, local governments, and so on. Pressure for changes in the distribution of power in major corporations or government bodies will require that people first experience new ways of making decisions on a smaller scale.

We need to build confidence in our ability to articulate viewpoints that have never had the opportunity to speak for themselves effectively. We need to learn that we can cope with far more open conflict of interests and values than we have in the past. We need to see that better decisions are made when all interests are truly represented, and that no single viewpoint can ever be either comprehensive or objective. We need to grow jealous of our right to speak for ourselves.

New social practices can spread in a community when they meet needs that may never have been adequately articulated before. In any social system there are some meanings that are never made, some connections that are never put into words, some actions that are not yet part of the social repertory because to make, say, or do them would be to change that system against the interests of those who regulate our social practices (see on the "system of disjunctions" in Lemke, 1984, pp. 131–150, 1985a). But such regulation, and the ideologies which rationalize it, only exacerbate the contradictions between what people do and what it is possible to say. This is a crucial source of the slippage between social action analyzed as semiotic practice and as material process.

We always do more than we recognize that we do. There are interests arising from patterns of social action that do not yet have social meaning or recognition. There is more potential meaning to every act than what its definition as a semiotic practice recognizes at any one point in history. Some significant social patterns are always "presemiotic" in this sense. The social power of the status quo is especially vulnerable to changes which articulate and make recognizable actions that express previously unarticulable interests. It is here that social semiotics can be a guide to effective political action.

What an individual or a group does only matters to the social system as a whole to the extent that it spreads and leads to changes in the relations among groups in the system. That is most likely to happen when what we do operates in the critical zones of vulnerability of the status quo: those places where its power is maintained by the absence of alternatives rather than by force.

It is in those areas where there seems to be no alternative to the status quo that any real alternative can begin to upset it. Constructing those alternatives means finding new ways to talk about problems that matter to people, ways that engage their real interests and their truest values. Constructing them often means adopting new points of view, fashioning new ways of talking about education and learning, about politics and decision making. In this, social semiotics offers far more than a new way of talking science, it offers what is inevitably a new way of making trouble, and hopefully a new way of making sense.

appendix A
The Activity Types of Science Classrooms

Pre-Lesson Activities

Before the Bell, or any noticeable efforts to get the lesson started, there are several common kinds of activities. They do not require a single dominant focus of attention for everyone in the classroom, and they may be going on simultaneously:

Teacher-Student Conferences. The teacher and one or a few students have a private discussion, usually at the front of the room, and usually about some aspect of the student's classwork.

Student-Student Conversation. In pairs or small groups, students talk privately to one another, usually at their desks, and usually not about classwork.

Settling in to Work. In some classes, students will have preassigned tasks, or know to begin tasks indicated on the blackboard, such as copying notes and/or assignments, working on a Do Now (see below), assembling and passing in homework, and so on. In other classes students may simply get out and open their notebooks or textbooks and wait for the teacher to begin. Or they may continue in Conversations until a Teacher Bid to Start.

Getting Started

As described in Chapter 1, the teacher makes one or more verbal and/or nonverbal Bids to Start, which are usually ratified by students. This creates a common focus of attention for classwork, the beginning of the Lesson in its widest definition.

Preliminary Activities

As described in Chapter 3, several activities commonly occur before the introduction of new subject-matter content (new thematics):

Do Now. Students work independently at their seats answering questions or solving problems which are indicated on the board from the start of the period. They write their results for discussion (see below).

Taking Attendance. The teacher may visually scan the class and note absences or Call the Roll; the teacher may ask other students for information about absentees, or they may volunteer it.

Classroom Business. The teacher may make Announcements regarding assignments, school or class projects, upcoming tests or special events, and so on. Students often raise questions about these matters.

Going Over the Do Now. This is usually a Triadic Dialogue activity (see below) in which the teacher asks for results of student seatwork on the Do Now (see above) assignment, students offer answers, and these are evaluated by the teacher.

Going Over the Homework. An activity in which the teacher asks for answers to the homework questions through Triadic Dialogue or the slightly modified activity structure of External Text Dialogue (See Chapter 3).

Collecting Homework. The teacher calls for the Homework, and students usually pass their papers to the front of the room where they are gathered by the teacher or by students helping the teacher.

Review. The teacher may either summarize in Teacher Monologue (see Chapter 3) or ask students questions in Triadic Dialogue about the previous Lesson's thematics (see example in Chapter 1).

Demonstration. The teacher may demonstrate some phenomenon or principle in front of the class. It may relate only tangentially to the main topic of the Lesson (Preliminary Activity), for the purpose of stimulating interest in the main topic, or it may introduce that topic directly (Main Lesson Activity, below). Students may assist in the demonstration.

Motivation. In addition to or in place of the Demonstration, the teacher may use a Teacher Narrative (anecdote, news story, joke) to motivate interest in the topic. This sometimes concludes with the teacher trying to "elicit" from students what they believe the topic or "Aim" of the lesson is to be (done by Triadic Dialogue).

Lecture. A less common but important optional preliminary activity is a teacher "lecture" to the class, admonishing students for their uncooperative behavior or poor achievement in the past and exhorting them to do better today and in future.

Diagnostic Activity

A teacher may make the transition to the thematics of a new topic by asking questions in Triadic Dialogue, or even as a written seatwork assignment, to learn what the students already know or think about the topic.

Main Lesson Activities

The teacher may signal the end of Preliminary Activities by a new Bid to Start for the Main Lesson activities (see Chapters 1 and 3). These deal with the new thematic topic of the Lesson:

Going Over the Do Now, Going Over Homework, Review, Teacher Narrative, and *Demonstration* may all occur as Main Lesson activities.

Teacher Exposition. The teacher may present new material intially in monologue, or may explain it further in response to student questions.

Triadic Dialogue. The most common activity structure of the Lesson. Teachers ask questions, call on students to answer them, and evaluate the answers. (See Chapter 1)

External Text Dialogue. This is a less common variation on Triadic Dialogue, in which the Teacher Question or sometimes the Student Answer is read from a written text. (See Chapter 3).

Student-Questioning Dialogue. An activity structure in which students initiate questions on the subject-matter topic and the teacher answers them. Often includes a series of questions by different students. (See Chapter 3).

Teacher-Student Duolog. A prolonged series of exchanges between the teacher and one student, in Triadic Dialogue or Student Questioning Dialogue.

Teacher-Student Debate. A prolonged series of exchanges in which students challenge or disagree with the teacher on a subject-matter issue, and the teacher defends a position. (See Chapter 2).

True Dialogue. An activity pattern in which teacher and students ask and answer one another's questions and respond to one another's comments as in normal conversation (i.e., with symmetrical status; see Chapter 3).

Cross-Discussion. A dialogue pattern in which students speak directly to one another about the subject matter, and the teacher acts as moderator or equal participant without special speaking rights (see Chapter 3).

Copying Notes. The teacher periodically writes on the board material students are expected to copy into their notebooks. The notes may be read aloud by the teacher or by students.

Media Presentation. Similar in function to Demonstration, but usually of longer duration. Teacher presents film, videotape, computer simulation, slides, and so on for viewing and subsequent or simultaneous discussion.

Seatwork. An activity in which students work independently at their seats on tasks specified by the teacher in a preparatory stage (e.g. the Do Now, above). Followed by Going Over Seatwork.

Boardwork. Students are asked to come to the blackboard and write their responses to tasks, or perform the tasks directly. Followed by Going over Boardwork.

Groupwork. Similar to Seatwork, but with small cooperative groups working on tasks. Less common except in laboratory work.

Labwork. Same as Seatwork or Groupwork if performed in the classroom, except that it involves the use of apparatus or specimens and other activities in addition to reasoning and writing on the part of students. Usually performed outside the classroom in a laboratory.

Teacher Summary. A monologue activity in which the teacher summarizes the thematics of the Lesson so far, or of the whole Lesson near its end.

Testing. Similar to Seatwork, but of longer duration, up to the full length of the period. Collected like Homework (and unlike most Seatwork), evaluated nonverbally and individually. Followed by Going Over the Test dialogue, on the same or next class day.

Interpolated Activities

At any time during the other Lesson activities, certain kinds of special situations may occur:

Interruptions. An intrusion into the classroom activity pattern by an outside participant or event (Loudspeaker Announcement, Class Visitor, Fire Drill) or by a class member (Request to Leave, illness, disruptive behavior). One can count Teacher Admonition Sequences (see Chapter 3) as one such Interruption.

Liminal Periods. Times between major activities in which there is no set common task or focus of attention and the Lesson breaks up temporarily into private conversations and activities.

Disorientation. Periods when all or part of the class is unsure what the activity structure is. Usually leads to Student Questioning (metadiscourse).

Confrontation. Serious exchanges of threats or defiance between teacher and one or more students.

Teacher and Student Strategies of Control

As described more fully in Chapter 3, these are the principal strategies commonly used by teachers and by students to control one another's behavior and the course of classroom activities. These are special strategies, above and beyond the means of control providing by simply following the rules of an activity structure such as Triad Dialogue.

Teacher Strategies: Structural Tactics

Signaling Boundaries. Teachers indicate the end of one activity or episode and the beginning of the next.

Terminating Student Discourse. Teachers close off discussion or debate of issues by students.

Interrupting Students. Teachers break into student's attempts to complete a move in the activity structure (e.g., question, answer).

Controlling Pacing. Teachers hurry students to get on to further topics or activities, or allocate limited time for student actions.

Admonition Sequences. Teachers interrupt the activity structure with comments to students signaling violations of classroom rules.

Retroactive Redefinition. Especially in Triad Dialogue, teachers may try to redefine the status of a student move after it has occurred but before the exchange is completed (see Chapter 1).

Teacher Stratgies: Thematic Tactics

Asserting Irrelevance. Teachers declare a student's answer or comment to be "off the topic" or not germane to "the question".

Marking Importance. Teachers indicate that the current discussion has a special importance.

Marking New/Old Information. Teachers signal that new information is being presented for the first time, or that the question under discussion in something the students should already know.

Regulating Difficulty. Teachers selectively pose easier or more difficult questions or directions as a means of controlling students.

Introducing Principles. Teachers introduce unfamiliar scientific principles as a way of asserting their authority in class discussions.

Creating Mysteries. Teachers create interest in a topic by temporarily withholding full information about it, offering only hints or clues to build suspense.

Being Funny. Teachers use humor in a variety of ways to encourage students to accept their use of other control tactics.

Getting Personal. Teachers make personal remarks about students or their behavior which may be humorous or potentially embarassing.

Student Tactics:

Calling Out. Students call out answers instead of waiting to be Nominated to answer.

Chorus Answer. Several or many students answer at once or in unison.

Questioning Answer. Student turns an Answer into a Question.

Declining to Answer. Student refuses or makes excuse for not answering a Teacher Question.

Asking Clarification. Student asks a question about the Teacher Question instead of directly answering it. Often a delaying tactic.

Student Questioning. Students take the initiative by asking teacher a question which may be only tangentially related to the topic (Digressive Questioning).

Student Challenge. Students openly disagree with the teacher on an issue of subject-matter content.

Metadiscourse. Students ask teacher to clarify the status of moves in the activity structure.

Agenda Enforcement. Students seek to keep teacher to a pre-set agenda for classroom acitivity.

Norm Enforcement. Student seek to enforce discourse norms on the teacher (see Chapter 5).

Disengagement. Side-talk or nonverbal behavior indicating the students are not paying attention to the teacher. May be Bid to end episode or lesson.

Semantic Relations for Thematic Analysis

In thematic analysis, a *semantic relation* describes how the meanings of two words or phrases (thematic items) are related when they are used together in talking about a particular topic. The same, or very similar, semantic relations can be expressed by different *grammatical* relationships between words and phrases. Sometimes grammatical terms are used to name the semantic relations. In the list below, I give some of the most common semantic relations along with their names in several different semantic and grammatical theories. For details, see Halliday (1985) and Lemke (1983a).

Nominal Relations:

ATTRIBUTIVE
Attribute/Carrier: The apple is red. Apple=carrier, red=attribute
Epithet/Thing: The red apple . . . . Apple=thing, red= epithet
A descriptive characteristic; quality, qualifier, modifier
CLASSIFIER
Classifier/Thing: a winesap apple; winesap=classifier, apple=thing
           the 2s orbital; 2s = classifier, orbital =thing
A type or kind of; an identifying characteristic of a subclass
QUANTIFIER
Quantifier/Thing: the three apples; three=quantifier, apples=thing
Numerative/Thing, Quantifier/Count Noun, Number
A quantitative characteristic like a number

Taxonomic relations:

TOKEN
Token/Type: John is a student. Token=John, Type=student
Member/Class, Instance/Category
An individual example of a type or class
HYPONYM (Hyponymy)
Hyponym/Hypernym: Any dog is a mammal. Hyponym=dog,
Hypernym=mammal
Subordinate class/Superordinate class, Subset/Set, Set/Superset
Name of a category that fits inside some more general category.

Co-*hyponyms:* two subcategories that belong to the same more general category

MERONYM (Meronymy)
Meronym/holonym: The drawer of a desk. Meronym=drawer, holonym=desk
Part/Whole
Name of a part belonging to some whole
Co-meronyms: two parts of the same whole

SYNONYM (Synonymy)
Synonym/synonym: Please go. Please leave. Synonyms: Go/ Leave
Equivalence pair; local equivalents; local synonyms
Two expressions that have the same meaning in context

ANTONYM (Antonymy)
Antonym/antonym: Please leave. Please stay. Antonyms: Leave/Stay
Contrast pair; local antonyms; local contrasts
Two expressions that have contrasting meanings in context

Transitivity relations:

AGENT (Agency)
Agent/Process: The man built the house. Agent=man, Process=built
Subject/Transitive Verb, Actor/Process
The entity that does or acts; the cause or instigator of a process

TARGET
Process/Target: The man built the house. Target=house, Process=built
Verb/Object; Process/Patient, Goal, Recipient, Affected
The entity that is done to or acted on; the object of the action

MEDIUM
Medium/Process: The jar broke. Medium=jar, Process=Breaking
The rain poured down. Medium=rain, Process=pouring
Intransitive subject/intransitive verb; Absolute subject
The entity in relation to which a process takes place

BENEFICIARY
Beneficiary/Process: He gave my aunt the jar. Beneficiary=my aunt
Indirect object/transitive verb
The participant to which or for which the action is done.

RANGE
Process/Range: He walked a mile. Range=mile
Extent; Cognate object
The limits, extent, or nature of what the process does

IDENTIFICATION
Identified/Identifier: The white part is the 2s orbital.
Identified=the white part; Identifier=the 2s orbital
POSSESSION
Possessor/Possessed: My aunt has the jar. Possessor=my aunt;
Possessed=the jar.

Circumstantial relations:

LOCATION
Location/Located: The pen is in the box. Located=pen,
                Location=box
                It rained outside. Located=rain, Location=outside
Expresses the spatial relationship of entities or processes.
Extent: how much space is involved (Distance, Volume, etc.)
TIME
Time/Event: I built it yesterday. Event=built, Time=yesterday
Expresses the temporal relationship of processes, events, entities
Duration/Frequency: how much time is involved/ or how often
MATERIAL
Material/Process: I built it of wood. Material=wood, Process=built
The matter or material involved in the process (mass nouns)
MANNER
Manner/Process: I made it with a saw. Manner=with saw,
                Process=made
                I made it slowly. Manner=slowly, Process=made
Quality, Means, Instrument
How, in what way, and by what means/instrument the process
occurred
REASON
Process/Reason: I left to get warm. Process=left, Reason=get warm
Cause, Purpose, Goal, Need
Why or for what reason the process took place

Logical relations:

ELABORATION
Item/Elaboration: "A, i.e. B" "A, e.g. B" "A, viz B" are the
three main subtypes: exposition, exemplification, and clarification
tion

ADDITION
Item/Addition: "A, and B" "not A, nor B" "A, but B" are the three *main subtypes:* conjunctive, negative conjunctive, and adversative

VARIATION
Item/Variation: "not A, but B" "A, but not B" "A or B" are the *three main subtypes:* replacive, exceptive, and alternative

CONNECTION
A miscellaneous category that includes the relations of the parts of various forms of argument, e.g., Cause/Consequence, Evidence/Conclusion, Problem/Solution, Action/Motivation, and so on.
(See discussion of Genres in Chapter 4).

Thematic Development Strategies

Thematic development strategies are the specific techniques used by teachers and students to build up a network of semantic relations among the key terms of a subject (a thematic pattern). The following are the most basic and common of these discourse strategies for using language to communicate the conceptual systems of science (see Chapter 4 and Lemke, 1983b for further details).

Dialogue Strategies

Teacher Question Series
A sequence of thematically closely related Teacher Questions in Triadic Dialogue that construct a series of linked semantic relations.
Selection and Modification
Restatement of selected Student Answer which may also modify it to fit a thematic pattern.
Retroactive recontextualization
Teacher Elaboration or comment on Student Answer places it in a different thematic context, retroactively changing its meaning.
Joint Construction
A thematic pattern is constructed jointly by contributions to dialogue from both teacher and students, with one completing or extending clauses begun by the other.
External Text Dialogue
A written or quoted text is assigned a 'participant' role in dialogue thematic development.

Monologue Strategies

Logical exposition
Monologue in which a series of thematically related logical connections are made between various thematic items and semantic relations.
Narrative
An account of a set of events or actions which establishes chronological and often also implied causal relations among them.
Selective summary
Summarization of prior discourse which includes only selected thematic elements and relations.

Foregrounding and Backgrounding
A repeat or summary of prior discourse in which certain themes are overtly marked as of greater importance and others implicitly as of lesser importance.
Anaphoric and Cataphoric Connection
Condensation (see below) or summary of themes and relations which establishes their potential or actual semantic relationship to prior themes (anaphoric) or to themes yet to be developed (cataphoric).

General Structural Strategies

Syntactic connection
Two thematic items or complex thematic elements are put into a semantic relationship by occupying corresponding functional parts of a grammatical structure (e.g., nominal group, clause, clause-complex).
Rhetorical connection
Two thematic elements are semantically related by being placed in particular roles in a rhetorical structure (e.g. Analogy, Exemplification, Syllogism-Deduction, Generalization-Induction, etc.).
Generic connection
Two thematic patterns are semantically interconnected by the functional relations of the parts of a Genre structure which they occupy.

Equivalence and Contrast

Apposition
Two expressions of the same thematic item or relation immediately follow one another as statement and restatement.
Tone Concord
Two expressions of the same thematic item or relation are spoken with the same intonational contour and vocal stress.
Glossing
An expression is immediately followed by a close synonym, or a formal or informal definition.
Contrastive stress
Expressions of two contrasting thematic items are spoken, one with and the other (often omitted) without a marked intonational contour and emphatic vocal stress.
Parallel environments
Two thematic items are indicated as contrasting by being placed in similar or identical thematic environments, realized by distinct expressions, without tone concord, and often with a sign of contradiction (NO, NOT, BUT, etc.).

Self-correction
Two thematic items or relations are shown to be in contrast by one replacing the other when the speaker corrects himself.

Global Thematic Strategies

Repetition with Variation
One or more repeats of the same partial thematic pattern, each with some items and relations similarly expressed and other differently expressed. Enables abstraction of pattern and flexible expression.
Condensation
Assigning a pattern of thematic items and their semantic relationships to a single new thematic item, that is, naming or designating the pattern. Condensations are then more easily connected to other themes.
Thematic nexus
The bringing together of themes expressed in different parts of the lesson or text into a single structural unit; a synthesis.
Theme-weaving (Cohesive harmony)
Establishing patterns of thematic interconnection by introducing thematic items and relations and bringing them together in different combinations across the lesson or text; usually leads to one culminative or through more than one intermediate thematic nexus.
Intertextual allusion
Establishing thematic relationships by implicitly or explicitly invoking a thematic pattern which is not explicitly expressed in the lesson or text, but which is known to the participants or can be located in some other text or occasion of discourse.

Other Strategies

Metadiscourse
Directly identifying or commenting on the structure or thematics of the discourse as a part of that discourse.
Marking Old Information
Various strategies for indicating that a thematic item or relation belongs to a thematic pattern that has been encountered before.
Marking Important Information
Various strategies for assigning relative importance or value to a thematic relation or pattern.
Framebreaking
Various strategies for denying the validity of a prior thematic pattern and recontextualizing an item or relation in a new pattern.

Methods Used in the Science Classroom Research Studies

DATA COLLECTION

In the study *Classroom Communication of Science*, sponsored during its initial stages (1979–1982) by the National Science Foundation (Research in Science Education, Project 79–18961), recordings and field-notes were made in 60 science classes, taught by 20 different teachers. Of these about two-thirds were observed in one junior and two senior high schools, and the others at a nearby public university. Only the secondary school data has been used in writing this book.

Most of the lessons followed the curriculum of grades 9–12 in biology, chemistry, physics, and earth science. All the teachers had volunteered to participate in the project and all were regarded by me and by their supervisor in the school as good science teachers. The classes were all of average to above-average ability students by the standards of the schools. None of the classes contained significant numbers of students with special problems. The classes were, in most respects, typical of such classes around the country, as I have observed them. They are not necessarily representative of classes where there are serious behavior problems, students with physical or emotional handicaps or learning disabilities, or students who are still learning English.

For each class, a preliminary visit for a full period lesson was followed by visits on two or more consecutive days. All lessons observed were tape-recorded (two recorders, one at the front and one at the back of the room). I myself made detailed fieldnotes on the events of the lesson as it occured, noting exact times for later collation of notes with tape transcripts. In about half the classes, I was accompanied by Shirley Brice Heath, an experienced sociolinguist and educator, who served as consultant to the project and made additional fieldnotes. We both paid special attention to the nonverbal signs of students' engagement (or lack of it) with the lesson.

For each class I also interviewed the teacher, usually before the lesson, on the nature of the class and the curriculum. In some cases students were also interviewed, and some teachers were interviewed after the last visit on their impressions of how representative the lessons had been of what usually went on in that class, and on their attitudes to student performance, the curriculum, and so on.

In a few classes, a special follow-up visit was made with a video camera to record students' reactions during a lesson. These tapes were mainly used to cross-check the reliability of the observers' fieldnote estimates of nonverbal indices of student engagement (see Chapter 5).

Fieldnote records contain such information as how many students were present, the ratio of males to females, the names of students speaking, items written on the board, visible objects and demonstrations referred to in the lesson, counts of numbers of students looking at the teacher or board vs. those talking to neighbors or looking out the window, the exact times at which events took place, the teachers' movements around the room, important gestures by teacher or students, significant nonverbal events, observer comments on class reactions to various events, and so on.

All fieldnotes were transcribed from rough to typed form by the observers, usually within a day of the observation visit. I myself made the transcriptions of dialogue from the tapes, using both tapes of each lesson, and listening to unclear passages up to a dozen times to get the most accurate transcription. Original transcripts indicate lengths of all pauses and include indications of unusual intonation patterns and other audible nonverbal phenomena (e.g., laughter, writing at the board, slamming of doors, general noise level, etc.).

Transcribing one's own tapes is a very laborious, but also very valuable procedure. You get to know their details intimately and when you read a transcript, you come to actually rehear voice qualities and intonation. The transcripts in this book have been edited to make them more easily readable. Nothing has been changed, but some of the nonverbal notations are omitted and shorter pauses have been indicated by standard punctuation when intonation patterns justified this. People do not really talk in sentences or use commas, but it is very hard to read a transcription that does not compromise a little with these conventions of writing.

DATA ANALYSIS

Transcription is already a preliminary kind of data analysis. Decisions have to be made constantly about what is important or how to interpret ambiguities. At the same time the transcriptions were made, outlines of the lessons were prepared, dividing them into episodes and parts of episodes based on changes in topic and/or changes in activity structure. This *segmentation analysis* was in some cases carried on to the level of detail at which one identifies the function of each utterance or line in the transcript as part of some larger whole.

The segmenting of the lessons into episodes was accompanied by a collation with the fieldnotes to include all information on nonverbal communication and communicative engagement. Notations were also made on the outlines of all the points where the stylistic norms of the language of science seemed to be strongly violated and of all points where student attentiveness to the lesson was markedly increasing or decreasing. It was this data that was relied on for the semiquantitiative analyses in Chapter 5.

The major work of the project became that of *discourse analysis.* Existing linguistic methods were refined and extended in order to perform two kinds of analysis on every transcript. First, episodes were analyzed to identify their activity structures and the specific moves and strategies employed by teacher and students in using the forms of Triadic Dialogue (Chapter 1), Teacher-Student Debate (Chapter 2), and so on. In the course of this, the various activity patterns listed in Appendix A were identified, along with some of the tactics of social control listed in Appendix B (both discussed in Chapter 3).

Secondly, episodes were analyzed semantically to uncover the thematic patterns of the science content and the typical thematic development strategies used by teachers (Chapter 4 and Appendices C and D). A fuller understanding of how thematic development works in the science class, especially over the length of a whole episode or lesson, took a few years of refining these methods (see Chapter 8).

Finally, selected episodes were analyzed to identify the stylistic norms of the language of classroom science and the ways in which teachers violated those norms in the course of teaching (Chapter 5). These results were combined with the fieldnote records and other audible indications of student engagement with the lesson to analyze when students listen more and when they listen less and what the relation is between attentiveness and the style of teacher language.

In the course of the analysis it also became clear that more than just science was being communicated in these classes, that a set of attitudes toward and beliefs about science, education, students' abilities, and society itself were being taught as well. In some cases teachers were aware of this, in others they were not. Sometimes they disagreed strongly with the beliefs that seemed to be implicit in the language of science teaching they were using. This led to the analysis of the mystique of science and its ideology. It was only a few years later that I make the further connection of this to the technocratic pattern in decision making.

This is an extremely brief overview of a complex research project. Further details on the data collection, transcription, and preliminary analysis stages are available in my report to the National Science

Foundation, *Classroom Communication of Science*, available from the Education Research Information Clearinghouse (ERIC) or the National Technical Information Service (NTIS), as listed in the Bibliography section of this book (Lemke, 1983b). Later developments and accounts will be found in the other references under my name in the References.

References

Althusser, L. (1971). Ideology and ideological state apparatuses. In *Lenin and philosophy and other essays* (pp. 127–186). New York: Monthly Review Press.

Bakhtin, M.M. (1981). Discourse in the novel. In M. Holquist (Ed.), *The dialogic imagination* (original work published in 1935). Austin TX: University of Texas Press.

Bakhtin, M.M. (1986). *Speech genres and other late essays* (original work published in 1953). Austin: University of Texas Press.

Bakhtin, M.M. [= Voloshinov, V.N.]. (1986). *Marxism and the philosophy of language* (original work published in 1929). Cambridge, MA: Harvard University Press.

Barthes, R. (1983). *The fashion system*. New York: Hill and Wang.

Bateson, G. (1972). *Steps to an ecology of mind*. New York: Ballantine Books.

Bloome, D. (1987). *Literacy and schooling*. Norwood, NJ: Ablex Publishing.

Bloome, D. (1989). *Classrooms and literacy*. Norwood, NJ: Ablex Publishing.

Boas, F. (1922). *Handbook of American Indian languages* (Bulletin No. 40, Bureau of American Ethnology). Washington, DC: Smithsonian Institution.

Bourdieu, P. (1972). *Outline of a theory of practice*. Cambridge: Cambridge University Press.

Bourdieu, P. (1979). *Distinction: A social critique of the judgement of taste*. Cambridge, MA: Harvard University Press (1984 edition).

Brown, G., & Yule, G. (1983). *Discourse analysis*. Cambridge: Cambridge University Press.

Cazden, C. (1986). Classroom discourse. In M. Wittrock (Ed.), *Handbook of research on teaching* (3rd ed., pp. 432–463). New York: Macmillan.

Cazden, C.B., John, V.P., & Hymes, D. (Eds.). (1972). *Functions of language in the classroom*. New York: Teachers College Press.

Chomsky, N. (1959). Review of *Verbal Behavior* by B.F. Skinner. *Language, 35*, 26–58.

Cook-Gumperz, J. (1986). *The social construction of literacy*. New York: Cambridge University Press.

Coulthard, M. (1977). *Introduction to discourse analysis*. London: Longman.

Crandall, J. (Ed.). (1987). *ESL through content-area instruction: Mathematics, science, social studies*. Washington, DC: Center for Applied Linguistics.

Douglas, M. (1984). *Food in the social order*. New York: Russell Sage Foundation.

Eco, U. (1976). *A theory of semiotics*. Bloomington: Indiana University Press.

Edwards, A.D. (1976). *Language in culture and class: The sociology of language and education*. London: Heinemann.

Edwards, A.D., & Furlong, V. (1978). *The language of teaching*. London: Heinemann.

Edwards, A.D., & Westgate, D.P.G. (1986). *Investigating classroom talk.* London and Philadelphia: Falmer Press.

Edwards, D., & Mercer, N. (1987). *Common knowledge: The development of understanding in the classroom.* London and New York: Methuen.

Eggins, S., & Slade, D. (1987). The structure of casual conversation. Paper presented at 14th International Systemics Congress, Sydney, Australia.

Emihovich, C. (Ed.). (1989). *Locating learning: Ethnographic perspectives on classroom research.* Norwood, NJ: Ablex Publishing.

Firth, J.R. (1957). *Papers in linguistics 1934–1951.* London: Oxford University Press.

Foucault, M. (1969). *The archeology of knowledge.* New York: Random House (1972 edition).

Foucault, M. (1976). *The history of sexuality.* New York: Random House (1978 edition).

Garfinkel, H. (1967). *Studies in ethnomethodology.* Englewood Cliffs, NJ: Prentice-Hall.

Garfinkel, H., & Sacks, H. (1971). On formal structures of practical actions. In J.C. McKinnery & E.A. Terakian (Eds.), *Theoretical sociology* (pp. 337–366). New York: Appleton-Century-Crofts.

Garvin, P.L. (1964). *A Prague school reader on esthetics, literary structure, and style.* Washington DC: Georgetown University Press.

Geertz, C. (1983). *Local knowledge.* New York: Basic Books.

Gilmore, P., & Glatthorn, A. (1982). *Children in and out of school: Ethnography and education.* Washington, DC: Center for Applied Linguistics.

Goffman, E. (1959). *The presentation of self in everyday life.* New York: Anchor Books.

Goffman, E. (1974). *Frame analysis.* New York: Harper and Row.

Goffman, E. (1981). *Forms of talk.* Philadelphia: University of Pennsylvania Press.

Gramsci, A. (1971). *Prison notebooks: 1929–1935* (original work published in 1935). New York: International Publishers.

Green, J.L., & Harker, J.O. (Eds.). (1988). *Multiple perspective analyses of classroom discourse.* Norwood, NJ: Ablex Publishing.

Green, J.L., & Wallat, C. (Eds.). (1981). *Ethnography and language in educational settings.* Norwood, NJ: Ablex Publishing.

Gumperz, J.J. (1984). *Discourse strategies.* London: Cambridge University Press.

Habermas, J. (1972). *Knowledge and human interests.* London: Heinemann.

Halliday, M.A.K. (1961). Categories of the theory of grammar. *Word, 17* (3), 241–292.

Halliday, M.A.K. (1975). *Learning how to mean.* New York: Elsevier.

Halliday, M.A.K. (1978). *Language as social semiotic.* London: Edward Arnold.

Halliday, M.A.K. (1985a). *An introduction to functional grammar.* London: Edward Arnold.

Halliday, M.A.K. (1985b). *Spoken and written language.* Geelong, VIC (Australia): Deakin University Press. [Republished 1989, Oxford University Press.]

Halliday, M.A.K., & Hasan, R. (1976). *Cohesion in English*. London: Longman.
Halliday, M.A.K., & Hasan, R. (1985). *Language, context, and text*. Geelong, VIC (Australia): Deakin University Press. [Republished 1989, Oxford University Press.]
Hasan, R. (1984a). Coherence and cohesive harmony. In J. Flood (Ed.), *Understanding reading comprehension* (pp. 139–154). Newark, DE: International Reading Association.
Hasan, R. (1984b). The structure of the nursery tale. In L. Coveri (Ed.), *Linguistica testuale*. Rome: Bulzoni.
Heap, J.L. (1985). Discourse in the production of classroom knowledge: Reading lessons. *Curriculum Inquiry, 15*, 245–279.
Heap, J.L. (1986). *Collaboration in word processing*. Toronto: Ontario Institute for Studies in Education.
Heath, S.B. (1983). *Ways with words*. London: Cambridge University Press.
Hjelmslev, L. (1961). *Prolegomena to a theory of language* (original work published in 1943). Madison, WI: University of Wisconsin Press.
Husserl, E. (1960). *Cartesian meditations: An introduction to phenomenology*. The Hague: Martinus Nijhoff.
Husserl, E. (1965). *Phenomenology and the crisis of philosophy*. New York: Harper and Row.
Jakobson, R. (1971). *Selected writings* (2 vols.). The Hague: Mouton.
Kress, G. (1982). *Learning to write*. London: Routledge and Kegan Paul.
Lemke, J.L. (1983a). Thematic analysis: systems, structures, and strategies. *Recherches Semiotiques/Semiotic Inquiry* (Toronto), *3*, 159–187.
Lemke, J.L. (1983b). Classroom communication of science. Final Report to the U.S. National Science Foundation. (ERIC Document Reproduction Service No. ED 222 346).
Lemke, J.L. (1984). *Semiotics and education*. Toronto: Victoria College/Toronto Semiotic Circle Monographs.
Lemke, J.L. (1985a). Ideology, intertextuality, and the notion of register. In J.D. Benson & W.S. Greaves (Eds.), *Systemic perspectives on discourse* (Vol.1, pp. 275–294). Norwood, NJ: Ablex Publishing.
Lemke, J.L. (1985b). *Using language in the classroom*. Geelong, VIC (Australia): Deakin University Press. [Republished 1989, Oxford University Press.]
Lemke, J.L. (1987a). Strategic deployment of speech and action: a sociosemiotic analysis. In J. Evans & J. Deely (Eds.), *Semiotics 1983: Proceedings of the Semiotic Society of America* (pp. 67–79). New York: University Press of America.
Lemke, J.L. (1987b). Social semiotics and science education. *American Journal of Semiotics, 5*(2), 217–232.
Lemke, J.L. (1988a). Genres, semantics, and classroom education. *Linguistics and Education, 1*(1), 81–99.
Lemke, J.L. (1988b). Discourses in conflict: Heteroglossia and text semantics. In J.D. Benson & W.S. Greaves (Eds.), *Systemic functional approaches to discourse* (pp. 29–50). Norwood, NJ: Ablex Publishing.
Lemke, J.L. (1988c). Towards a social semiotics of the material subject. In T.

Threadgold (Ed.), *SASSC Working Papers, Volume 2* (pp. 1–17). Sydney: Sydney Association for Studies in Society and Culture.

Lemke, J.L. (1988d). Text structure and text semantics. In R. Veltman & E. Steiner (Eds.), *Discourse and text: Explorations in systemic semantics* (pp. 158–170). London: Pinter.

Lemke, J.L. (1989a). Social semiotics: A new model for literacy education. In D. Bloome (Ed.), *Classrooms and Literacy* (pp. 289–309). Norwood, NJ: Ablex Publishing.

Lemke, J.L. (1989b). Making text talk. *Theory into Practice, 28*(2), 136–141.

Lemke, J.L. (1989c). Semantics and social values. *WORD, 40* (1–2), 37–50.

Lemke, J.L. (In press-a). Technical discourse and technocratic ideology. In M.A.K. Halliday, J. Gibbons, & H. Nicholas (Eds.), *Proceedings of the 8th World Congress of Applied Linguistics, Sydney.* Amsterdam: John Benjamins.

Lemke, J.L. (In press-b). Intertextuality and text semantics. In M. Gregory & P. Fries (Eds.), *Discourse in society: Functional perspectives.* Norwood, NJ: Ablex Publishing.

Lemke, J.L. (In press-c). Heteroglossia and social theory. In New York Bakhtin Circle (Eds.), *M.M. Bakhtin: Radical perspectives.* Minneapolis: University of Minnesota Press.

Lemke, J.L. (In preparation). The development and evolution of social semiotic systems.

Malinowski, B. (1923). The problem of meaning in primitive languages. Supplement I to C.K. Ogden & I.A. Richards (Eds.), *The meaning of meaning* (pp. 296–336). New York: Harcourt Brace.

Malinowski, B. (1935). An ethnographic theory of language. Part 4 of *Coral gardens and their magic* (Vol.2, pp. 4–78). London: Allen and Unwin.

Mann, W., & Thompson, S. (1983). *Relational propositions in discourse.* Marina del Rey, CA: Information Sciences Institute.

Mann, W., & Thompson, S. (1987). *Rhetorical structure theory: A theory of text organization.* Marina del Rey, CA: Information Sciences Institute.

Martin, J.R. (1985a). Process and text. In J.D. Benson & W.S. Greaves (Eds.), *Systemic perspectives on discourse* (Vol. 1, pp. 248–274). Norwood, NJ: Ablex Publishing.

Martin, J.R. (1985b). *Factual writing: exploring and challenging social reality.* Geelong, VIC (Australia): Deakin University Press. [Republished 1989, Oxford University Press.]

Mehan, H. (1979). *Learning lessons: Social organization in the classroom.* Cambridge, MA: Harvard University Press.

Merleau-Ponty, M. (1962). *The phenomenology of perception* (original work published in 1945). London: Routledge and Kegan Paul.

O'Toole, L.M. (In press). A functional semiotics of painting and architecture. In T. Threadgold (Ed.), *Constructing a critical social semiotic theory.* Toronto, Victoria University: Toronto Semiotic Circle Monographs.

Peirce, C.S. (1958). *Collected papers* (original work published in 1908), 8 vols.

C. Hartshorne and P. Weiss (vols. 1–6), A. Burks (vols. 7–8), Eds. Cambridge MA: Harvard University Press.

Preziosi, D. (1983). *Minoan architectural design: Formation and signification.* New York: Mouton.

Propp, V. (1968). *The morphology of the folktale* (original work published in 1928). Austin, TX: University of Texas Press.

Rorty, R. (1979). *Philosophy and the mirror of nature.* Princeton, NJ: Princeton University Press.

Salthe, S. (1985). *Evolving hierarchical systems.* New York: Columbia University Press.

Salthe, S. (In press). Self-organization in hierarchically structured systems. *Systems Research.*

Sapir, E. (1921). *Language.* New York: Harcourt Brace.

de Saussure, F. (1959). *Course in general linguistics* (original work published in 1915). New York: Philosophical Library/ McGraw-Hill.

Schutz, Alfred. (1967). *The phenomenology of the social world* (original work published in 1932). Evanston, IL: Northwestern University Press.

Sinclair, J., & Coulthard, M. (1975). *Towards an analysis of discourse.* London: Oxford University Press.

Stubbs, M. (1980). *Language and literacy: The socio-linguistics of reading and writing.* London: Routledge and Kegan Paul.

Stubbs, M. (1983). *Discourse analysis: The sociolinguistics of natural language.* Chicago: University of Chicago Press.

Thaiss, C.J. (1983). *Learning better, learning more: In the home and across the curriculum.* Washington, DC: Dingle Associates.

Thibault, P. (In press). The cognitive hypothesis: A critical comment. In *Text, discourse, and context: A social semiotic perspective* (pp. 26–43). Toronto, Victoria University: Toronto Semiotic Circle Monographs.

Threadgold, T. (In press). *Constructing a critical social semiotic theory.* Toronto, Victoria University: Toronto Semiotic Circle Monographs.

Trueba, H.T., Guthrie, G. P., & Au, K. (1981). *Culture and the bilingual classroom: Studies in classroom ethnography.* Rowley, MA: Newbury House.

van Leeuwen, T. (In press). Music and ideology: Towards a sociosemiotics of mass media music. In T. Threadgold (Ed.), *Constructing a critical social semiotic theory.* Toronto, Victoria University: Toronto Semiotic Circle Monographs.

Ventola, E. (1987). *The structure of social interaction: A systemic approach to the semiotics of service encounters.* London: Frances Pinter.

Walter, B. (1988). *The jury summation as a speech genre.* Philadelphia, PA: John Benjamins NA.

Whorf, B.L. (1956). *Language, thought, and reality.* Cambridge, MA: MIT Press.

Wilkinson, L.C. (1982). *Communicating in the classroom.* New York: Academic Press.

Wittgenstein, L. (1967). *Philosophical investigations* (original work published in 1949). Oxford: Blackwell.

Transcripts of Lesson Episodes

"CHEMICAL PERIODICITY": DRS-27-NOV
(Includes "Atomic Orbitals" Episode)
"TERRESTRIAL RADIATION": LG-26-NOV
(Includes "Light-Heat Debate" Episode
and "Solar Heating of the Earth")
"LONGITUDINAL WAVES": EL-20-NOV
"GIANT CELL": JR-29-OCT
"CRUSTAL MOVEMENT": SC-20-MAR

INTRODUCTION TO THE TRANSCRIPTS

Appendix E describes the general background of the project in which these lessons were recorded. Each lesson lasted a full 40 minute period and was recorded in its entirety. These transcripts are minimally edited versions of the research transcripts and present episodes or portions of episodes within each lesson that are referred to in a significant way in the previous chapters.

Each transcript begins with a context note describing the content of the lesson which preceeds the point at which the transcript begins. Some transcripts are divided into episodes when these are separated in time by more than a few minutes. Minor boundaries of topic or activity shift within an episode are not shown here, except that a new segment may begin on its own line. There are context notes within and at the end of transcripts to indicate what happens in the remainder of the lesson.

Some conventions of the transcripts should be noted. Commas are used to represent brief pauses in the flow of speech, and appear only when there are such pauses. Triple dots (. . .) do not mark omissions, but pauses of about 1 second. Longer pauses are indicated by duration (e.g., [2 sec]). A short dash at the end of a word indicates that the rhythm of speech was broken off or interrupted. Double dash (=) indicates a linking of two words spoken as one. Material enclosed in square brackets was added during transcription; material in parenthesis is unclear dialogue. Underscore or italics indicates verbal emphasis on the part of the speaker, usually marked by intonation.

Simple punctuation has been added to improve the readability of transcripts and the detailed timing of interruptions and overlapping speech has been omitted. Hesitations, false starts, repeats, mispronunciations, and dialect variants are all represented in the transcripts. Spoken language is very different from written text and takes some getting used to. There is much to be learned from studying its special characteristics.

FROM "CHEMICAL PERIODICITY" LESSON: DRS-27-NOV

EPISODE 1: Atomic Orbitals Review
This is an 11th grade Chemistry class. We are at the beginning of the lesson period. The class is just settling down. There is a complex colored chalk diagram of atomic orbitals left on the board from the previous period's class by the same teacher. He begins speaking to the class:

Teacher: Before we get started . . . Before I erase the board . . .
Students: Sh!
Teacher: Uh . . . Look how fancy I got . . . [looks at board]
Students: Sh!
Teacher: This is a representation of the one S . . . orbital. S'pozed to be, of course, three dimensional. . . . What two elements could be represented by such a diagram? . . . Jennifer?
Jennifer: Hydrogen and helium?
Teacher: Hydrogen and helium. Hydrogen would have one electron . . . somewhere in there, and helium would have . . .?
Student: Two electrons.
Teacher: Two. . . . This is . . . one S, and . . . the white would be . . .? Mark?
Mark: Two S.
Teacher: Two S. And the green would be . . .?
Janice: Two P.
Teacher: uhh . . .
Janice: Two P [louder].
Teacher: Janice.
Janice: Two P—[less loud, interrupted]
Teacher: Two P [Overlapping Janice]. Yeah, the green would be 2P x and 2P y. If I have one electron in the 2Px, one elctron in the 2Py, . . . two electrons in the 2S, two electrons in the 1S, what element is being represented by this configuration? [High pitched sound] Oo! That sound annoys, doesn't it? [Laughter] Ron?
Ron: Boron?
Teacher: That would be—That'd have uh . . . *seven* electrons. So you'd have to have one here, one here, one here, one here, one here . . . one here—

Student: Carbon.

Teacher: Who said it? you? What's—

Students: Carbon! Carbon!

Teacher: Carbon. Carbon. Here [points to Period Table]. Six electrons. And they can be anywhere within those—confining—orbitals. This is also from the notes from before. The term orbital refers to the average *region* transversed [sic] by an electron. Electrons occupy orbitals that may differ in size, shape, or space orientation. That's- that's from the other class, we might as well use it for review. [6 second pause]

INTERLUDE.

Tutoring. With Miss Kitchener, Thursday, period 3.

Student: Tutoring with who?

Teacher: Miss Kitchener. Nice? She help you?

Student: Yes.

Teacher: Good. [2 sec] Tutoring with Mr. Forbes, Wednesday and Thursday, period 2. [5 sec]

EPISODE 2: Going Over the Homework

Teacher: Please take out your, homework, Homework, 10.

Student: Sure it's number 10?

Another: It's supposed to be, number (12, not) 10. We had two homeworks in between.

Teacher: But I didn't collect them. I didn't collect those two homeworks. So. . . [7 sec] OK, it was page 69. [7 sec] Question number 7 . . . A. [Reads staccato:] "What-is-an-electron-cloud?" Sheldon?

Sheldon: [Reads from Homework paper:] The portion of space about a nuculus [sic] in which the electrons may most probably be found.

Teacher: Fine. These are kind of, representational diagrams, of electron cloud, theory. Of course, that's like most of the time, Sheldon said. . . If you uh, 99% of the time. Theoretically it can be *anywhere*, except in the nucleus. Electron can exist anywhere in space, except the nucleus. [3 sec]

OK, number, letter B. "What properties does the electron cloud give an atom?" *Janice.*

Janice: Gives it—size and shape.

Student: Shape and size [interrupting].

Teacher: Your name Janice? Is your name Janice?

Student: No. [Student is male. Other males joke, "It is!"]

Janice: Size and shape.

Teacher: Size and shape. Thank you. Also space orientation, a little bit? Whether it's, uh, going this way, or that. . . [Gestures] [2 sec] OK. Question number 8.

[Dialogue continues in this fashion through the homework questions for the next six minutes. We resume with the last two questions:]

Teacher: Uh. . . 11. "May two electrons in the same atom have exactly the same set of four quantum *numbers*?" *Joanne.*

Joanne:	No.
Teacher:	Thank you.
Student:	"Why?" Why do they ask "why?"?
Teacher:	Why do they ask "why?"? Why? Sam?
Sam:	I think it has something to do with the electron spin? That they always run, ah, *spin* in opposite directions.
Teacher:	It happens to be called the, *Hund* [guttural], rule, that, if, two electrons, had exactly the same four quantum numbers, in an atom, it would mean, that they were, in the same place, at the same time. And in reality, two things cannot, be in the same place, at the same time. So they have to be, slightly different. [2 sec] OK. Uh. . . "May two electrons occupy the same space orbital?" [5 sec] Huh? [4 sec] If one's here, what must the other one in the orbital have to be doing? [3 sec, Students gesture answer] Spinning in opposite directions. . . *Fine.* And. . . *12,* "Distinguish between an atom in its ground state, and an, excited, atom." . . . *Mario.*
Mario:	"When an atom is in its ground state, its electrons hold the lowest possible energy. When an atom is in- when an atom is excited, it absorbs energy. Therefore an excited atom hold more energy than an atom at its ground state."
Teacher:	OK. What you're saying. . . Anybody else say it differently? [To Mario:] You know what you're saying?
Mario:	Yeah.
Teacher:	Cheryl?
Cheryl:	Um. . . the ground state is at a lower energy—
Teacher:	No *added* energy.
Cheryl:	And the excited is—
Teacher:	You *add* something, like thermal energy, like heat. Electrons jump to another shell, another kind of higher energy orbit. . . and, uh, they're *excited.* Eventually they fall back, and when they fall back, what happens? *Destina.*
Destina:	They fall back?
Teacher:	Yeah. When they fall back from a higher energy level to the ground state, what happens?
Destina:	They, uh, lose energy.
Teacher:	They lose energy, but exactly how much energy? Sam?
Sam:	A photon.
Teacher:	A photon. Which gives a special characteristic wavelength (to them). Pass these forward [i.e., homework]. First person hold them. The teacher will, collect them from the first person.

[The teacher answers a question about when the next test is scheduled and then begins to do a sample problem from the newly assigned homework. There are a series of student questions on orbitals, and the lesson concludes with a brief discussion of chemical periodicity for the halogens and the coinage metals.]

FROM THE "TERRESTRIAL RADIATION" LESSON: LG-26-NOV

This is a 10th grade Earth Science class. We are about 14 minutes into the 40–minute period. The teacher has made a few announcements and done a demonstration of breaking sunlight into the colors of the spectrum with a prism. He then asked a few questions to relate this back to the new unit begun the week before. It leads into a study of weather through an analysis of the Earth's response to solar radiation. He summarized the answers to these questions but did not build on them. Instead he has written the Lesson Aim on the board and begins with it as a new topic:

Teacher: Let's get to the main question for today, and we'll take what you just said, and let's talk about, *The Earth*. We talked about the *sun, reaching* the earth, with it's *energy*. [2 sec] Let's talk about what happens afterwards today. [34 sec, Writing at board] And this says, "What are some factors which affect *terrestrial*, radiation." [6 sec] And there are two words in this Aim. . . that I think we better make sure we understand *first*, so we can go *on* from there, and answer the question I *hope*, by the end of the period. [4 sec] What is a *factor*? [1.5 sec] What do you think the word *factors* means here? It can mean a *lot* of things, but in this, *sense*? [2 sec] Yes.

Gary: It's—it's cert—it's *things* affected.

Teacher: What, Gary? a little *louder*.

Gary: It's like, certain things.

Teacher: O=K [rising tone]. Anybody else? Tommy?

Tommy: Does it have to do with like, the subject you're talking about?

Teacher: O=K. David?

David: The main elements?

Teacher: OK. In other words there are a lotta ways to describe it, but as long as we understand the key idea: the *things* that have an *effect*. [2.5 sec] *Effect, change* in something. In other words what we're really asking is what changes, *terrestrial* radiation. Except we didn't figure out what this word, terestrial means. Except all of you who watch, Star Trek and. . . Planet of the Lost Chicken, and all of those terrific programs, must know what that means already. Monica?

Monica: Um, it refers to the sun and—

Teacher: *Frank*, did you hear Monica?

Frank: No.

Teacher: Why not?

Frank: She hasn't—

Teacher: Aaaah. Always bored with a good lesson. Be quiet. [Laughter] Monica, tell us again.

Monica: I asked you if it had to do with the *sky* or the heavens.

Teacher: Mmm, no. You're setting your sights too high, Monica. [4 sec] David?

David: Something that has to do with the Earth.

Teacher: *The Earth.* OK. Now let's take off our pretty picture here [Erasing the board], and we'll get started. [5 sec] And we're gonna use some simple questions to get at some complicated ideas. First of all. [2.5 sec] And this is, literally, something I expect you to *remember* from last week, so it should be a snap. [Writes at board, 24 sec] And what form of radiant energy do we get from the sun? Scott?

Scott: Sunlight. *Sunlight.*

Teacher: OK, I'm gonna kinda capsulize that, and write down, *light*, energy. [8 sec] *Light* energy essentially. David?

David: Solar energy?

Teacher: OK. That's another way of saying light energy from the sun. Yes.

Student: *Heat.*

Teacher: Well [hesitating], I'm *not* . . . Yeah, you're right. But a very *small* amount, compared to the light, OK? For example, you know it's *daylight* today, because the sky is lighter than it is at night, not much, because it's pouring out. But you don't feel any heat from the sun today. [4 sec] *Light* energy, *essentially*. [2 sec]

           And now we come to another question. And something people, I think very few people realize, but now *you* will, and maybe you'll tell all your friends. [2 sec, Students commenting] [Aside, to one student:] Shows how scientifically oriented *you* are. [2 sec, then to class:] Let's take this sunlight. . . And let's look at a little picture. [5 sec, drawing at board]

Student: Um, do we gotta *draw* this? [8 sec, Teacher still drawing]

Teacher: That's the earth's surface. This is the inside of the earth. Here's the sky. And here's. . . *light energy* coming down from the sun. [8 sec, drawing] Now from what Mr. Scott [their Student Teacher] said last week, what happens, *when*, this, energy, hits the earth? Charley?

Charley: The earth absorbs it?

Teacher: OK. Erin?

Erin: It also reflects it.

Teacher: There's some reflection. [6 sec, drawing] Let me ask you something, from what Charley, and Erin told us. . . what determines, the amount of absorption, or the *amount*, of reflection? And I'd like to make *that*, the next question. [4 sec, Writing] Oh! I started with "A". I'd better go to "B" instead of "2" [Referring to his outline notes on board]. [Writes at board, 17 sec] *Well*. A new *hand*. Chris.

Chris: Uh, the seasons.

Teacher: Partially right.

Scott: Varies with the different color of the object.

Teacher: Yes it does.

Student: What do you mean, "yes it does"?

Scott: Uh. . . the light colors reflect light and the darker colors absorb 'em.
            And. . . if it's a cloudy day, there's not gonna. . . the—, earth's sur-
            face isn't gonna be absorbing that much because, it's—the clouds
            are reflecting some of the light.
Teacher: Thank you, Scott. You hit on a key idea.
Student: Earth's surface.
Teacher: Thank you. [Writing at board, 12 sec] OK. "The surface composi-
            tion." Is it *water* we're talking about? is it *land*? Is it, *open* land? Is it
            land covered with a *forest*? with a *city*? [4 sec] And now we come to
            another question. [Writes it on board, 11 sec]
            Let's say the earth has absorbed this radiation. To a certain extent,
            some places more, some places less. [Writes, 26 sec] What happens
            to the surface area that *absorbs*, the light energy? [8 sec] Rosie.
Rosie: The *ground* gets hot.
Teacher: Yes. Not sometimes—not hot enough, to *feel* the heat. Sometimes—
Erin: *What* gets hot?
Teacher: Rosie, would you repeat that?
Rosie: The *ground* gets hot.
Teacher: Thank you. Did you hear that, Erin? Good. If you weren't, whisper-
            ing to *Scott*, [Loudly:] you mighta heard her in the first place! Thank
            you. [2 sec] The ground gets hot sometimes, in fact at trhe beach in
            summertime, if you walk around barefoot, pretty tough sometimes.
Rosie: Yeah, my *feet* get burned!
Teacher: You have to do the dance of the crazed student sometimes, while
            you're running to the blanket from the water. Sometimes, it's *not* too
            hot, it stays pretty cool. Sometimes on a day like today, it isn't hot.
            But *essentially*, we're talking about, what kind of energy now?
Students: Light! Light!
Others: Heat! Heat! Solar energy!
Teacher: Yeah, *originally*. And Rosie?
Rosie: *Heat* energy.
Teacher: Yeah. [12 sec, Writing at board] The *ground* is now creating *heat*
            energy, *from* the light energy. Erin, you have a question?
Erin: Yeah, how can it be the ground creates the heat energy, if the *sun*
            creates the heat energy?
Teacher: *Well*, on the *sun*, and *in* the sun, the sun *is* creating a tremendous
            amount of heat energy. But it's sending most of its energy here as
            light, traveling through space.
Erin: But light is *hot*, light is heat.
Teacher: No! Some light is not hot at all. When I turned on these flourescent
            lights today, I haven't roasted yet.
Student: The bulb has heat.
Erin: Yeah, but when the bulb is on you get—the bulb gets hot.
Teacher: And essentially—
            most energy from the sun comes here in the form of light, and *not*
            heat.

Erin:	So the ground can't be *creating* heat. Because if the ground wasn't dark, then it wouldn't absorb the light, and the light, is heat, so it's not *creating* it.
Teacher:	No. Light is *not* heat. The light is light energy.
Erin:	Yeah, and *heat* is heat energy. [Students laugh]
Teacher:	And if you remember back—to the eighth grade—and you should've learned a *rule*, and if you didn't it's OK, we'll learn it now.
Student:	What was it—[Interrupted by teacher]
Teacher:	You can change energy from one form to another, but you can't create or destroy it. Well, I don't know if that's true anymore either. But you can *change* it, from one form to another. And that actually happens. The ground creates heat energy, from the light, which causes something very interesting. [Turns and writes a Question for student notes on the board]

[Lesson continues with a discussion of how the heat that is now re-radiated from the ground is trapped by clouds to warm the atmosphere.]

FROM "LONGITUDINAL WAVES" LESSON: EL-20-NOV

This is a 9th grade General Science class in a senior high school. We begin 9 minutes into the 40–minute period. The teacher began with a fable designed to remind students of the need to work harder to improve their test grades, then he did some business routines, and now begins the main lesson:

Teacher:	Yesterday, we were talkin' about, uh, *wave* motion. And we said that *sound* was a particular *kind* of wave motion. Can anybody remember what kind of wave motion sound *is*? [To student with hand raised:] D'you remember? [Student indicates she only wants the pass to the bathroom.] Why should I give you a pass? [4 sec, Laughter] When you can't answer a question like that? [2 sec, then to class:] What kind of wave motion is sound?
Student:	It's—it's a *wave* motion.
Teacher:	Sound is a *wave* motion. What *kind* of wave motion?
Student:	Sound wave.
Teacher:	Sound is a wave, what *kind* of wave?
Another:	Vibration.
Teacher:	What *kind* of vibration?
Student:	Waves.
Teacher:	What *kind* of waves?
Eugene:	Are you askin' which one of those four?
Teacher:	M=hmm.
Eugene:	Oh. . . um, uh long- long-i-tud-inal, wave.

Teacher:	Eugene is correct. [Others comment, whistle] [31 sec, Writing at board]
Jimmy:	Hel-*lo* there.
Teacher:	No! . . . If you coulda answered this question I'd a said *yes.* [2 sec]
Jimmy:	*Can I talk to you?*
Teacher:	What kinda- it's not a question of- *stay* there! [Students laugh nervously] No. No.
Jimmy:	No *what?* You don't even know what I was gonna ask you.
Student:	[Mimics teacher:] What was the answer to the question?
Jimmy:	I can't *see.*
Teacher:	Tough. T-U-F-F. [2 sec] When you can be *quiet.* I can hear you up here, OK?
Jimmy:	(How can I learn if-)
Teacher:	So *flunk!* That's what you're telling me, OK? All=right. You'll have to listen very well back there, OK? [Laughter] *Sorry.*
Jimmy:	(But I can't see-)
Teacher:	That's *your* problem.
Jimmy:	But it's your problem because you won't even let me-
Teacher:	Right. It's your problem though. It's your problem. See me after class and I'll *talk* to you.
Jimmy:	OK.
Teacher:	OK? I'll *talk* to you. [2 sec] Because it doesn't make any difference *where* I put you. As of right now, you have a U, an Unsatisfactory, a flunking mark.
Student:	Whew!
Teacher:	If you change your way of livin', you'll *pass,* but not right- not the way you've been doin'. Alright? Now let's look at longitudinal waves. (9 sec) [Aside:] Control yourself! [To class:] Alright. Now what, if we take a spring, and we *compress* it, as we did here in class, you get a pulse to go down the spring, that looks something like this. [5.5 sec, Draws diagram] And so forth, going down the spring. [7 sec, drawing]
Student:	We gotta draw that?
Another:	No.
Teacher:	Now I'm putting this up for *you* and not for *me.* If I put it on the board, since, you do not have as yet a textbook, it's a good idea, to put it in your notes. You don't *have* to, I'm not making you. You'll, be taking it next term if you don't get it this term. It's up to you. [13 sec, draws and writes at board; student sidetalk] Now. If- [Aside:] Felicia please. . . Felicia! [To class:] If you compress, a spring, as you saw in here, what we did, last week, what we did, before yesterday. If you compress a spring, a pulse goes down that spring. [2 sec, demonstrates] Now notice that the *spring* does not move, from me to the door, say, if I have it attached to the door. The spring *is* between me and the door. But something *does* move, if I push that spring, something *does* move between me and the door. What moves, William?

William: A wave.

Teacher: Alright. A pulse *does* move. Now notice that the wave motion *goes* to the right, from me to the door, if I push it in that direction. So the wave *motion* is toward the door. [Writes on board] Which way does the *spring* move? Paul?

Paul: The opposite.

Student: It's not moving.

Teacher: But it *is*. If you recall that spring, it *did* wiggle. Which way does the spring move?

Student: The same way.

Teacher: If it didn't *move*, there would be no wave *traveling*.

Paul: The opposite.

Teacher: The opposite to what?

Paul: The way the wave goes.

Teacher: It does? What a- what- which direction is th'opposite?

Paul: Goin' right from the lens.

Teacher: Are you sayin' that the spring moves back *this* way? Yes it does. Does it move in any *other* direction? [4.5 sec]

[The teacher now draws a diagram of the movement of spring and pulse and elicits that the spring moves both parallel and antiparallel to the direction of the pulse. He uses this as a definition for the term *longitudinal wave*. A few minutes later he asks a "new" question:]

Teacher: What's an *example* of a longitudinal wave?

Student: Uh, a telephone call?

Teacher: Say that out loud.

Student: When you *call* someone on the telephone.

Another: Good God! [Students laughing]

Teacher: What is it that goes through the *wire* when you call somebody?

Student: Electricity.

Teacher: OK, now—*that*, uh, is not a longitudinal wave. Uh, sorry about that. It's uh—I know you might think that the electricity goes from *my* house to *yours*. It really doesn't. The electricity goes back and forth. Uh—you might not *believe* this, but the individual electrons in a wire travel slower than you can walk. Give you an example of that. If I take this piece of *pole* here [laying the window pole along the demo table], push on one end of it. . . [2.5 sec] What happens to the other end?

Student: It's goin' *down*.

Teacher: OK. This is the way *electricity* is. When you *punch*, an electron in on one end of the wire [pushes on pole], one pops out on the other end. OK? So this is [repeats] the, way the *electricity* moves through a wire. But, you might say that this *pulse*, travels instantaneously, this is if this pole were hundreds of miles long, and I pushed one end of it, the other end would move *almost* at the same time. Not quite, but *almost* at the same time. Electricity is like *that*. When I push electrons into *one* end of a [repeats] wire, another one pops out on the *other* end, and the pulse pops out. But the individual electrons travel slower than you can walk. The *current* travels at the speed of *light*. So it's not a longitudinal wave motion. It's somethin' quite different. Can you give me an *example* of longitudinal wave *motion*? *Please*. [3 sec] OK?

Student: Like when a wave comes *in*, y'know on a beach, like just a- wave, 'n it goes back out.

Teacher: That's- No that's a *water* wave. That's traveling in a *circle* more than, in a, longitudinal wave. [Draws] This is- this is *not* a longitudinal wave. A water wave is *not* a longitudinal wave. It's not *quite* transverse either. It's a different kind of thing, *water* is. But uh, can anybody in the room give me an example of a longitudinal wave? [2.5 sec] Victor, how 'bout it? [3 sec] What've we been *talking* about?

Victor: Water waves?

Student: The spring.

Teacher: What else? What's the *topic*, what're we on?

Students: Waves/ Wave motion/ *Sound*/ Sound=wave

Teacher: Yeah! Who said sound first?

Gary: Me!

Teacher: Y'did? Alright, Gary, you're right. It's *sound*. Soundwave is a perfect example of longitudinal wave motion.
[10 sec, Writing at board]
Now what we did yesterday was the same sort of thing as the *spring*, when we taked about compression of *air*. Instead of compressing a *spring*, let's compress *air*, instead, and watch what happens. If you could *see* molecules of air-

Student: Can you?

Teacher: You can't, they're invisible, if you *could*, you would see . . . [Makes dots on board] magnified billions of times, little dots. Now I'm going to draw a line, so *you* can see it, and represent a molecule of air. Alright, now there's billions and billions on this line, and there's another molecule right beside it, and another one right beside it, like this, with no sound at=all. Now as soon as you make a sound, *pulse-*

Andrew: [Aside:] Michael-

Teacher: You *with* us, Andrew? OK. [Resumes:] As soon as you make a sound *pulse*, you cause these *air* molecules here to move, along, in *this* direction, to stretch apart. And to make a compression, here. And air molecules that *were* over here, will move *sideways*, in *this* direction, to make a, compression. And as the pulse *travels*, it gets compressed again over *here*, and then the air molecules stretch apart. They get compressed again. And they stretch apart. So now notice what happens is exactly the same thing with a seel- a steel spring. Here I have a pulse, that causes the spring to stretch togeth- uh compress together and stretch apart.
Now. Which *way*, are these air molecules *moving*, if the sound moves to the *right*? Sound wave goes in this direction, which way does the, *air*, move?

[A new discussion ensues in which students again have trouble with the notion that the medium moves both forward and back as the wave moves forward. Finally this is established, and the connection made again to the definition of longitudinal waves. The last 10 minutes are devoted to transverse waves.]

FROM THE "GIANT CELL" LESSON: JR-29-OCT

This is a 10th grade Biology class. We are about 14 minutes into the 40 minute lesson period. The teacher has returned homework and quiz papers, taken attendance, and described his grading policies. Students asked a few questions about assigned work. The main body of the lesson now begins:

Teacher: OK. Um, there's a movie that was made . . . quite a while ago with Steve McQueen in it about this tiny- . . . thing that

Martin: -Planning the Great Escape!

Teacher: came from another planet, called the Blob. . . . And that is- you probably *all* saw it, it's been on the 4:30 movie a million times.

Victor: Scott! [Laughter]

Teacher: This tiny blob goes around, and what it does is it eats people, and uh, by the end of the movie this little blob that started out about *this* big . . . is big enough so that it's covering an entire diner. OK, and there's a couple people trapped inside, and it's very dramatic, and finally they freeze it and send it off to Alaska. That's not what-

Martin: It's a one-celled animal, isn't it?

Teacher: Well, it's, it's sort of like a one-celled animal. You don't really know because they don't tell you.

Victor: Giant condensed *soup*!

Martin: They *said* that.

Victor: Why can't he explain *science* in a scientific way!

Teacher: The question is . . . can a one-celled animal reach the size that this blob did in the movie? Could a one-celled animal

Student: No!

Teacher: be as big as a *diner*? . . .

[INCONCLUSIVE DISCUSSION OF THIS QUESTION FOLLOWS FOR 4 MINUTES.]

Teacher: Well, let's use this analogy.

Martin: I know, they *could* be that size, there *is* no reason why not.

Teacher: No, there *is* a definite reason why they couldn't be this size. [1.5 sec pause] If you think about it, um don't- . . . Well, use this analogy. Instead of thinking of a large cell, think of a large group, of people. OK? If we had a huge crowd of people, . . . [6 sec, drawing diagram at board] Today, there's a rally on Wall Street to stop nuclear reactors, OK? There's supposed to be a tremendous turnout of people. Let's say we have this huge crowd of people. [Makes many, many chalk dots to represent people in diagram]

Victor: We're getting the point, Mister Jorro. [Laughter]

Teacher: What problems would some of the people face?

Martin: Cops!

Teacher: [4 sec] Yeah Ron?- Larry! C'mon, I mean I was looking at you when you *did* it [threw something]. Be a little *subtle*. [3 sec] OK, Ron.

Ron: They'd be all crowded together, and not be able to move around. *You* know.

Teacher: OK. So say they were comfortable there. Say that they had to stay there for a *while*. Like this rally's gonna be there the whole day. What problems would y- people face? Aside from traveling.

Student: They'd get *hot*.

Teacher: OK.

Ron: People would start to stink! [Laughter, comments]

Teacher: Frank! Siddown. Whad you say, Ron? That was a good-

Ron: Want me to say it again? People would start to smell.

Student: There'd be so much. . . *odor*!

Teacher: See now that was- he gave sort of a silly answer there, but it turns out that that *would* be one of the problems. The people in the *middle* would be dying from the smell. [Laughter] Because all these. . . people, all this living material, would be producing a lot of waste products. [Aside:] Andrew! And if you have a lot of waste produced, the poor people in the middle, are stuck.

Student: Um, they can't get the *food*.

Teacher: What other problems would these poor slobs in the middle have? [Laughter]

Student: They can't get the food, they can't get any food.

Teacher: OK. You have this huge crowd of people. The hot dog vendors would be around the *out*side, [Laughter] and even if the people in the mid- middle y'know would give the guy next to 'em some money and pass it down, or along- First of all the money would disappear, [Laughter] but even if it, it did reach out here [Points to diagram], where the hot dogs are, by the time the hot dog got back- nobody likes it cold.

Victor: Hey, I think they *get* the point, Mr. Jorro.

Teacher: OK, the people in the middle have a problem with getting *food*, and they have a po-problem getting rid of their wastes

Student: Air!

Teacher: . . . and if the crowd was big enough, they'd have a problem getting air. The same thing would happen to a huge cell.

Student: It'd *die*!

Teacher: Food can only enter along the outside edge.

Victor: So if it has- if it's *bigger*, then more food should be able to get in, but . . .

Student: It can't get into the middle.

Teacher:	Right. The *outside*, the material on the outside of the cell, would use up the food and the nutrients before the living material in the center could *get* it. So the stuff in the center, would end up *dying*.
Martin:	But the stuff in the middle would be bigger-
Teacher:	Go ahead.
Martin:	It would be like more proportion. It would be like bigger, than it was in the other.
Teacher:	Say that-
Victor:	Can I say it?
Martin:	Like all in the nucleus, and the little stuff, that's in there, would be bigger, than it was, if it was in a *little* cell.
Student:	They'd be to *scale*.
Teacher:	Well it turns out that the organelles are, their particular size because, they function best at that size. OK? So they, making them bigger wouldn't really, help things out.
Martin:	Yeah, but like with DNA-
Victor:	If the outside were, if the outside was this big and the inside was this big, and it grows to be *this* big, then its insides would be *this* big [using gestures]. It would- it would keep, like if there's a difference of five inches, it would just double it, if it doubles its size. Y'know what I'm trying to say?
Teacher:	Uh, that's a good point. The thing that, turns up here, I didn't want to bring it up because it gets into geometry, and I don't know if you've had this in geometry yet. . . but, as the area of- we're talking not about a circle now, we're talking about a *sphere*. OK? A *ball*. As the area of a ball. . . as the size of the ball gets bigger, the *volume*, the space *inside*, gets larger a lot faster, than the surface area. OK? the area along the *outside*. So that, even though the outside area would be getting bigger, maybe, a greater, proportion of, material in the middle-
Martin:	Yeah but the stuff in the middle, wouldn't it be bigger *also*?
Student:	The whole *thing* would grow.
Martin:	Like with a *person*, the *outside* grows and so does the *inside*. So that the cell-
Robert:	Mr. Jorro. Why is the cell's size limited?
Teacher:	*That's* what we're trying to figure out.
Martin:	Yeah but Mr. Jorro- Like with a person, I mean like we'll grow and so will the *inside*. So with a cell. so if the cell grows big, the insides will grow big to compensate for the size and-
Teacher:	OK, what we're saying is that, the organelles of the cells don't grow bigger as the cell grows bigger.
Martin:	But how do you know that if there's never a cell that size?
Teacher:	We know it by observing, *small* cells grow, [Coughing and pounding] cells of a different size, and you can compare a smaller cell and a larger cell.
Student:	One that's changing in size?

Teacher:	Right. The size of the nucleus is usually the same, the sizes of the organelles are usually the same.
Martin:	But in something like you know like, if the DNA goes berserk or something like that-
Teacher:	But it- Well let's not get into a whole, type of cell theory. Basically, Robert, to answer *your* question, the reason the cell's size is limited is because as the cell gets, larger and larger and larger, the proportions in- the living material in, the very center of the cell, is deprived of food and oxygen. So a cell *can't* just become, larger and larger and larger and-
Victor:	Who says the Blob was one cell?
Teacher:	What we're uh. . . trying to get at here, someone brought it up before, is why cell division *has* to take place. And one of the reasons it *has* to take place, is because cells just cannot grow, indefinitely. So *that's*, it took a little while to get around to it, but that's our Aim for today. [9 sec, Writing official Lesson Aim on board, reads:] "Why must cell division . . . occur?" [7 sec]
Students:	[Crosstalk, copying from board]
Teacher:	And we saw that cell size was limited because as the cell got larger. . . the center of the cell had a harder and harder time getting the things it needs to stay alive. [3 sec]
Victor:	When the cell divides, does it get any smaller?
Teacher:	[Writing, 4 sec] Hold on a second, OK? [Writing, 8 sec] So the reason the cell size is limited. . . because as the cell *gets* larger [Writing, 5 sec], it becomes harder and harder for the, central part of the cell to get, the things it needs to stay alive. [Writing, 24 sec]
Victor:	Mr. Jorro
Teacher:	Yeah, hold on. . . let me just, finish writing, then I'll get to you. [Reads:] "It becomes harder for the center of the cell to get the necessary. . . materials." [Writing, 9 sec] Materials like food, oxygen. . . [Writing, 6 sec]. OK. *Yes.*
Victor:	When a cell divides, it gets smaller, right? So, wouldn't it- would not function as well as the perfect size, OK? Now you're saying *that's* the perfect size, OK?
Teacher:	No, I'm *not* saying this is the perfect size. What I'm saying is the cell could *never* reach, a size this big.
Victor:	No-o-o! I'm just proving, you know. . . Assume that you've got the ideal size.
Teacher:	OK, let's assume there's an ideal size for a cell.
Victor:	That's the ideal size. Now split it in half. Draw a line right down the middle. [2 sec, Teacher complies] Now it won't function as well, cause it only has *half.* [2 sec]
Teacher:	OK. You have a good point. Now what happens is, after the cell splits in half, each of the two halves, will grow again.
Victor:	But how long would that take?

Teacher: It depends on the cell. Some cells take 20 minutes to, double their size. Some take *hours*, OK? [2 sec] *but-*
[Martin interrupts to ask question about how well cell works before it has grown back to normal size. Teacher takes one more question, then closes off discussion of these issues and goes on to a related topic for remainder of lesson.]

FROM LESSON "CRUSTAL MOVEMENT": SC-20-MAR

This is the same class, approximately, as for the "Terrestrial Radiation" lesson, in the second semester of a year-long Earth Science curriculum. The teacher is not the same as in the other lesson. We are about 12 minutes into the 40–minute period. The teacher has completed class routines and reviewed definitions of a number of terms that students had just written out as a Do Now. The last of these terms was *fossil*. The main part of the lesson now begins:

Teacher: I'd like to go on with what we were talking about. And we were talking about *fossils*, that are used as *evidence*, that the earth's crust has moved. Now what did we say about these fossils, how do they help us- *know* that uh, the earth's crust has been moved? Vito.

Vito: Like, if y'find, *fish*, fossils on top of a mountain, you know that once there was water, up there 'n the, land *moved* or somethin'.

Teacher: OK, and what else, besides, finding fossils at high elevations of marine, that were marine at one time. Tony?

Tony: They get transported to different, different areas, or whatever? These, these things 're done by tran- they're *all* transported and that's how you know that they're moved? and they were in that, one area? or-

Teacher: OK let's remember that, it's not the *fossils* that are actually moved. It's the *earth* that's being moved. OK? Monica?

Monica: If you find the original *area*, with, um, things that belong on land, or vice versa, in water, if you find the opposite of what the environment is, you know, that it was, just th' opposite.

Teacher: OK. What Monica said is right, but what would be an *example* of what she said?

Student: What'd she say? you can't *hear* her.

Teacher: Alright. *Shh!* She said, that you might find, *fossils*, in environments where they originally, they- they definitely didn't come from, the- those environments. So what's an example of this? Scott?

Scott: Well in a *glacier*, or uh, an area that was once wa- underneath water or something, and they, y'know, or- or a bunch of *us* underneath the water- like that.

Teacher: That's, that's good but it, just, doesn't- uh Paula?

Paula: I think you could use the big *dome*, and maybe then there'd be- by *intrusion?*

Teacher: Well. . . I think I'm gettin' off the track. Let me help out a little OK? Just let me help you out a little. Remember I told you that we might find, *shallow* water fish, fish that are known to be found in s- shallow waters, very low waters, we find these, *fossils* in deep, oceans. OK that's when the subsistence- *subsidence* happens.

Author Index

Subject Index

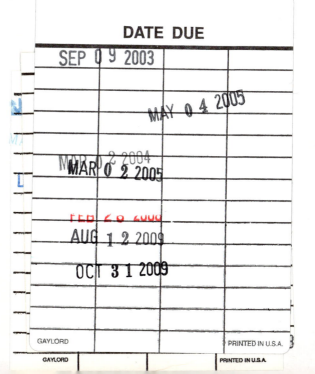